UNIVERSITY OF NORTH CAROLINA
STUDIES IN THE ROMANCE LANGUAGES AND LITERATURES
Number 94

THE MAJOR THEMES OF EXISTENTIALISM
IN THE WORK OF
JOSÉ ORTEGA Y GASSET

THE MAJOR THEMES OF
EXISTENTIALISM IN THE WORK OF
JOSÉ ORTEGA Y GASSET

BY

JANET WINECOFF DÍAZ

CHAPEL HILL

THE UNIVERSITY OF NORTH CAROLINA PRESS

PRINTED IN SPAIN

DEPÓSITO LEGAL: V. 3.702 - 1970

ARTES GRÁFICAS SOLER, S. A. - JÁVEA, 28 - VALENCIA (8) - 1970

TABLE OF CONTENTS

ACKNOWLEDGEMENTS

The writer is particularly indebted to Dr. Richard L. Predmore of Duke University for his counsel during preparation of portions of this manuscript. Thanks are also due the University of North Carolina Research Council, whose generous grant made this publication possible.

INTRODUCTION AND BIOGRAPHICAL NOTE

There certainly need be no explanation or apology for having chosen José Ortega y Gasset as a worthy subject for study. He is a familiar figure, not only to those initiates of Spanish literature, but to anyone interested in, or involved in, the cultural life of the twentieth century. Not since Cervantes has a Spanish author been more widely translated in Europe, or so influential beyond his national boundaries. With the possible exception of Unamuno, Ortega is unrivaled as the Hispanic intellectual leader of this century.

Ortega's critics and commentators have devoted thousands of words to the problem of whether or not he is "really a philosopher" and whether or not he "created a system" of philosophy. Philosopher or no, Ortega is undisputedly the foremost Spanish thinker of his generation. The purpose of this study is to consider him in the light of this generation's most provocative, most publicized, and perhaps most significant philosophy: existentialism.

Is Ortega an existentialist? The answer of his disciples and of the majority of his critics is no. Lest this be misleading, however, it should be stated that the majority of his critics do not deal directly with the question. Among those whose orientation is primarily philosophical rather than literary, there seems at first glance to be a conspiracy to avoid the subject. But those who deal with existentialism explicitly in connection with Ortega are most frequently concerned with showing that no connections exist. Both García Morente and Julián Marías (see Chapter II) have made much of the fact that Ortega enunciated certain ideas at least ten years before Heidegger.

One needs only a superficial grounding in existentialist ideas to note a number of parallels in Ortega's work. These are most often parallels of concept rather than of terms; but existentialists do not agree among themselves as to terminology. Other readers of Ortega have recognized these similarities, among them Guillermo de Torre: "La vida como proyecto, la obligación de elegir, la dimensión de la libertad frente a la fatalidad del ser... he aquí algunas ideas personales anticipadas por Ortega, que años más tarde el existencialismo propagaría." [1] But Guillermo de Torre does not pursue the subject further. Nor has any critic compared the ideas of Ortega with the corresponding existentialist concepts to determine the nature and extent of similarities or differences. Are the resemblances superficial? Are they no more than the result of their authors' breathing the same intellectual atmosphere? Or is there in fact a significant similarity of spirit and purpose? Is it the differences (i. e., of vocabulary) which are superficial?

These are questions which this study will attempt to answer. The problem involved is twofold: Ortega's most important philosophical ideas must be identified and understood; and a working definition of existentialism must be found. As is not unusual with dynamic, still-evolving philosophies, there is no consensus as to the meaning of existentialism. A wide and frequently contradictory range of critical notions exists, and there seems to be no reconciliation possible. The best which can be hoped for is a common denominator, or a number of ideas which are present in the works of several of the more important existentialist writers. This common core of ideas, the "skeleton" of existentialism, will serve as a standard to which to refer the apparently related ideas of Ortega.

In the tradition of the writers of the "Generation of '98," most influential during his formative years, Ortega's chief vehicle of expression is the essay. His influence as a prose stylist has been noted by almost all his commentators, who seem virtually unanimous in acclaiming his excellence. This vein of criticism has added consider-

---

[1] Guillermo de Torre, "Ortega y su palabra viva," *Atenea*, CXXIV (1956), 25.

ably to the bulk of writings about Ortega, but both because of its relative homogeneity and its almost total irrelevance to questions herein to be considered, no detailed treatment of stylistic criticism is undertaken.

The scope and extent of Ortega's writings necessitate certain further omissions in order to narrow the focus to the major problem. For example, *La deshumanización del arte e ideas sobre la novela,* dealing primarily with the area of aesthetics, is of no more than peripheral relevance. Chapter III deals with the works of Ortega, and explanations are given for the omission of a number of his writings.

The principal problem of Chapter I is the definition of existentialism. Ambiguities and conflicts in definition are noted, and historical origins briefly outlined. A "common denominator" of existentialism is the goal, and both primary and secondary sources are consulted.

Chapter II reviews critical works, including books and articles written in Europe, Latin America and the United States. No claim is made to exhaustiveness, although it is felt that the criticism discussed is thoroughly representative of publications appearing up to the time of termination of initial research on this study in 1961. A subsequent check of works published after that date discloses, first, that the flood of secondary material produced in the years inmediately following Ortega's death has abated considerably, and almost without exception tends to reiterate positions already established in the sources included. The avid seeker of bibliographical data is referred to Arturo Gaete's compilation in his *El sistema maduro de Ortega* (Buenos Aires: 1962) which contains citations from a 1915 review by Antonio Machado through 1960.

Chapter III contains a study of Ortega's major ideas in comparison with the major tenets of existentialism as outlined in Chapter I. The philosopher's major works are approached from the perspective of a positive hypothesis of existentialist concepts, with an attempt made to relate his principal publications to an overall philosophy of life. The posthumous works included are those published during the first seven years following Ortega's death, the premise being that these are the works left most nearly complete or most clearly organized, while works appearing later would be those requiring a larger degree of contribution by editor Julián Marías. Whether or not this supposition is justified, the number of works consulted and included is certainly amply representative. Then too, Julián Marías and others have shown quite convincingly that most of Ortega's major ideas were enunciated rather early in his career and developed over a period of time, so that the latest posthumous works should hold few surprises indeed.

Chapter IV is devoted to a summary and conclusions.

BIOGRAPHICAL NOTE [2]

José Ortega y Gasset was born in Madrid on May 9, 1883, the son of a wealthy and influential newspaper family. He was educated at the Jesuit Colegio de Miraflores del Palo in Málaga; at Deusto, also a Jesuit school; and received his doctorate in philosophy and letters from the Universidad Central in Madrid in 1904. About this time he published his first essays in "Los Lunes," literary section of *El Imparcial.* In the latter part of 1904, Ortega studied at the University of Leipzig, and at the University of Berlin in 1906. Later he studied in Marburg with the prominent Neo-Kantian philosopher, Hermann Cohen, who considerably influenced his intellectual development. He returned to Spain briefly in 1908, married, and taught philosophy in the Escuela Superior del Magisterio in Madrid. He then returned to Germany to renew his studies with Cohen.

Upon his return to Spain, Ortega introduced Neo-Kantian principles to a group of young intellectuals. He won through competitive examination the chair of metaphysics at the Universidad Central in Madrid, which he was to hold for a large part of his life. In 1914 he published his first book, *Meditaciones del Quijote,* and later in the same year *Vieja y nueva política,* a series of lectures which he delivered as spokesman for the League for Political Education.

---

[2] This material is not footnoted since it contains nothing not easily available in numerous other sources. The following authors (listed in the bibliography) provided biographical background: Marías, Salmerón, Salaverría, Chabás, and Ceplecha, who has the best biographical summary in English. The reader is especially referred to the introduction of María's *Circunstancia y vocación,* probably the best and most detailed biographical sketch.

First published in scattered newspapers and reviews, *Personas, obras, cosas* (1916) is a collection of articles and essays dating from 1902. In 1916 Ortega made his first trip to America. He taught and lectured in Buenos Aires. In this same year he began the publication of *El Espectador* which continued until 1934. The series grew to eight volumes of essays on issues of the day, on literary criticism, on philosophy, on travel and lighter themes.

Toward the end of the first World War, Ortega founded the weekly *España,* a review of progressive character which observed a lay attitude in religious questions, supported Europeanization in national education, showed considerable appreciation of new artistic movements, and vacillated politically between a republican regime and a reformed constitutional monarchy.

The Worker's Socialist Party was gaining power in Spain during these years. Labor unions were increasing in strength, and there was growing resistance to the government after its repression of the general strike of 1917. The problems and unrest of the years 1917-1921 led to Ortega's publication in the latter year of *España invertebrada,* an analysis of the lack of effective leadership in Spain.

In 1922 Ortega left the weekly *España* and began to write for *El sol,* a newly-organized liberal democratic daily, which represented the interests of a young industrial capitalism, as opposed to those of the great aristocratic landowners and the high clergy. In 1923 Ortega founded the *Revista de occidente,* a periodical of mixed literary, scientific, and philosophical character. It became influential immediately in literary circles and for over a decade was Spain's major contact with contemporary European intellectual and artistic movements. Shortly afterward, its work of cultural diffusion was amplified and a publishing firm organized under Ortega's direction. This was to be complementary to the *Biblioteca de ideas del Siglo XX* of Espasa-Calpe, an enterprise also under Ortega's management. The publishers aimed to introduce throughout Spain the important new ideas of the century. Their ambitious undertaking involved the translation, annotation, and critical analysis of many of the significant literary, historical, and philosophical works produced during a quarter of a century. This was a most noteworthy cultural influence upon succeeding generations of students.

Ortega continued to write for *El sol,* most often on themes of national reconstitution. These articles are collected in *La redención de las provincias.* Ortega resigned his chair of metaphysics at the Universidad Central in the period 1923-1930, years which saw the dictatorship of Primo de Rivera.

In 1923 Ortega published *El tema de nuestro tiempo,* his ideas on the philosophy of history, on epistemology, and on life and culture. *La deshumanización del arte e ideas sobre la novela* followed in 1925. Three years later, Ortega returned to Argentina to lecture at the University of Buenos Aires.

During the last years of the military dictatorship of Primo de Rivera, Ortega associated with a heterogeneous group of intellectuals calling themselves the "Defensa de la República," certain of whom joined with him in February of 1931 in signing a manifesto calling for the uniting of the intelligentsia and professionals willing to place their services at the disposal of the Republican cause. It appealed to youth, art, letters, science, even to religion, and caused considerable embarrassment to the government because of its wide publicity.

In 1930 Ortega published *La rebelión de las masas,* and shortly afterward, *La misión de la universidad.* The former book has been translated into nearly every modern language and is Ortega's best-known work in America where for several years it headed the non-fiction best-seller lists.

With the fall of Primo de Rivera ending the monarchy (1931), there was general recognition of Ortega's contribution to the new regime. In the early days of the Republic, he was elected as a representative to the Cortes Constituyentes and became a proponent of equanimity and a calm, constructive sense of nationalism. He counseled that a state cannot be forged by shouting revolution and warned against following the futile pattern of change in name only. Later in 1931, Ortega was named ambassador of the Republic to Berlin. Also at this time, he wrote of the impending tragedy of the young Republic in *Rectificación de la República.* He was a member of the electoral college in the Presidential elections of December, 1931 and was summoned for advice during the acute cabinet crises of the summer of 1933. Several attempts to form a cabinet failed, and effective Republican unity was at an end. Ortega seems to have been disappointed in his companions and in the course the Republic was taking, for he drew away from politics after this and wrote no more political works. At the beginning of the Civil War in 1936, Ortega was distant from both sides. He went first to France and later to Argentina.

Ortega lived in voluntary exile in Buenos Aires, writing for newspapers and periodicals, lecturing, and teaching at the University until the beginning of World War II. During the years in Buenos Aires he published *Ensimismamiento y alteración* and *Estudios sobre el amor* in 1939, and *El libro de las misiones* and *Ideas y creencias* in 1940. *Mocedades, Historia como sistema,* and *Esquema de las crisis* appeared in 1941.

In the years of the second World War, when most European intellectuals sought liberty in America, Ortega returned to Europe and took up residence in Portugal. *Teoría de Andalucía* and *Del Imperio Romano* were published in Madrid in 1943 and *Dos Prólogos* in 1944. After this time Ortega wrote little, but waited for the day when he could return to Spain. He made a few brief, desultory visits across the border before his definitive return in January of 1949, when he resumed residence in Madrid with Franco's permission, subject to the stipulation that he adhere strictly to "cultural" subjects. Ortega founded a short-lived Instituto de Humanidades in Madrid and gave free courses to lovers of philosophy from the stage of the Barceló theater. He continued to be in demand as a lecturer and was a guest in the United States in 1949 at the Goethe festival in Aspen, Colorado. In 1950 he resumed his teaching at the Universidad Central in Madrid. José Ortega y Gasset died in Madrid on October 18, 1955.

Ortega left much work unfinished at his death, and several important books have been published posthumously. Although not a complete list, these include *El hombre y la gente, ¿Qué es Filosofía?, Meditación del pueblo joven, La idea de principio en Leibniz,* and *Idea del teatro.*

From these few facts, it is clear that Ortega was no "ivory tower" philosopher. Journalist, publisher, lecturer, teacher, diplomat, statesman, political theorist, literary critic and voluminous essayist, this multifaceted personality lived very much (in his own phrase) "at the level of his time." He was definitely concerned with the present, with his own generation, and he wrote for his contemporaries. He used the newspapers to reach the widest possible audience; almost all his books of essays first appeared as newspaper articles. That this was deliberate, part of a conscious plan, is indicated by Ortega's many references to "taking philosophy into the market-place." His lifelong loyalty to this method may be a significant clue to understanding his work as a whole.

CHAPEL HILL
1968

CHAPTER I

DEFINING THE EXISTENTIALIST ETHIC

It has become an intellectual commonplace today to talk of existentialism, but this best-known or most publicized philosophy of modern times is perhaps the least understood. "Existentialist" is perhaps most frequently taken as synonymous with "beatnik" or "Bohemian," and the followers of existentialism are thought of as bearded habitués of cellars or garrets on the Left Bank, pessimists, whose gloomy atheism serves them as *carte blanche* for all sorts of strange and devious behavior, perversions, and flying in the face of convention. Many college students consider existentialism a belief in "free thinking" and "free love." The layman thinks of it as intriguing or revolting, and accordingly praises or defames, exalts or attacks, but is probably unable to name even one of the basic tenets.

Among the experts, or professional critics of existentialism, the lack of any real agreement would indicate that there is a comparable degree of misunderstanding, if not of ignorance. This lack of consensus is evident in such divergent definitions of existentialism as the following:

> Existentialism is
>
> a modern philosophy arising largely from the works of Sören Kierkegaard, though influenced considerably by Karl Jaspers and Jean-Paul Sartre. It claims basically that Existence cannot be conceived, i.e., cannot become an object of thought, but that it may be experienced and lived. Man is thought to be both *free* and *responsible*. [1]

---

[1] Michael H. Briggs, *Handbook of Philosophy* (New York, 1959).

Existentialist philosophy
determines the worth of knowledge not in relation to truth,
but according to its biological value contained in the pure
data of conscience when unaffected by emotions, volitions,
and social prejudices. Both the source and the elements of
knowledge are sensations as they "exist" in our consciousness. There are no differences between the external and
internal world, as there is no natural phenomenon which
could not be examined psychologically; it all has its "existence" in states of the mind. [2]

Existentialism: A term applied to a group of attitudes
current in philosophy, religion, and artistic thought during
and after World War II; which emphasizes existence rather
than essence, and sees the inadequacy of human reason to
explain the enigma of the universe as the basic philosophical question.... Basically, the existentialist assumes
that the significant fact is that we are and things in general
exist, but that these things have no meaning for us except
as we, through acting upon them, can create meaning. [3]

L'existenzialismo ha, come tratto comune, un atteggia-
mento polemico verso la ragione, cioè verso quel metodo
che conduce la propria ricera con procedimenti analitico-
deduttivi e determina l'essere attraverso la mediazione dei
concetti ... Il problema del *senso* dell'essere è la questione
centrale posta dall'esistenzialismo. La finitezza dell'esistenza
è *contingenza*: esistere significa venire all'essere da, emer-
gere da nulla, e, dunque, possibilità di non essere ... Tutta
l'ontologia dell'esistenzialismo ha un'intonazione etica. ... [4]

It is possible to find more extreme philosophic disagreement;
it is doubtless also possible to find certain areas of agreement among
existentialism's critics. That no unanimity of interpretation has been
reached is too obvious to require any exhaustive demonstration, nor
is such the purpose of this chapter. Rather, the present goal is to
locate and to bring together the points of agreement between the
critics of existentialism (and of tangency between various existentialists) and to interpret the whole thus formed.

---

[2] *Dictionary of Philosophy,* ed. Dagobert D. Runes (New York, n.d.).
[3] *A Handbook to Literature,* ed. William F. Thrall et al. (New York, 1960),
pp. 192-93.
[4] *Enciclopedia Filosofica* (Roma, 1957).

In order to restrict the problem to manageable dimensions, it has been necessary to consider only those expressions of existentialism which are primarily philosophical (treatises and essays) and to eliminate those which are primarily literary (novels and plays). A not inconsiderable amount of background reading in existentialist literature has been done, but no attempt will be made to survey it for its relevance to the problem at hand.

If one reads more than a very limited number of criticis of the "philosophy of existence," one is faced with the problem of just where in history to begin. In other words, while many consider existentialism a phenomenon of the twentieth century, there are those who trace its origins to Kierkegaard (*Either/Or,* 1843); to Neitzsche some thirty years later; or, with Sartre, to Descartes in the seventeenth century, insofar as his famous "I think, therefore I am" is also one of the "discoveries" of existentialism. But other critics find the beginnings of existentialism in places as remote, and, at first glance unlikely, as the ideas of Socrates and St. Thomas Aquinas. Among professional philosophers (particularly the more esoteric) it is not unusual to find existentialism referred to as "neothomism." [5]

The major affinity between St. Thomas and Sartre (certainly a strange alliance) is a belief in the priority of existence over essence, or that existence precedes essence. In the words of Marjorie Grene,

> As Sartre and numerous others have repeatedly insisted, there is, in fact, no need for all this vagueness and obscurity, since an extremely simple, literal, and precise definition of existential philosophy is easy to come by ... Existentialism is the philosophy which declares as its first principle that existence is prior to essence. [6]

What the eager searchers for philosophic sources have perhaps failed to emphasize is that in asserting the principle that existence precedes essence, St. Thomas was concerned mainly with the genesis

---

[5] For an example of this in an eminent contemporary Spanish philosophic writer, see Julián Marías, "El hombre y la historia" in *Obras,* IV (Madrid, 1959).

[6] Marjorie Grene, *Introduction to Existentialism* (Chicago, 1959). Hereafter referred to as Grene.

of human knowledge. He would certainly have been appalled at the extension of the idea to the metaphysical realm.

Descartes, likewise, can be excluded as a legitimate precursor of existentialism, since he never intended to reduce metaphysics to the fact of individual existence. Like St. Thomas, his preoccupations were epistemological, and though he and Sartre may both take the fact of personal existence as a point of departure, their paths separate immediately thereafter.

Although they disagree among themselves as to whether he is really an existentialist, most contemporary historians of existence philosophy begin with Sören Kierkegaard. This is true, for example, of H. J. Blackham, [7] of F. H. Heinemann, [8] and of Walter Kaufmann, [9] who considers Dostoevsky an "overture" though chronologically following Kierkegaard. Marjorie Grene [10] also begins with Kierkegaard; and Karl Jaspers [11] and Martin Buber, [12] both with claims to consideration as existentialist philosophers in their own right, see Kierkegaard as an origin of the contemporary philosophic situation.

In addition to the authors above, Sabino Alonso-Fueyo [13] might be mentioned in support of the determination to begin a consideration of existentialism with Kierkegaard. Other names could be added, but this seems unnecessary. Those cited above are sufficient evidence of precedent.

Having established a starting point, the next step is to set the outer limits. Who are the existentialists? The list of men so labeled could be extended almost indefinitely. It we consider for the moment only the seven critics cited previously, the roster (mentioning only the better-known) would include the fallowing: Dostoevsky, Kierke-

---

[7] *Six Existentialist Thinkers* (New York, 1959). Hereafter referred to as Blackham.

[8] *Existentialism and the Modern Predicament* (New York, 1958). Hereafter referred to as Heinemann.

[9] *Existentialism from Dostoevsky to Sartre* (New York, 1957). Hereafter referred to as Kaufmann.

[10] See note 6.

[11] *Reason and Existenz* (New York, 1960). Hereafter referred to as Jaspers.

[12] *Between Man and Man* (Boston, 1957). Hereafter referred to as Buber.

[13] Sabino Alonso-Fueyo, *Existencialismo y existencialistas* (Valencia, 1949). Hereafter referred to as Alonso-Fueyo.

gaard, Nietzsche, Rilke, Kafka, Jaspers, Heidegger, Sartre, Camus, Berdjaev, Marcel, Husserl, Tillich, Barth, Buber, Scheler, and Dilthey. There are socalled "schools of existentialism" in Russia and Italy, and in Spain Unamuno, Ortega and Zubiri have been considered, at least superficially, as existentialists.

In order, therefore, to reduce the problem to manageable dimensions, only those four most frequently included by critics as existentialists will be surveyed here. It should be clear from the outset, however, that a critical unanimity, or near unanimity in selection of a given philosopher as an existentialist does not presume a like unity of interpretation.

Since all of the authors mentioned above use Kierkegaard as a point of departure, his inclusion is automatic. With the exception of Jaspers, who deals primarily with Kierkegaard and Nietzsche, the inclusion of Heidegger is also unanimous. Excepting Buber (and he is more philosopher than critic) the critics under study all include Jaspers and Sartre. Five of the seven include Nietzsche, and because of Ortega's acquaintance with Nietzsche's works, some later reference to him could prove fruitful. Unfortunately, the scope of the present study precludes detailed consideration at this time.

Checking the list of names so derived against the choices of another important critic, the selection would seem to be ratified by Reinhardt, who studies the "main themes and phases of existentialism" [14] and includes these philosophers among his array of six existentialists.

The Existentialists, [15] another significant study, covers all of them in its investigation of seven existence philosophers. The *Handbook of Philosophy* refers to Kierkegaard, Jaspers, and Sartre in its definition: the *Enciclopedia Filosofica* to Heidegger, Kierkegaard, Jaspers, and Sartre. The definitions of existentialism found in the *Dictionary of Philosophy* and *A Handbook to Literature* refer to Kierkegaard, Heidegger and Jaspers in the former instance and to Kierkegaard, Heidegger and Sartre in the latter.

---

[14] Kurt F. Reinhardt, *The Existentialist Revolt* (Milwaukee, 1951). Hereafter referred to as Reinhardt.

[15] James Collins, *The Existentialists* (Chicago, 1951). Hereafter referred to as Collins.

It is therefore apparently justifiable to conclude that the works of Kierkegaard, Heidegger, Jaspers and Sartre constitute a sort of "core" of existentialism, and ideas which may be found to be common to them all will form the skeleton of existentialism, the major themes which will be evidence of existentialist thought or influence in other writings.

Regardless of its metaphysical implications, the orientation of existentialism is not primarily metaphysical. In other words, the "heart" of existentialism is not its theology or metaphysics, as is clearly indicated by the lumping together of such opposites as Kierkegaard's Protestantism and Sartre's atheism, Jaspers' non-denominational religiousness and Nietzsche's impassioned anti-Christian views. The tendency among some contemporary critics to distinguish "Christian" and "non-Christian" schools of existentialism is another case in point. According to Reinhardt, "It is, roughly speaking, a different anthropology which accounts for the metaphysical and ontological differences between theistic existentialism (Kierkegaard, Jaspers, Marcel), on the one hand, an the non-theistic or atheistic forms of existentialism on the other (Heidegger, Sartre)." [16]

Collins explains the philosophical bases for the relegation of the supernatural to a secondary plane as follows: "Existence cannot be predicated of the eternal, immutable Being, since to exist means to be engaged in becoming, time, freedom and history." [17] He sees the existentialist quandary as how to relate existential thinking to the Divine Being, who is by definition beyond the existential order. "Man is not only central in existence: he is the only truly existential being." [18]

Though further arguments both pro and con might be introduced, there seems to be sufficient ground for beginning the search for the common ideas or major themes of existentialism in areas other than the metaphysical.

One approach to the business of locating the major existentialist themes would be to read all the important works of each of the philosophers most frequently considered existentialists. While this

---

[16] Reinhardt, p. 15.
[17] Collins, pp. 14 ff.
[18] Collins, pp. 14 ff.

may be the most thorough and respectable approach, to choose it would be to complicate the problem tremendously, and to lose sight of the primary focus of this study. In the interests of cogency, it seems preferable to follow the method previously used for selecting the major existentialists, and to decide on the basis of a "majority vote" by several critics. Since all the critics follow a chronological or man by man pattern, convenience dictates a similar procedure.

Although the purpose of the following survey of critics is a search for major themes of existentialism, it is also obviously desirable to give some idea how these themes are used. This will necessitate quotations of occasionally greater length than would otherwise be the case, but will have the advantage of presenting a more under-standable picture of individual philosophies than would a mere listing of themes.

No attempt is made, however, to give a complete outline of each of the four existential philosophies considered, nor to explain or harmonize inconsistencies between them or within the thought of a given philosopher. The sole purpose is to identify primary themes and major concepts and to explain their use in the existentialist context.

KIERKEGAARD

> Gradually but inevitably Kierkegaard centered his exis-tence in the alternative indicated by the title of his first great book: *Either/Or* (1843). Either wholehearted obedi-ence to God's law or open rebellion against it; either for or against Christ; for or against Truth; either hot or cold, but never lukewarm or halfhearted! [19]

This author asks,

> What is the meaning of "existential truth" in Kierkegaard's life and work? It is a translation of the abstract into the concrete ... an active practice and realization rather than any doctrinal knowledge, a "how" rather than a "what." It is the actual living of all that one believes, teaches, and preaches. [20]

---

[19] Reinhardt, p. 24.
[20] Reinhardt, p. 39.

> The authentically existing individual will always be in-
> finitely interested in himself and in the realization of his
> destiny. That infinite interest Kierkegaard calls the *passion*
> *of human freedom.* This passion forces upon the individual
> a decisive *choice,* but a choice which always involves the
> incertitude of a risk. [21]

Reinhardt continues with the theme of insecurity, which is present
because the existing individual is constantly in the process of becoming. He mentions the element of paradox in Kierkegaard's work
and his view of existence, which includes positive and negative, is
a synthesis of finite and infinite, eternal and temporal. This leads
to the themes of contingency and death, anguish and fear. "Authentic human existence is, however, never a real unity or synthesis but
a togetherness of opposites, a paradoxical and ambiguous junction
of contrasting elements whose vital tension finds its expression in
existential *anguish.*" [22]

Finally Reinhardt returns to Kierkegaard's initial contention that
"the deadly disease of the modern age was the divorce of thought
and life. He complained that philosophy had become highly abstract,
lifeless ... that life had been emptied of real content to such a
degree that human beings no longer knew what it means to 'exist.' " [23]

Collins distinguishes the following main themes in Kierkegaard's
work: (1) The individual versus the collective—a reaction to the
social phenomenon of the industrial revolution. (2) The acceptance
of neither rationalism nor irrationalism. (3) Existence is not predicated of things but of persons in their moral dispositions. "Existential truth, for Kierkegaard, is a moral and religious state of being
rather than a purely cognitive perfection. It rests on the attempt to
shape one's conduct in accord with what one knows about the
purposes of freedom." (4) The relation between metaphysics and
ethics, or the metaphysical foundations of moral theory. [24]

The first theme singled out by Collins is echoed by Grene's title
of the chapter on Kierkegaard: "The Self Against the System." As
this author sees it, "his thought centers in the problem of the in-

---

[21] Reinhardt, p. 42.
[22] Reinhardt, p. 54.
[23] Reinhardt, p. 57.
[24] Collins, pp. 11 ff.

dividual and his personal or subjective existence, his existence as 'inwardness'. ..." [25] Kierkegaard's whole thought is seen in terms of a reaction to Hegelian idealism. She also mentions (1) "a strong indictment of empirical science"; (2) the belief that understanding one's self is the only important understanding; (3) a belief in turning "from tautology to paradox," from systems of impersonal "truth" that are, because they are impersonal, "as superficial and trivial as they are consistent, to the one passionately realized subjective truth that is profoundly meaningful because it is profoundly self-contradictory—because it is absurd from start to finish." [26] (4) For Kierkegaard, there is no one totality of human nature which could be directly and systematically described. There are just human existences, whose inner quality the subjective thinker can attempt to communicate only by the most devious sorts of indirection. (5) The "awareness that here and now may be the last moment is, for Kierkegaard, as for contemporary existentialism, a central and terribly serious motif in the interpretation of human life." [27] (6) Kierkegaard tries

> to face the puzzle of the human individual in ... contrasts between time and eternity, infinite and finite, ... often in a character sketch or parable that sharply stresses some aspect of the general problem that forms the main preoccupation of existential philosophy—the theme of the contingency of human life. [28]

Death is cited as the most dramatic example of such contingency, but, more generally, "what Kierkegaard and existentialism are concerned with is the stubbornness of fact not as data to be understood but as the necessity for free beings to be just this and not that; the impingement of the sheer brute givenness of each person's history on his aspirations as an individual." [29] (7) What is "peculiar and important ... is the stress on the discontinuity of personal existence that Kierkegaard everywhere displays." [30]

---

[25] Grene, pp. 15-40.
[26] Grene, p. 20.
[27] Grene, p. 23.
[28] Grene, p. 30.
[29] Grene, p. 32.
[30] Grene, p. 37.

According to Buber, Kierkegaard "grasped like no other thinker of our time the significance of the person"; [31] Kierkegaard means "true responsibility"; [32] he describes the "ethical as the only means by which God communicates with man." "The crowd is untruth" expresses the relation of the person to the aggregate. Recurrent use of paradox, the ideas of decision and anguish, and the theme that the only truth is subjective, are especially singled out by this critic.

In the opinion of Kaufmann, Kierkegaard "confronts us as an individual." He not only "*was* an individual but tried to introduce the individual into our thinking as a category." [33] Kierkegaard rejected belief in the eternal verities, as well as Plato's trust in reason as a kind of second sight. Ethics for him is not a matter of seeing the good but of making a decision. He attacked theology, ethics, and metaphysics as self-deception, as an effort to conceal crucial decisions. "The self is essentially intangible and must be understood in terms of possibilities, dread and decisions. When I behold my possibilities, I experience that dread which is 'the dizziness of freedom' and my choice is made in fear and trembling." [34] Kierkegaard focuses attention on decision. He was, says Kaufmann, a "man in revolt."

As did Grene and others, Blackham regards Kierkegaard's works as a philosophical revolt against "the System" of Hegel. "The titles are in themselves characteristic hits at the elaborate system established under the rule of Hegel. Existentialism begins as a voice raised in protest against the absurdity of Pure Thought, a logic which is not the logic of thinking but the immanent movements of being." [35] He explains Kierkegaard's hostility to objective system-building "because it provides a life-long escape from the real problems of individual existence." [36]

This author does not search for major themes, but certain words recur frequently in his treatment: "tension," "individuality," "discontinuity between faith and reason," "paradox," "uncertainty," the idea of the incapability of human reason to know "Truth," decision,

---

[31] Buber, p. 37.
[32] Buber, pp. 40 ff.
[33] Kaufmann, p. 16.
[34] Kaufmann, p. 17.
[35] Blackham, p. 13.
[36] Blackham, p. 19.

risk, "possibility," "subjective passion," "ethics," "despair." His work is largely limited to selected quotations from Kierkegaard on these topics. Finally, he touches upon the theme of "individual versus collective," but makes it clear that Kierkegaard did not see this in terms of conflict:

> He lacked the historical interest and understanding for an adequate analysis of the social situation, but he was saved from a merely literary treatment of it and from personal petulance by his firm anchorage in the religious and philosophic conception of the human situation and the permanent function of the individual in saving and realizing the distinctively human. It is from this point of view that later existentialist thinkers have elaborated their analysis of the modern problem of depersonalization in a mass industrial society. [37]

Heinemann concentrates primarily on the epistemological aspects of Kierkegaard's thought, and introduces him as representing "a reaction against, and a break with, the whole of modern philosophy from Descartes to Hegel." [38] He calls Kierkegaard's attitude to the philosophy of consciousness "paradoxical," and notes that: "He rejects abstract consciousness and abstract thought for the sake of the concrete spiritual individual, with his inwardness and subjectivity." [39] Kierkegaard, he says, "defends the Particular against the Universal," but is "more concerned about the human condition as such and the singularity of the individual." [40] He gives particular attention to Kierkegaard's protests "against the levelling brought about by the phantom of public opinion, the ascendancy of the mass and of mass-man, socialism, the demon of collectivism. . . ." He explains that "Levelling destroys the singularity and qualitative difference of the Self, and therefore the order of value and of status. A sort of external alienation arises; the individual disappears in the mass." [41] Heinemann pursues the idea of alienation, seeing it as a "self-estrangement of the mind." This means: "Man has lost his

---

[37] Blackham, p. 21.
[38] Heinemann, pp. 30-46.
[39] Heinemann, p. 33.
[40] Heinemann, p. 34.
[41] Heinemann, p. 40.

self, has ceased to be man, has suffered dehumanization. Having become 'objective,' he fails to be a subject."[42] For Heinemann, Kierkegaard "heralds the Age of Anxiety" by describing the state of alienation as anxiety (apparently his translation of *Angst,* which other critics or translators have rendered as "anguish"). For Heinemann, Kierkegaard goes one step further and "transforms anxiety into despair," which is the sickness unto death. This marks the point where modern doubt and scepticism turn inward, focus on the self, and lead to despair. Kierkegaard believed that one had to start with despair, and proceed from there to again become oneself.

Heinemann continues in some detail, and mentions the ideas of paradox, possibility, of authenticity (not pretending), of existence as "becoming": "To be human is not a fact, but a task." He lists the following "propositions": (1) All essential knowledge concerns existence; (2) all knowledge which does not relate itself to existence, in the reflection of inwardness, is essentially contingent and inessential; (3) Objective reflection and knowledge has to be distinguished from subjective reflection and knowledge. The former, and objective truth, are seen as indifferent, for (4) the only reality which an existing being can know otherwise than through some abstract knowledge is his own existence. (5) The essential truth is subjective or internal; or "truth is subjectivity."

Alonso-Fueyo's treatment of Kierkegaard is very brief, but the following two fragments serve very well as summaries of topical or thematic ideas:

> Kierkegaard comienza a revalorizar lo singular frente a lo universal, lo concreto frente a lo universal, y traslada el problema de la realidad al problema de la existencia, que se centra en el hombre, en el individuo que cada uno es: con sus ansias y sus esperanzas, con su angustia, con su visión peculiar de la vida y de la muerte.[43]
>
> Los avances existencialistas de Soren Kierkegaard han sido resumidos en los seis puntos siguientes: 1.° Aversión al idealismo hegeliano. 2.° Valoración del individuo singular sobre las entidades colectivas y universales. 3.° Anti-conceptualismo y exaltación de la fe desesperada como

---

[42] Heinemann, p. 41.
[43] Alonso-Fueyo, p. 48.

único camino para ponerse en contacto con la existencia auténtica. 4.° Antiburguesismo y odio a la liviandad en la manera de vivir. 5.° Valoración de la angustia ... 6.° Distinción de estadios en la vida: estético, moral, religioso. [44]

Before turning to Heidegger, it should be emphasized that this is not an attempt at a complete or systematic exposition of the thought of any of these existentialists, but only to locate common preoccupations and ideas. In any case, individual philosophies would necessarily remain incomplete with the omission of the religious element for the reasons mentioned earlier.

HEIDEGGER

Reinhardt treats Heidegger jointly with his teacher Husserl (with whose works Ortega was acquainted). According to this critic,

> While the contemporary philosophy of existence presents in most of its discussions modern variations of the major themes of existential thinking of the past, the orchestration of these themes as well as the technical nomenclature used in their elaboration stems to a large extent from the German philosopher Martin Heidegger. ... This in spite of the fact that Heidegger himself has repeatedly disavowed his association with 'existentialism' insisting that his philosophy is primarily concerned with 'being' rather than with existence. [45]

The existentialist themes, discussed by various authors in the terminology coined by Heidegger, include, says Reinhardt:

> the contingency, insecurity, self-estrangement, and dereliction of human existence (Dasein); its ultimate meaning; its "temporality," "historicity," and "authenticity"; its "care," its "dread," and its encounter with the abyss of "nothingness"; its "being-toward-death"; the interrelation of "being" and "existence," "being" and "truth," "being" and "nothing," "being and transcendence." The

---

[44] Alonso-Fueyo, p. 49.
[45] Reinhardt, p. 121.

connotations implied in these philosophical and anthropo-
logical concepts and the conclusions educed from them vary
according to the theological and metaphysical convictions of
individual authors, but the questions and problems to which
they refer are essentially the same. [46]

Reinhardt notes another common characteristic: "The method
which is adopted by most of the contemporary existentialist thinkers
for the analysis and elucidation of these basic problems is similarly
uniform: it is the 'phenomenological method' which was first developed by Edmund Husserl. ..." [47]

While much of the philosophical rationale for this method is not
particularly relevant, certain remarks about its use are enlightening:

This method in application to analysis of contents of human consciousness demands simple, unprejudiced observation and description of those phenomena which are actually
encountered. ... As his starting point, Husserl chooses the
point of view of everyday life with its experience of a
surrounding external world. [48]

The relevance of this method to existentialism is certainly evident.
Returning to Heidegger and his avowed disassociation from
"existentialism," Reinhardt contends:

It is true nevertheless that the central concept in the published part of *Being and Time* is "existence," not "being,"
and it is this fact, among others, that has led to the adoption
of the term "existentialism" to designate certain trends in
contemporary philosophy that show the influence of Heidegger's major work. [49]

Why then Heidegger's protestation that he has no affiliation with
existentialism? Because, says Reinhardt, for him, "existence" and
"man in existence" or "existence in man" is merely a starting point
and a "means for the illumination of *being as such,* that is, for

---

[46] Reinhardt, p. 122.
[47] Reinhardt, p. 127.
[48] Reinhardt, p. 131.
[49] Reinhardt, p. 140.

the elaboration of a *universal and fundamental ontology.*" [50] This critic supports the view that Heidegger's philosophy begins where that of Sartre ends. While that would be difficult to demonstrate (and it is not demonstrated) it serves at least to emphasize the point that Heidegger meant to go beyond the individual existence.

Because of its relation to the themes of "the individual and the mass" and of "self-estrangement" it is worthwhile to include a fairly lengthy explanation of *Das Man* and some of Heidegger's related terminology. Abridging from Reinhardt: In order to point out the difference between authentic and unauthentic existence, Heidegger proceeds from an analysis of the banality of everyday life and refers to a potentiality of human *Dasein* which he terms *das Verfallen* (the "falling away, disintegration). Who is this, he asks, who in "everydayness" exists in the world and with others? It is not the individual, private ego with its genuine intentions, endeavors, and possibilities, but an anonymous and featureless public ego (*das Man*), the "one-like-many," shirking personal responsibility and taking its cues from the conventions of those who live *en masse*. *Das Man* thinks, believes, speaks, behaves as "one does" and expresses the conformist leveling which characterizes the average human life. *Das Man* has fallen prey to the things in the world and has become alienated from authentic human purposes and possibilities. It expresses itself and communicates with others not in genuine speech but in conventional, superficial chatter. To exist authentically, Reinhardt continues, "does not mean, however, that one has to disown or discard all the attitudes of everyday life. Authentic existence is something decisively different from everyday life, nevertheless, because it makes man capable of seeing his everyday life in an entirely new perspective." [51]

A new theme or new area of emphasis is introduced in the concepts of "temporality" and "historicity." Heidegger asserts that to envisage *Dasein* or human existence as a whole, it is necessary to understand it as "being-toward-death." Death, being the "end" of *Dasein,* completes it. And this is related to "authentic" existence. As Reinhardt explains it,

---

[50] Reinhardt, p. 140.
[51] Reinhardt, p. 147.

In virtue of the "resoluteness" with which I face my own death I am freed from the bondage of those inconsequential concerns and activities which engulf the everyday existence of *das Man*. By overcoming in my "freedom-toward-death" the self-delusions of *das Man,* I can at last arrive at an understanding of my *Dasein* as a whole. [52]

"Historicity" is the ground of "authentic understanding of 'Being.'" Existence must be understood in the frame of the social and national community.

The final important theme elaborated by Heidegger has to do with the nature of "nothingness," viewed as a metaphysical category and in relation to the problem of "Being." In the words of Reinhardt:

The specific mood in which "nothingness" is experienced is "dread" (angst). Once man has been threatened and stirred to his depths by the engulfing terror of nothingness, he is prepared for a new and radically different approach to reality. Things, after having been tested in the contrast to nothingness are revealed in the total "otherness" of their being. [53]

He quotes Heidegger's "Nothingness is the veil of Being." After considerable exposition and analysis, however, the critic concludes:

One question of great importance is in the end left at least partially unanswered by Heidegger: the question as to how "Being" is related to "nothingness." It seems to be Heidegger's conviction that, since what at first appears as "nothingness" is ultimately revealed as "Being," all existents are ultimately grounded in that immense realm of "Being" which reveals itself behind the veil of nothingness and which restores to man all things and beings, including his own authentic *Dasein.* [54]

Kaufmann's treatment of Heidegger is limited to a discussion of his differences of interpretation of Nietzsche and Kierkegaard, as related to the interpretations made by Jaspers, and aside from re-

---

[52] Reinhardt, p. 151.
[53] Reinhardt, p. 153.
[54] Reinhardt, p. 155.

ferring to the themes of "Being" and "nothingness," neither confirms nor adds to the exposition by Reinhardt.

Buber also makes mention of the importance of the teachings of Husserl and of his "phenomenological method" in Heidegger's work, and sees that work as an "attempt at a philosophical anthropology." [55] Buber is concerned primarily with the problem "What is Man?" [56] He notes that Heidegger recognized that social "connexions were primary but treated them esentially as the great obstacle to man's attainment of himself." He states that in order to illustrate his own problem, he deals mainly with that part of Heidegger's work which "treats of man's relation to his death." He refers to the theme of *das Man,* the ideas of "transcendence" and "self-being" and of "care." He compares Heidegger's ideas of anxiety and dread to Kierkegaard's, and their ideas of "one" and the "crowd" or the "levelling" of society. The ideas of "possibility," "becoming" and "responsibility" are used but not developed. Buber's purpose is a comparison of Kierkegaard's man and Heidegger's man.

Blackham also comments on Heidegger's dissociation from existential philosophy, but remarks: "For all that, he is inescapably put amongst the existentialists because he is one of them in his themes and ideas and in his treatment of them and in the language he uses..." [57] He says that Heidegger's philosophy proposes to raise the question, "What is Being, what is what is?" He notes that methodologically Heidegger is indebted to Husserl. "Human existence is obviously indicated as the starting point." [58] The biggest part of his essay is devoted to *Dasein,* which he defines as "the mode of existence of the human being," noting that it is generally accepted as an untranslatable technical term. He quotes Heidegger that "The essence of *Dasein* is in its existence" which to him means that human reality cannot be defined, because it is not something fixed or given. "A man is possibility, he has the power to be. His existence is in his choice of the possibilities which are open to him." [59] These

---

[55] Buber, p. 159.
[56] Buber, pp. 163-181.
[57] Blackham, p. 88.
[58] Blackham, p. 89.
[59] Blackham, p. 94.

possibilities are limited both by death and the givenness (historicity) of the individual's situation, which results in a sense of "finitude," of "dereliction," of "solitude and abandonment." Language he sees as possibly communicating truth, but in everyday, constant use, it loses touch with the objects to which it refers. "Language then spreads untruth and establishes inauthentic existence." [60] This is the same idea as Kierkegaard's anti-abstractness. Alienation or hiding from oneself (covering truth with language), taking refuge in impersonal existence is inspired by "dread." (This is the concept which Kierkegaard called "anguish.") Blackham's analysis of the concept of dread and its effects is very good, but a little too lengthy for inclusion. Another theme is that of "care," or concern for what is to come. "Care expresses my being in the grip of particular relations and preoccupations in this world." [61]

The themes of death, authenticity, possibility, and responsibility recur frequently throughout Blackham's treatment.

> Authentic personal existence resolves not only to live steadily in the light of its sovereign possibility which devalues everything but also to accept what has been determined by the actualities of individual inheritance and past actions and what is determined by the social actualities which sustain everyday life in the world. ... Authentic personal existence is a synthesis of the imposed and the willed. ... [62]

The meaning which a "resolved personal existence gives to itself and to the world transcends the intelligible world of everyday meanings as this in turn transcends brute existence. [63] Blackham last deals with the themes of "Being" and "Nothing" but adds little to Reinhardt's treatment of them.

Heinemann entitles his chapter on Heidegger "Heroic Defiance." [64] He deals to a considerable extent with Heidegger's influence in France and Germany, and the question of whether or not he is

---

[60] Blackham, p. 96.
[61] Blackham, p. 100.
[62] Blackham, p. 102.
[63] Blackham, p. 103.
[64] Heinemann, pp. 84-108.

an original thinker and as such a spiritual leader. He refers to the "Heidegger problem" or the "contradiction in the man himself" which he sees resulting from Heidegger's reinterpretation, late in life, of his earlier works.

The themes of possibility, authentic and unauthentic existence, self-estrangement, the individual and the crowd (*das Man*), and the "close connection between existence, being and time" he considers particularly noteworthy. Heinemann calls Heidegger the "rebel among contemporary philosophers, in revolt against all philosophers of the past." Heidegger, he says, "is opposed to logic," but is "quite right in defending himself against the slander that he wanted to install irrationalism." The ideas of "Nothing" and negation, and his own previous utterances on the subject occupy much of the rest of Heinemann's treatment, although he returns to Heidegger in the end for a mention of the ethical implications of his thought. As other critics (including Reinhardt and Blackham) have done, he pays rather special attention to Heidegger's penchant for language, returning to original roots, archaic meanings, or redefining his words for his own special use.

Alonso-Fueyo is brief in his treatment, [65] but attempts to be comprehensive, and hence is perhaps especially fruitful as a source of major themes. He mentions the "meaning of being" as the central problem of Heidegger's philosophy, sought through phenomenological analysis of human existence. The ideas of "being-in-the-World," of authentic and unauthentic existence, "care," anguish, *das Man* and the problem of understanding (language) are explained. Man is not a complete being, but a plan (*un proyecto*). Nothingness (*la nada*) occupies perhaps the greatest part of his treatment. "*Existir* significa *mantenerse en la nada*." [66] "Being-toward-death" and transcendence and temporality complete his coverage of ideas.

Grene presents some difficulties for inclusion here, since she treats Heidegger and Sartre together. In her two essays, "Sartre and Heidegger: The Free Resolve" and "Sartre and Heidegger: The Self and Other Selves" it is frequently not possible to tell whether ideas referred to are those of one or the other or both. What she

---

[65] Alonso-Fueyo, pp. 63-74.
[66] Alonso-Fueyo, p. 70.

distinguishes as important themes will serve, of course, to re-emphasize the selections of other critics, but since her double treatment need only be included once and lends itself well to summary, it is perhaps preferable to leave it as a conclusion to the listing of themes in Sartre.

JASPERS

> Among all those thinkers, past and present, who may roughly be classified as "existentialists," the German philosopher Karl Jaspers comes closest to a systematic and integrated presentation of his philosophic creed. This is so despite the fact that, in contrast to Heidegger, Jaspers does not acknowledge the need for an ontology, or fundamental discipline embracing the totality of being. The "philosophy of existence"—a title to which the philosophy of Jaspers definitely lays claim— must be satisfied with the illumination of the possibilities of the individual, concrete existence in its freedom, uniqueness, and ineffability. [67]

Philosophy begins for Jaspers, says Reinhardt, "not with an inquiry into the problem of being but with an inquiry into the specific *situation* in which the philosopher finds himself in the world." [68] He explains this philosopher's view as follows:

> I know from experience that everything is transitory. ... I am anxious to find in this incessant flux a statically fixed point which would permit me to arrive at some objective certainty concerning myself and the world. I am looking for an answer that will give me a firm hold on myself and on life, because the incertitude of my present situation fills me with doubt and anxiety. I have come out of one darkness in which I was not yet, and I am on my way into another darkness in which I shall be no more.
>
> In my search for a secure anchor of being, I am thrown back on my own concrete self. ... I must accept my concrete situation in its entirety and its necessity, and I must try to "illuminate" it as completely and as profoundly as

---

[67] Reinhardt, p. 177.
[68] Reinhardt, p. 178.

possible. Here, if anywhere, do I have a chance of finding my search for "being" answered. ... What is this personal, concrete "existence" in a given situation? It is, says Jaspers, the hidden ground of my self, that which never becomes an object and which therefore can neither be rationally known nor conceptually defined. [69]

This lengthy quotation is justified since in it are mentioned the themes of flux, doubt, anxiety, necessity, and the "personal, concrete existence" all of which are basic to Jaspers' philosophy. Reinhardt comments that the meaning of existence is further "illuminated" when it is contrasted with *Dasein,* the simple "being-there" of empirical reality, which "signifies the pure givenness of the temporal life and the conditions of the world as experienced by all." Human *Dasein,* according to Jaspers, is of the same order as the universal *Dasein* of the world: it can be regarded as an "object" and thus can be analyzed, described and explained. Human *Dasein* is not "existence," says Jaspers, but man in his *Dasein* is "possible existence." Man is "that being who is not but who can be and ought to be and who therefore decides in his temporality whether or not he is to be eternal."

And how does "possible existence" realize itself? As Reinhardt explains it, it is "by the decision of an existential choice. Existential consciousness is the consciousness of personal freedom of choice." [70] He quotes Jaspers that "Existence is real only as freedom... Freedom is... the being of existence." [71] In the act of freedom "everything lies ahead of me in a fluid state of possibility, and it is I who... impart actuality to one possibility or the other. I break out of the limitations of my *Dasein* and decide what I choose to be. The act of freedom is thus an absolute beginning, a spontaneous source and origin of true personal authenticity." [72]

For Jaspers, to be free means to be one's self, a self with a history, and the act of freedom is the fulfillment of the self's "historicity." The "historicity" narrows somewhat the margin of individual freedom.

---

[69] Reinhardt, p. 179.
[70] Reinhardt, p. 180.
[71] Reinhardt, p. 181.
[72] Reinhardt, p. 182.

> The unity of existence and *Dasein* in the concrete, historical self signifies for Jaspers the fusion of the "eternal" and the "temporal." "Eternity" is ... not the infinite extension of temporal existence, nor an infinite duration of human existence after death in a life beyond: "eternity" becomes incarnate in "time"; it manifests itself in the fulfilled moment. [73]

In the act of freedom, existence not only takes possession of itself but also enters into communication with existences. According to Jaspers, I cannot really become myself in isolation, but only in communication and collaboration with others. Existential communication does not "lead to a fusion of existences" such as would entail the submersion of the individual in the collective, but rather respects and preserves the distinctions between individuals and their existential truths. Jaspers, like Kierkegaard and Heidegger, is aware of the dangers which threaten human existence when it surrenders its "inalienable personal prerogatives" to the impersonal anonymity of the mass.

Reinhardt summarizes Jaspers' themes of freedom, communication, and truth, and deals with his ideas on "revealed religions," atheism, and "philosophic faith," a sort of religion without dogmas. "Although philosophic faith differs in many respects from religious faith, both are grounded in 'transcendence,' and a philosophy without faith in transcendence ceases to be philosophy in the true sense." [74] Transcendence is an important part of Jaspers' philosophy, but since he uses it in much the usual philosophic meaning of the word, lengthy elaboration of the concept is unnecessary.

Man is faced throughout life with the alternative of the conquest or loss of his self. In view of the posibility of self-annihilation, he is overcome by dizziness, fear, and "dread" (anguish). "There is no freedom without the threat of possible despair." [75]

In human existence there are contradictions ("antimonies") which cannot be resolved, opposites which cannot be reconciled. There is,

---

[73] Reinhardt, p. 185.
[74] Reinhardt, p. 190.
[75] Reinhardt, p. 190.

for example, no good without some evil, no truth without falsehood, no happiness without grief, no life without death. This produces a perpetual "tension" of human existence, of which, says Jaspers, "the ultimate is shipwreck." (This is a term also used by Kierkegaard.)

> Human existence in the world is destined to suffer ship-wreck.... But man is capable of giving a meaning to shipwreck and existential despair: existence uses both to gain access to "Being" and "transcendence." Ultimate ship-wreck thus becomes the supreme "cipher" which imparts value to all the others. [76]

Reinhardt emphasizes that Jaspers' existentialism is a philosophy of "becoming" rather than a philosophy of "being," valuing more highly the endless seeking and striving than the tranquility of possession. Jaspers' existentialism is

> equally opposed to determinism, positivism, and scientific materialism, on the one hand, and to Cartesian and Hegelian idealism, on the other. Jaspers centers his philosophy in the concrete situation of the concretely existing and unique individual, emphasizing the elements of personal courage, risk, and venture, and the anguish which the individual experiences in view of imminent shipwreck and death. What counts ... is the unique and irreplaceable value of human personality. [77]

Alonso-Fueyo concentrates on some specific differences between Jaspers and Heidegger, and in this instance can offer nothing relevant to the present problem.

Grene places Jaspers first of all in "the increasing group of those who lament the mechanization of personality that has accompanied the mechanization of industry." [78] She refers to his "polemics against technocracy," an attack on the *Massemensch*. "Jaspers finds the failure of our age in the human analogies to mass production: in the levelling-down of human differences and therefore of the only significant human achievements, to fit the cheap and shoddy pattern

---

[76] Reinhardt, pp. 197-98.
[77] Reinhardt, pp. 200-201.
[78] Grene, p. 122.

of the massproduced average man." [79] As much as sustaining individuality, he is objecting to "the universal predominance of mediocrity as fact and standard in our society." He turns, says Grene, "to existential concepts as reminders of those aspects of human nature which should not and cannot be mechanized." [80]

She notes that Jaspers deals extensively with positivism and idealism, but feels that both have failed because they did not recognize their limitations, although they may be useful to existential philosophizing if those limitations are recognized.

The three volumes of his *Philosophie* "deal with three essential aspects of human experience: the knowable objective world open to science; the experienced, but unknowable process of the individual's inner history; and the equally unknowable, yet inexhaustible, symbols of cosmic meaning variously interpreted in art, religion, and metaphysics." [81]

Some of Jaspers' concepts are familiar from Kierkegaard, notes Grene, who then lists the unconditioned character of the existential resolve as against the conditioned nature of the objectified sensory world; the individual's history as union of time and eternity; the absoluteness of my freedom and the guilt which it entails. Other themes briefly covered are death, suffering, struggle, "the particular historical determination of my particular existence" and the "relativity of all that is real, its self-contradictory character as being always somehow what it is not." These Grene calls common existential stock-in-trade, and notes that what distinguishes Jaspers' views from those of other existentialists is his particular emphasis on communication and transcendence. The remainder of her essay is devoted to an exposition of these concepts.

Heinemann calls Jaspers the "great Psychopathologist-Philosopher of our age," noting that he excels in the description of abnormal personalities as individuals and as types. Like the critics considered previously, he notes Jaspers' concern for the person in danger of becoming a "mere cog within the enormous machine of the modern welfare state," and states that the philosopher "wants to

---

[79] Grene, p. 124.
[80] Grene, p. 125.
[81] Grene, p. 132.

show the way from the unauthentic existence of the mass-man to the authentic existence of the self." [82] He sees this philosophy as "essentially *therapeutic*," an appeal to every individual to take care of "his historical substance *qua* self."

He deals with the themes of reality and possibility, and then lists Jaspers' fundamental philosophical questions: (1) What is science? (2) How is communication possible? (3) What is truth? (4) What is man? (5) What is transcendence? These, says Heinemann, are metaphysical problems, based on "the view that Science, Self and World have to be transcended." He notes the themes of "being" and "becoming" and the importance of the concepts of freedom, choice, and the "concrete, historical situation, and the concrete, individual self." Change, risk, and uncertainty are menitoned next, and the theme of "philosophical faith." This critic says that: "Jaspers' existentialism is all-comprehensive without accepting anything as final. It would be true and false to call it Platonic, neo-Platonic, Kantian, Schellingian or Hegelian, for it incorporates elements of these systems, but rejects each system as such." [83] He says that Jaspers' work could rightly be characterized as transcendental existentialism. "Philosophy of existence, says Jaspers, is a way of thinking which uses and transcends all material knowledge, in order that man may again become himself." [84]

Heinemann compares Jaspers' philosophy to what he calls Heidegger's Philosophy of Finiteness, noting that for Jaspers all authentic being, whether of God or man, is indefinite or infinite. "Exclusive reality and truth cannot be claimed for that which discourse and objective thinking have made determinate and hence finite." Further inverting existential concepts, Jaspers continues: "What seemed an abyss, become space for freedom; apparent Nothingness is transformed into that from which authentic being speaks to us." [85]

This points to the illusoriness and transitoriness of earthly experience, and no doubt results from the philosopher's belief (derived from Kierkegaard) in the subjectivity of truth.

---

[82] Heinemann, p. 60.
[83] Heinemann, p. 68.
[84] Heinemann, p. 68.
[85] Karl Jaspers, *Way to Wisdom*, in Heinemann, p. 69.

According to this critic, Jaspers "really aims at the inner experience of essential Being or of Being in itself." He states that his central thesis is that

> the philosophy of existence reaches a state of perfection, fails, and is transcended in Jaspers' last writings. It reaches a state of perfection or it finds its fulfillment, because once more it turns full cycle. The religious motives of its origin are again coming to the fore. It is a return to Kierkegaard, to Biblical religion and to a quasi-medieval system of axioms. [86]

The remainder of the chapter attempts to demonstrate his thesis.

Kaufmann treats Jaspers largely in respect to his relation to Heidegger and his ideas on Nietzsche. Kaufmann's work is, of course, primarily an anthology with lengthy introductions. His selection of portions from Jaspers' works would tend to support the range of themes outlined by Reinhardt.

Blackham considers the importance of the influence of Kierkegaard and Nietzsche, and deals with Jaspers' attitudes toward reason and science (the theme of the limitations of positivism and idealism). Beginning with personal existence, turning from the external world to the private world, the themes of liberty (freedom), choice, solitude, dread, anguish, possibility and becoming are explained and interrelated. The ideas of limitations of liberty in terms of personal situations, necessity of choice, of authenticity, and Transcendence, of polarities (paradox) and tension follow. In connection with liberty and self-determination, Blackham deals more fully than have other critics with the existentialist concern with "the subtle and complex relations between law and liberty, the objective norms of ethics and the subjective reality of the self and its exigencies." [87]

The themes of death, suffering, conflict, fault (guilt), and risk lead Blackham to conclude: "In Jaspers' view imperfection, failure, fault inhere in the human situation as fatally as death, suffering and conflict." [88] Turning from these general human limitations to the "concrete historical situation," Blackham notes Jaspers' concern with

---

[86] Heinemann, p. 76.
[87] Blackham, p. 51.
[88] Blackham, p. 53.

the "depersonalizing tendencies of the present age of masses and machines." He supplies an omission of other critics by a thorough consideration of the place of the State in this part of Jaspers' thought.

> The State is the most formidable of all the objectivities which are indispensable but which enclose personal existence with the threat of lifeless emptiness. Because of its authority and power, as collective will manifesting the character of personal will ... because of its identification with duty and high ideals and the sweets of virtue ... its claim to transcend its members ... is hard to resist. The individual has somehow to come to terms with the State, to find his vocation and his destiny within it, and to find himself the source of criticism of its aims and ideas and its actual policies. ... the State can never give meaning and value to personal existence but only stimulus, scope, and opportunity. The individual needs the State for becoming himself. ... The State mediates the participation of the person in history. [89]

The themes of communication, the relation of the self and "the other," authenticity, and autonomy, together with discussions of Transcendence and "philosophic faith" complete the chapter.

SARTRE

Reinhardt considers *L'être et le néant* (*Being and Nothingness*) Sartre's "major philosophical work." His goal is a "phenomenological ontology" centered in human existence.

Existence for Sartre is pure contingency. It means simply "to be there; existents appear; they are encountered, but they can never be inferentially deduced. ... No necessary Being can explain existence. There is not the least reason for our 'being-there'. ..." [90] Every existent is *de trop*; superfluous, absurd. People try in vain to hide behind the idea of law and necessity; "every existent is born without reason, prolongs its existence owing to the weakness of inertia, and

---

[89] Blackham, pp. 54-55.
[90] Reinhardt, p. 157.

dies fortuitously." [91] The massive "extramental universe" is sym-
bolized in the seemingly insignificant objects of everyday life. The
"brute reality of existing things strikes and overwhelms, in contrast
to the phantomlike reality of ideas." The experience which makes
man aware of the "being-there" of existence is nausea, the "great
disgust." What makes this experience terrifying is the fact that dead
objects have the power of limiting the freedom of a human being.

> All being spends and wastes itself on a prodigious scale, but
> gratuitously, without any meaning or purpose. Man faces
> the fearful sight of this colossal, inert mass of being, and
> simultaneously experiences himself as the only existent that
> is aware in his consciousness of the extent, the weight, and
> the ultimate meaninglessness of this gigantic realm of
> being. [92]

One characteristic element of human consciousness, according to
Sartre, is negation, the capacity of saying "no." The "nothingness"
of negation, the possibility of not-being, "is lodged like a worm in
the very core of being: Nothingness haunts being." [93]

Sartre distinguishes two basic elements in life or the world: the
En-soi, being-in-itself, the objective world of things, undivided, im-
pregnable, massive; and the Pour-soi, human consciousness, the
world of ideas. The goal of all human striving is an ideal "self,"
combining the fulness of being with the fulness of consciousness.
Man, says Sartre, is nothing but this striving to become "l'en-soi-
pour-soi." But the goal is impossible. It attempts to unite two types
of being which exclude each other by their very nature.

Why, then, does man continue this hopeless race? Because, answers Sartre, he cannot do otherwise. "To exist means for man to
realize himself in action, to storm ahead toward an impossible goal.
Man is condemned to a freedom which weighs upon him like an
inescapable fate." [94]

"Man is his freedom, and therefore this freedom is absolute. It
extends to anything and everything; it leaves no room for any kind

---

[91] Reinhardt, p. 157.
[92] Reinhardt, p. 159.
[93] Reinhardt, p. 159.
[94] Reinhardt, p. 161.

of determinism. No one can relieve me of this burden: neither I myself, who am this freedom, nor any of my fellowmen, nor a god, because there is no God. . . ." [95] Human freedom is thus not a blessing but a curse.

"Constantly checkmated in his projects, thrown back on his fragile momentary existence, man, in his dereliction, experiences dread and aguish. He knows that he is completely alone, absolutely on his own, under the fearful pressure of his own responsibility." [96] Attempts to escape by shifting this responsibility to some super-human power, religious or materialistic, Sartre sees as essentially dishonest and doomed to failure. "Man is what he makes himself, and he alone is responsible for what he makes himself." [97]

"Not only in love and lust but in all human relationships, my own projects may at any time be crossed and paralyzed by the projects of 'the other.' Therefore, claims Sartre, the original and natural attitude among human beings is not love, harmony and peace, but hate, conflict and strife. [98]

Death is seen as something which can neither be experienced nor anticipated; it can never become part of human projects. It is, in short,

> not encountered among the possibilities of my existence. It is simply the nonsensical destruction of all human possibil-ities, the absurd annihilation of the human self. Far from imparting any meaning to human life, death rather reveals most clearly that life in its totality is absurd. It is meaning-less that we were born; it is meaningless that we die. [99]

Reinhardt here comments that it would seem that man's sorry lot, condemned to a life of futility and absurdity might plunge him into abysmal despair. "But the conclusions at which Sartre arrives are quite different. Beyond despair, entirely new perspectives are opening up, perspectives which even impart an ethical substance to human action." [100] The critic is for several pages more concerned

---

[95] Reinhardt, p. 161.
[96] Reinhardt, p. 162.
[97] Reinhardt, p. 162.
[98] Reinhardt, p. 162.
[99] Reinhardt, p. 163.
[100] Reinhardt, p. 164.

with a refutation of Sartre's theses than further exposition. For present purposes, however, variations on the themes are insignificant in comparison to the repeated use of the same themes themselves.

Collins terms much of Sartre's work "technical phenomenological studies on the imaginary, imagination, and the theory of emotions,"[101] following the technique of Husserl and Heidegger, whom he studied. Much of this critic's treatment is extremely technical and esoteric, and concerned with showing the shortcomings of Sartre's "ontology." Certain themes, however, recur: existentialism as the doctrine which maintains the primacy of existence over essence, and takes its start from human subjectivity; nausea; "complete contingency of everything"; meaninglessness of being; the *En-soi* and the *Pour-soi*; consciousness as the power of negation; and consciousness or will as the force which gives structure to the world we experience. The characterization of man as a useless passion, futile thirst to be God, leads to absurdity, defeat, despair. For Sartre, "denial of God is the beginning of man's self development."[102] The only necessity man need admit is that of being free. "He is condemned to freedom—cannot *not* be free." "The gaining of authentic freedom is the sole prize of life."[103] Sartre is apparently aware that unqualified acceptance of this view would lead to a glorification of power, and to chaos. Hence, observes Collins, "under cover of the new existentialist terminology, he is obliged to restore some common objective standards. He says that one 'ought' to act authentically and 'ought' to respect the liberty of others."[104]

What authenticates an individual's act of choice? As Collins sees it, Sartre offers two criteria: that it be done with perfect lucidity, and that it involve an acceptance of responsibility for other men as well. "If these conditions are fulfilled, then the act is unconditionally free, value-creative, and authentic or good."[105] Lucidity is not clearly defined, and as the critic rightly observes, there could also be cases of a diabolical lucidity.

---

[101] Collins, p. 40.
[102] Collins, p. 51.
[103] Collins, p. 53.
[104] Collins, p. 75.
[105] Collins, p. 75.

Buber does not consider Sartre, and Kaufmann is rather more literary than philosophical in the orientation of his treatment. Aside from details mostly biographical, and a lengthy exposition of the *En-soi* and the *Pour-soi,* he contributes only a defense of Sartre from some criticisms he feels to be unjustified.

Alonso-Fueyo sees in Sartre the epitome of the "approximation of philosophy to literature" which he considers a dominant trend of existentialism. As highlights he touches on the ideas of nausea, "necessary" freedom, and being and nothingness.

Blackham deals primarily with what he calls the two modes of being, consciousness and its object, the *pour-soi* and the *en-soi.* Negation, temporality, the future as project, the rejection alike of realism and idealism, the body as concrete center of reference, liberty, and relation to "the other" are discussed in their relation to these two main categories. Sartre's idea of an aboriginal state of conflict between human beings, and that one limits or is limited by "the other" leads to everyone being *de trop* in relation to "the other." The individual's relation to the crowd or society is treated by Sartre in a slightly different way: Merging in the crowd is seen as a way of escape for the individual consciousness anxious to forget its liberty, isolation and responsibility.

The critics have frequently noticed the penchant of existentialists for psychology (with its various modern extensions) and their apparent delight in the abnormal, the devious and perverse. Blackham underscores these observations.

Heinemann entitles his essay on Sartre "The Philosophy of Commitment" and so emphasizes an aspect of this philosopher's work which has been rather overlooked by some other critics. The concept of commitment is a logical extension of the idea of existial choice, which is common to all the philosophers considered.

> Sartre occupies a specific place in the history of Existentialism. He represents the stage where self-estrangement seems to have reached its highest possible degree, that is to say, where the pressure of the group has become so great that the individual is almost forced to live in self-estrangement as the natural state of affairs.
>
> ... ...
>
> Sartre has an uncanny appreciation of the contemporary condition, combined with a gift for analysing, almost

> brutally, its weakness and the negative and destructive
> forces prevalent in human society.... His reaction to this
> situation differs fundamentally. ... Sartre, longing for
> change and liberation, experiences his freedom in this
> same situation. [106]

The concepts of absolute liberty, total responsibility and solitude, and the sentiment of absurdity are seen as permeating Sartre's work. The concepts of liberty, situation and negation, says Heinemann, must be understood if one wants to understand Sartre. Consciousness, Being, Nothingness, are interrelated, for "Consciousness has the power of reducing to nothing" (negation).

> Man is conceived as a contradictory being, as an *Ego* de-
> pending on the existence of others and including inter-sub-
> jectivity as a condition of his existence, but these others
> depend likewise on him. He is a being in a situation which
> is biological, economic, political and cultural, and therefore
> dependent on it, and nevertheless "choosing himself in a
> situation" and therewith the situation itself. [107]

By choosing, man becomes what he makes himself. He is his own project. He is thus responsible for what he is, and by his choice, committed.

"Sartre adopts Kierkegaard's imperative, with God left out, deprived of its religious flavour and transformed into the principle of commitment." [108] Sartre's is essentially a philosophy of action. It is not intended as mere theorizing but as a basis for decision. "Committed philosophy does not arise *in vacuo*; it is written for others and in interrelation with others, in a particular historical situation. The writer must be fully conscious of this situation and able to express it." [109] The critic continues that it is no accident that all commitments imply value judgments. "Commitment represents Sartre's specific response to the challenge of his time."

As noted earlier during the consideration of Heidegger, Grene treats Sartre jointly with this philosopher. Her two essays are entitled: "Sartre and Heidegger: The Free Resolve" and "Sartre and

---

[106] Blackham, pp. 111-12.
[107] Blackham, p. 124.
[108] Blackham, p. 129.
[109] Blackham, p. 130.

Heidegger: The Self and Other Selves." These concepts are the keynotes of the respective treatments, but naturally involve several other themes. "Self-creation—the making of one's essence from mere existence— is demanded of each of us because ... there is no *single* essence of humanity to which we may logically turn as standard." [110] The importance of the situation is emphasized, but, "though there is no self apart from this particular economic, social, physical situation, such a situation does not constitute the self." [111] Sartre's philosophy is seen as an attempt to reinterpret human nature in terms of human subjectivity, an "attempt to show how human values are derived from a totally human—in fact, a desperately human— situation. ..."

Of sheer circumstances (external objects) and their relation to consciousness, Grene says, "Circumstances become circumstances only for the consciousness that tries to make of them something other than mere circumstances." [112] Solitude, freedom, responsibility, action, failure, guilt, all are related to consciousness, and to the existentialist "dread" before emptiness, nothing, death. A full realization of these latter is necessary for authenticity, decision, and the creation of values. As Grene sees it, Sartre characterizes conventional existence as fraudulent. These ideas complete the recounting of themes, inasmuch as her treatment of the relations between the "self" and "others" serves only to reinforce what has already been abstracted from other critics.

SUMMARY

From the foregoing, certain shared themes emerge. All place primary emphasis on the importance of choice or decision, and all their metaphysical or "ontological" allegations serve to provide the necessary facts on which the individual is to base his existential decision. So seen, it is clear that the principal orientation of existentialism is ethical.

---

[110] Grene, p. 41.
[111] Grene, p. 44.
[112] Grene, p. 48.

The point of departure for each of these philosophers is individual existence, and this can be shown to be not only the point of departure, but the major concern of existentialism. All are concerned with the relation of the individual to the collective, and with the dangers of mechanization and depersonalization. The individual, concrete existence is the center of existentialist philosophy: freedom, dread (anguish) and responsibility, as well as death, are all extremely individual matters. Another case in point is the subjective nature of truth. None of these philosophers endorses either rationalism or irrationalism, science or idealism. All of their philosophies are seen by critics as revolts or reactions against preceding philosophy; all are characterized by the use of paradox, and by their concern with its presence in life (whether they call it paradox, polarity, or absurdity). All are anti-abstract. None of them believe in a fixed human "nature" or essence; all insist upon the importance of contingency ("historicity," the "situation," human limitations and the ultimate certainty of death) as prime factors in the decision to be oneself. The themes of freedom of choice (within situational limits), or responsibility, of "authenticity" and the impossibility of transferring decision to any other are likewise common to all these philosophers.

The variations on the themes are numerous, and individual vocabularies do not always coincide. But there are other points of similarity, in addition to the many common preoccupations. For example, there is the "literary" character of the movement as a whole, and the interest of most existentialists in style, in words as such, an the essay as the dominant form. There is also the pronounced interest in psychology, in communication, and the whole range of aberrations. The philosophy of existence is first and always a philosophy of Man.

CHAPTER II

THE CRITICAL REACTION TO ORTEGA

Only a few years ago, little had been written about Ortega's work. Today there exists an impressive quantity of secondary material, although much of it is in the nature of *homenajes,* published in the year or two following his death. Many of the *homenajes* have little value as criticism, being primarily tributes to Ortega the man or the writer, or else personal reminiscences by various former students and friends who recount a conversation, an encounter, or some anecdote. These, however, contribute little of the insight into Ortega's work which one might expect his friends or students to possess.

Of the essays which are critical in nature, many deal with literary aspects: Ortega's style or stylistic contributions, and his aesthetic theories, particularly on art and the novel. There are others which involve a more detailed, linguistic approach, dealing with his writings from the point of view of metaphor and vocabulary innovations. Other authors have emphasized the historical, sociological (or social) and political elements of Ortega's philosophy. Most of these are expository only; a few involve comparison with other theoretical writings, particularly in history. There is, in addition, a somewhat heterogeneous group of miscellaneous essays in "philosophical" criticism. Nearly all critical articles touch on two great points of controversy regarding Ortega, whether as a major or minor theme:

1) Is Ortega really a philosopher, a mere *literato,* or a combination of both?

2) Did Ortega create a systematic philosophy, or only a rambling, incoherent group of essays? Can his numerous works be related in

some logical fashion, do his ideas show "evolution," or did he write at random, inspired only by events of the day?

A large number of the articles on these themes have little direct relevance to the question of whether or not Ortega is an existentialist. The problem receives explicit mention on a very limited number of occasions. There is, however, occasional implicit recognition of existentialist traits. In other words, with no apparent realization that he is doing so, a critic may explain Ortega's writings in existentialist terms. Some reference will be made to this type of criticism, but in the interests of coherence, the greater part of the articles which deal primarily with literature, aesthetics, history, politics, or the two arguments mentioned above will be relegated to an appendix. The treatment which seems most appropriate for this irrelevant body of criticism is a division along the following lines:

A. *Homenajes*: Tributes to the man and writer, and personal reminiscences and anecdotes;

B. *Aesthetics*: Essays dealing with style, literary criticism, and Ortega's aesthetic theories;

C. Essays dealing with Ortega's ideas on history, his social and political theories, and his sociology;

D. Miscellaneous philosophical criticism, including articles dealing primarily with Ortega's "system" or lack thereof, and the question of whether he is really a philosopher.

The style of the appendix will be similar to that of an annotated bibliography, with the subject or theme of each article noted where it is not clear from the title. In addition, the more interesting and original articles will be noted, and mention made of those with a bearing on the two major critical controversies mentioned above.

Books will be divided into two groups, those that deal primarily with Ortega, and those which contain some lesser study of him, from a chapter to a brief reference. The books of which Ortega is the chief subject will receive some individual attention. The others, unless particularly relevant, will be treated in the appendix.

Surprisingly few articles or books have a direct relevance to the question of existentialism in Ortega's thought. It appears in many cases that the only relevance is a negative one: either the question has been deliberately ignored, or it has not been recognized as an issue. The latter explanation fits several cases:

1) those critics who consider Ortega primarily a *literato*;

2) those who see him primarily as an aesthetic theorist;

3) those who interpret his work mainly as political and conservative.

The other possibility, that the question has been deliberately ignored, is suggested strongly in the work of certain excellent philosophical critics such as Julián Marías, José Ferrater Mora, and José Gaos. These men possess a common specialization in Ortega (although to varying extents), and all are sympathetic in their criticism. This latter point may be of significance, since Ortega seems to have found few indifferent reviewers. Most of the secondary writings may be rather broadly divided according to whether the author is an attacker or a supporter of the philosopher. Examination indicates that those critics favorable to Ortega have, in general, been more fair and objective than his attackers. However, most times that the question of Ortega's existentialism (or of existentialism's influence upon him) has been the principal critical theme, the criticism has been unfriendly. It may be for this reason that Ortega's "disciples" have chosen to play down the issue. Existentialism has had a generally "unfavorable press" in Spain, where its Protestant aspects have been emphasized perhaps more strongly than its atheistic tendencies, both at the expense of any other elements of this philosophy.

It is not reasonable to assume that men like Marías and Gaos are unacquainted with contemporary philosophic thought to a degree such as to be unable to recognize similarities between Ortega's philosophy and that of other recent writers. Their own writings belie such a possibility. One need glance at only a few titles among the many by Marías: *Historia de la filosofía, Introducción a la filosofía, Biografía de la filosofía, Idea de la metafísica.* Like Ortega, his principal interpreters are men of considerable philosophic culture and erudition.

This makes their avoidance of the issue of existentialism even more intriguing. If Ortega was *not* influenced by the strongest philosophical current in Europe during his maturity, this fact in itself would seem to require explanation.

Neither the demonstration of Ortega's originality nor of others' influence on him is the object of the present study. The primary concern is the investigation of his ideas themselves, and a comparison to similar or related themes. Without, therefore, assuming any of the critical stances which follow, let us examine what the critics say (and omit) about Ortega's philosophy.

JULIÁN MARÍAS

No other among the critics of Ortega can compare with Julián Marías, either in sheer bulk of critical output, or in excellence. If one adds to this Marías's own personal stature as a philosopher in his own right, his long years of specialization in Ortega, and the fact that he was (and is) Ortega's student, personal friend, collaborator, disciple, continuer, and editor of his unpublished works, it must be considered that, in the interpretation of Ortega, Marías constitutes a class by himself.

A chronological order (by date of publication) is not in this case the best order for dealing with Marías's works. Because of their bulk, the best approach appears to be one based on the chronological order of Ortega's works, or an ordering of Marías's writings according to the volumes by Ortega with which they deal.

Marías is extraordinarily thorough. He begins by pointing out in the prologue to *Ortega, I, Circunstancia y vocación,* the importance of Ortega's theory of circumstances. Everything that man does, he does *en vista de las circunstancias,* and thus Marías devotes almost half the ponderous volume to an exposition of Ortega's "circumstances." This includes the historical and political situation of Spain from the late 19th century (immediately preceding Ortega's birth) up until the Spanish Civil War. Most particular attention is paid to the "Generation of '98," and its members are seen as Ortega's most important formative "circumstance." One chapter dealing with the intellectual crisis in the years after 1898 is significantly entitled "El naufragio como punto de partida," [1] a thoroughly "existentialist" evaluation.

Much of the introductory material is important to an understanding of Marías's picture of Ortega, and particularly to a grasp of his

---

[1] Julián Marías, *Ortega, I, Circunstancia y vocación* (Madrid, 1960), p. 67. Hereafter referred to as *Circunstancia y vocación.* This was Marías' most recent volome on Ortega when research for the present study was done.

presentation of the philosopher as a man with a mission, a mission concretely determined by his circumstances and vocation. The concrete historical situation in Spain was part of Ortega's *circunstancia*; equally important was the intellectual situation:

> El desnivel con Europa, la falta de una producción intelectual original en España, la total ausencia de algo que se pueda llamar "crítica," la inexistencia, incluso, de la mera *publicidad* en la mayor parte del tiempo, se traduce en una consecuencia no suficientemente subrayada: la *irresponsabilidad*. Casi todo lo que se dice y escribe en España durante los tres primeros cuartos del siglo xix es puro capricho y arbitrariedad. [2]

The titles given by Marías to this background material are often revealing and significant. The above selection is from a section entitled "España como desorientación."

Most of Marías's introductory study emphasizes the political and intellectual aspects of the years preceding and following the crisis of 1898. The intellectual and emotional atmosphere of the psychological reaction to Spain's defeat of that year begins to emerge as Ortega's single most significant "circumstance."

The words with which Marías describes the "generation of '98" could hardly be more existentialist:

> Los hombres del 98 hacen literatura, arte, historia, ciencia, *porque no tienen más remedio,* porque parten de un naufragio y necesitan saber a qué atenerse. Ninguna razón externa —conveniencia económica, prestigio social, facilidades políticas, automatismo de las instituciones— los lleva a la vida intelectual; ésta emerge en ellos desde dentro, desde los senos más profundos de su autenticidad, porque la necesitan *para ser ellos mismos en esa realidad española que han aceptado.* [3]

The passage could be applied verbatim to an explanation of Kierkegaard's or Sartre's ideas of a beginning "beyond despair." The use of the concept *naufragio* is identical to Kierkegaard's use of

---

[2] *Circunstancia y vocación*, pp. 50-51.

[3] *Circunstancia y vocación*, p. 68. Italics in all quotations are those of the author cited unless otherwise noted.

"shipwreck"; the introduction of the idea authenticity in this context is particularly striking, as is the *necessity* of a certain life to "be oneself."

In the second half of the Introduction, Marías analyzes and summarizes the situation of European philosophy about 1900. He gives particular attention to anti-Hegelianism, and to neo-Kantian idealism, but also makes brief reference to a number of currents of lesser importance. One of his most important points has to do with what might be called a time lag between the first elaboration of a philosophy and its coming to the intellectual forefront. The point is made in connection with the phenomenological method of Husserl (called the principal method of existentialism by several of the critics in Chapter I):

> se sabe que la fenomenología de Husserl data de 1900; y en vista de ello y de que a nosotros nos parece de extremada importancia, se tiende a pensar que la filosofía de los dos primeros decenios de este siglo era principalmente la fenomenología. Las cosas son algo distintas. ...[4]

Marías explains that as late as 1920, books on contemporary philosophy, adequate treatments, could be written without so much as a mention of phenomenology. Therefore, this philosophy was not *vigente,* or operative. It was not necessary to reckon with it. "Si se hubiera de buscar un término que expresara la vigencia común de la filosofía en los primeros años de nuestro siglo, habría que recurrir al de *criticismo.*"[5] But there is more than a common critical attitude: "La innovación capital que acontece a la filosofía es el haber parado su atención en la realidad de la *vida humana.*"[6] Marías remarks that it seems paradoxical that this theme, soon to be the first and at times exclusive philosophical preoccupation, should not have reached such importance until late in the 19th century. His following words may help to explain his avoidance of the term "existentialism":

---

[4] *Circunstancia y vocación,* p. 84.
[5] *Circunstancia y vocación,* p. 88.
[6] *Circunstancia y vocación,* p. 89.

> el descubrimiento de la vida humana como realidad y por
> tanto como problema filosófico ha venido oscurecido por el
> hecho de que se ha rehuído esa denominación desde los
> comienzos. Fue Kierkegaard, como es sabido, el que intro-
> dujo el término "existencia," alternando su sentido tradi-
> cional, para denominar la realidad de la vida humana.
> Quería apuntar con él al carácter de ser "una síntesis de
> lo infinito y lo finito, de lo eterno y lo temporal," pero el
> uso, ciertamente arbitrario, de esa expresión, cargada desde
> siempre de una significación bien distinta, ha enmascarado
> durante mucho tiempo en la mayor parte de la filosofía
> europea la vida que se había descubierto, la ha "encubierto,"
> a la vez. [7]

Thus Marías deplores the use of "existence" as arbitrary, charged
with different meaning(s), and concealing the true problem. He continues: "La cuestión no era simplemente de terminología: la deno-
minación es ya una intepretación, es el *escorzo* en que se presenta
una realidad." [8] This idea is not further developed, but it is clear
that Marías believes that words have a significance beyond the
semantic: they represent a point of view, or an interpretation of
the reality they represent. (Ortega's ideas on this subject were very
similar.)

Marías is well acquainted with modern and contemporary philosophy; he has written on "existencialismo en España"; and the
existential elements in his own writings are occasionally very striking. His complete and consistent avoidance of the word in any connection with Ortega must be assumed to be deliberate, and while
Marías may have other reasons for doing so in addition to those
above, the reasons already adduced seem a sufficient explanation.

However, changing the name does not mean that the reality under
discussion is different. This is implicity recognized by Marías in the
following excerpt, even though he is arguing against a use of any
except *le mot juste*:

> Pero aun en los casos en que no aparece (la vida) "disfra-
> zada" —bajo la especie de "conciencia," "voluntad," etc.—,
> aparece ya interpretada teóricamente desde ciertos puntos

---

[7] *Circunstancia y vocación*, pp. 89-90.
[8] *Circunstancia y vocación*, p. 90.

> de vista que impiden el acceso a su nuda realidad, precisa-
> mente a lo que Ortega descubrirá como "realidad radical,"
> *por debajo de todas las teorías.* [9]

The implication is clear: regardless of the name or the interpretation it implies, the underlying "radical reality," life, is the same. Thus, Marías's use of *vida* is essentially equivalent to the use of "existence" by the existentialists.

Following the Introduction, the book is divided into three major parts. The first deals with Ortega's family background, his youth, his education, his relation to his "circumstances." The second treats of the writer: matters of style, metaphor, literary *genre,* rhetoric, early themes. In the third, Marías begins to show the evolution of Ortega's philosophy, from his earliest writings through the *Meditaciones del Quijote.* The book stops just short of Ortega's "discovery" of *la razón vital,* to which Marías has devoted a book and several essays. Most of Ortega's later writings were covered in other works by Marías, with the exception of parts of the most recently published posthumous books.

Marías's biography of Ortega is excellent and detailed, with occasional familiar insights reflecting his long intimacy with the philosopher. Seen as a whole, the biography attempts, whether consciously or otherwise, to show Ortega's as the ideal life of the "life philosopher"—a life lived, in Ortega's words, at "the height of his times," "authentically," "historically "or "circumstantially." A few excerpts will serve to demonstrate: "Pocas cosas fueron indiferentes a Ortega. Su vida fue un continuo apasionamiento, y si se olvida esto no se la puede entender. El entusiasmo, la exigencia, la decepción, la confianza, rigieron y dominaron su vida." [10]

> Cuando algo o alguien le importaba —y casi todo lo
> que pasó cerca de él y entró en el área de su vida le im-
> portó entrañablemente—, se lo veía mirar con atención,
> lleno de tensa esperanza, afanoso de verlo cumplir su pro-
> mesa, con los ojos encandilados ante el acierto y la buena
> andadura. ... [11]

---

[9] *Circunstancia y vocación,* p. 90.
[10] *Circunstancia y vocación,* p. 162.
[11] *Circunstancia y vocación,* pp. 163-164.

The biographical section as a whole is entitled "Ortega y su circunstancia," with a second major part bearing the title, "La circunstancialidad del pensamiento orteguiano." Marías gives considerable emphasis to the importance of Spain and of being Spanish in Ortega's life, attitudes and thought. "Ortega se sintió desde su comienzo arraigado en España. No hay un solo momento en toda su obra en que desaparezca esa condición, en que se enfrente con la realidad desde 'fuera' de su circunstancia española." [12]

One's particular circumstances are the necessary beginning of philosophy or knowledge:

> Saber, en su sentido primario y radical, es "saber a qué atenerse" respecto a la realidad, y esto quiere decir respecto a la situación en que uno se encuentra; por tanto, sólo desde la circunstancia propia es esto posible. Esta idea lo acompaña (a Ortega) durante toda su vida.
> ... ...
> Por raza entiende Ortega una manera histórica de interpretar la realidad, una versión original de lo humano. Sólo aceptando la circunstancia se puede tener un conocimiento *real* y no utópico, abstracto; más aún: sólo en ella, radicándose en ella, se puede ser quien se es auténticamente. [13]

It is only through constant mental reference to Ortega's "raza" (nationality) and particular historical circumstances, says Marías, that one can understand Ortega's fight against provincialism, for example, as shown by his zeal for *europeización*.

The generation of '98 had been preoccupied with Spain as no other; as a generation it is identified by this theme. "Ortega es heredero de esta posición; en este punto, su actitud es 'cumulativa,' continuadora. ..." [14] Marías devotes many pages to Ortega's preoccupation with Spain, and its theoretical relevance to his philosophy. He notes, however, that the national circumstance is not the only or sufficient consideration for intellectual orientation: "por el carácter circunstancial de la realidad, la consideración de España es absolutamente insuficiente para entender España: 'Toda circunstancia

---

[12] *Circunstancia y vocación,* p. 175.
[13] *Circunstancia y vocación,* p. 176.
[14] *Circunstancia y vocación,* p. 178.

está encajada en otra más amplia'. ...." [15] This attitude, which Marías calls *pensar circunstancial,* is considered a cornerstone of Ortega's philosophy.

> Pensar —esto va a sentir desde el principio el joven Ortega— es precisamente afincarse en la circunstancia, hundirse en ella, usarla como instrumento para salvar nuestra propia realidad y así escapar a lo que esa misma circunstancia tiene de limitación y opresión. Sólo se libera uno de su propia circunstancia aceptándola, haciéndola funcionar como tal, convirtiéndola, de prisión que era, en recurso de liberación. [16]

The existentialist ring of these last words is unmistakable.

Many critics of Ortega have emphasized the importance of his studies in Germany, and some have accused him of being a germanophile, of lacking patriotism. Marías devotes some thirty pages to the subject of "Ortega y Alemania," beginning with a glance at the effect of German culture on Spain in the 19th century. He concludes that the idea that France was the only important cultural influence during this period is erroneous, though French influence was most significant. He emphasizes that Ortega's early "culture" was French, and points out that in some respects the influence was a continuing one. "Las más enérgicas influencias que se ejercen sobre el joven Ortega son sin duda Chateaubriand, Barrès y Renan," [17] says Marías. However, in most respects, Ortega later reacted against his early French formation: "Ortega vuelve a pedir *una introducción a la vida esencial*; es lo que no encuentra en Francia, que en lugar de lo esencial propone la *nuance,* en lugar de pan, *brioches.* España desde luego, pero Francia también, necesita otra cosa." [18]

The young Ortega came to feel that German culture was the only introduction to "la vida esencial," says Marías, adding Ortega's words "Pero esto no basta." Much of the remainder of the section is devoted to Ortega's experiences as a student in Germany, and to exaggerations or misinterpretations of Ortega's enthusiasm for

---

[15] *Circunstancia y vocación,* p. 179.
[16] *Circunstancia y vocación,* p. 187.
[17] *Circunstancia y vocación,* p. 200.
[18] *Circunstancia y vocación,* p. 203.

German culture, in preference to the "Mediterranean." Marías attempts to explain away these misinterpretations, and concludes with these words of Ortega's, followed by a final statement of his own:

> "Pero hay una forma de la cultura peculiar al Sur de Europa, un modo mediterráneo de amar a Dios, de contar los cuentos, de andar por las calles, de mirar a las mujeres y de decir que dos y dos son cuatro." No cabe duda de que Ortega, aunque no renunciara a lo germánico, lo hizo todo en su vida de este modo. [19]

In the following chapter, Marías continues to relate Ortega's life to his circumstances in the best existential manner:

> Ortega hace depender su programa juvenil de la situación española; es ella, si bien no ella *sola*, la que va a decidir "lo que hay que hacer" ... Ortega actúa mucho: como articulista, promotor de revistas nuevas, crítico, conferenciante, profesor. Todas esas actividades le parecen necesarias, solicitadas por la situación en que vive. [20]

Living "at the height of the times" can bring conflicts between the national circumstances and the larger (world) circumstances, but for Ortega the Spanish reality was always paramount:

> Cuando haya desnivel entre varias exigencias de "altura de los tiempos" —la suya personal, la de España, la general europea o incluso de Occidente—, Ortega optará por la española y a ella sacrificará las demás. Creo que este punto de vista ilumina extraordinariamente su biografía y la significación de su obra entera. [21]

Marías's message is clear: Ortega never failed to accept his Spanish circumstances or lived "inauthentically," but managed to transcend his situation by his acceptance of it. Be his intent as it may, the effect of Marías's version of Ortega's biography is completely existential.

---

[19] *Circunstancia y vocación*, p. 222.
[20] *Circunstancia y vocación*, p. 225.
[21] *Circunstancia y vocación*, p. 231.

Marías next turns to matters of style and aesthetics, to which he devotes some 100 pages. If it were not that he relates these closely to philosophical considerations, the material would be largely irrelevant. A very few excerpts will illustrate:

> La importancia del estilo literario viene de que es una manifestación —la más visible y patente— del estilo vital. Tiene un valor "fisiognómico," como la expresión de un rostro.
>
> ... ...
>
> En un filósofo, el estilo suele parecer secundario y casi irrelevante; creo exactamente lo contrario: el estilo —o su "ausencia" en ocasiones, que es una forma peculiar de estilo— es el supuesto básico de toda filosofía, pues en esa "instalación" y en ese "temple" se dan la primera vivencia y la primera interpretación de la realidad. ... [22]

Marías considers the literary *genres* employed by Ortega, affirming that he could have written poetry; his work is full of a "personal lyricism"—but he felt poetry "insufficiently justified" for him. As for novel and memoirs, the case is less clear-cut. From several references in his work, he believes that Ortega meant to write these. Marías points out several "novelistic characters" and themes which run through a number of Ortega's essays. However, Ortega confined himself to essays, and particularly to newspaper articles, because of a duty he felt to his public. Philosophical treatises and books, as such, he did not write; these are less accessible to the layman.

Marías analyzes several early literary and critical articles from the point of view of style and thesis, and relates many of the early themes and stylistic devices to Ortega's mature work, showing a consistency of thought and a persistent recurrence of similar philosophical preoccupations. This is very likely intended as a response to the many critics who have contended that Ortega had no system.

The section dealing with metaphor is interesting and very well done. Marías states that Ortega "hace una teoría filosófica de la metáfora" [23] and that the metaphor is for him a philosophic ex-

---

[22] *Circunstancia y vocación,* pp. 264-266.
[23] *Circunstancia y vocación,* p. 286.

pression of reality. It is, in other words, an interpretation of a given reality. From here Marías turns to Ortega's lectures "Las tres grandes metáforas," and while the entire argument is much too lengthy to follow here, he shows how this idea of the metaphor as an interpretation of reality is subsequently applied to philosophical systems. The "three great metaphors" are realism, idealism, and (much later) "vital reason."

In the last two-fifths of the book, Marías deals with Ortega's early literary and philosophical motivations and themes. The time span is from 1902 to 1914, but more particularly from 1908 to 1914. (The latter date is that of the publication of *Meditaciones del Quijote.*) Within a framework which at first appears descriptive, Marías's work is to a large extent interpretative. He emphasizes the interrelatedness of Ortega's juvenilia and mature work, and his overall object is to show how it all fits together to bring about the evolution of *la razón vital.* However, he points out the error of giving too much emphasis to early glimpses of later ideas:

> hablar del "pensamiento" de Ortega antes de 1914 es ya sumamente equívoco: no se puede llamar "pensamiento" de un autor a lo que piensa en cierto momento. Si Ortega hubiese muerto en 1913, nunca se hubiera podido hablar de su *pensamiento,* por ricas que fueran sus ideas juveniles. ... [24]

Marías feels that it is not without significance that Ortega's first important philosophical work was published in the year 1914. Ortega had just become thirty, the age at which, according to his own philosophy, "se inicia la actuación histórica *sensu stricto.*" [25] The time had come for him to begin independent action in the name of his generation and for himself.

> Pero hay otras razones de índole estrictamente teórica, que hay que tener en cuenta. En 1913 se publican dos libros, enormemente distintos y distantes, pero —y atender a esto es lo característico de la consideración histórica— muy próximos en la perspectiva vital de Ortega: las *Ideen*

---

[24] *Circunstancia y vocación,* p. 357.
[25] *Circunstancia y vocación,* p. 360.

de Husserl y *Del sentimiento trágico de la vida* de Unamuno. [26]

According to Marías, the *Ideen* means the theory of phenomenology, which he sees as "el idealismo de la *conciencia* pura." Unamuno's work is for Marías "la formulación más intensa y vibrante del irracionalismo, la oposición más apremiante, enérgica y aguda, entre la razón y la vida." [27] The impact between these precipitated Ortega's personal philosophy, in Marías's opinion. *La razón vital* is thus an attempt to synthesize the two opposites.

However, obviously there can be other interpretations of the importance of these two books for Ortega's philosophy. It will be remembered that phenomenology is the "method of existentialism"; it is *Del sentimiento trágico de la vida* which has led many critics to class Unamuno as an existentialist. A reader whose prime point of departure was human existence would not necessarily see the relationship between the two books as antithetical; rather his reaction might logically be an attempt to harmonize the two using life as the "radical reality," exactly as Ortega did.

It was intrinsically necessary from a theoretical point of view, says Marías, that Ortega begin his philosophy with a book of reflections on the *Quijote*. His argument to this effect may be abbreviated and summarized in his own words:

> 1)   Se trata de *saber a qué atenerse,* de alcanzar la orientación necesaria para poder vivir. ...
> 2)   Para ello hay que salir de sí mismo, recurrir de mí sólo a lo que Ortega va a llamar... *la circunstancia.* Esta circunstancia es primariamente España. ...
> 3)   España se hace inteligible en ciertas experiencias esenciales, y acaso la mayor es el *Quijote.* ... Y Cervantes es una plenitud española. ... [28]

Marías devotes a chapter to the idea of "circunstancia," and the meaning of the concept in Ortega's philosophy. He believes that the idea as used by Ortega is unique: "Que yo sepa, nunca había

---

[26] *Circunstancia y vocación,* p. 361.
[27] *Circunstancia y vocación,* p. 361.
[28] *Circunstancia y vocación,* pp. 374-375.

sido utilizado antes en filosofía, ni después lo ha sido sin referencia a Ortega o a sus continuadores." [29] He analyzes the philosophical antecedents of the concept, considering Comte's "milieu" and the same word as used by Taine; "environment" as used by William James; and "Umwelt" as used by a German biologist, Jakob von Uexküll, whose influence on Ortega he says was considerable. Actually none of these have any real relevance, and it is difficult to see why they were included. It should be evident to a critic of Marías's stature that the failure to find antecedents of a concept in the exact, literal translation proves little. He looked only for a word for word equivalence and not for similar *meanings*. Actually, Marías's main preoccupation is the demonstration that the prior users of the word "circumstance" or its exact translated equivalents were not sources for Ortega. In his desire to show Ortega's originality, he may have overlooked legitimate influences or sources of inspiration in writers who used similar concepts but different terms.

The concept of circumstance in Ortega is articulated along with that of perspective, a pairing which Marías considers essential. One must find for his individual circumstance the proper place in the world perspective. The classic antecedent of this idea, says Marías, is Leibniz, whom Ortega studied, along with Nietzsche's ideas on the same subject. The object of Marías's analysis of these two thinkers is likewise to show wherein Ortega is different from them and this portion seems to fall below his usual level of objectivity and excellence.

Finally returning to the idea of perspective in Ortega's philosophy, Marías concludes:

> En Ortega, la idea de perspectiva tiene otra radicalidad. Sin salir del nivel de las *Meditaciones del Quijote* y "Verdad y perspectiva," es decir, en torno a 1914-16, cuando por primera vez toma posesión filosófica de su intuición originaria, encontramos que la palabra "realidad" carece de sentido para nosotros fuera de la perspectiva en que se constituye y organiza, en que *es real*. Podemos decir que para Ortega *la realidad sólo existe como tal perspectivamente,* y en ello se funda la posibilidad de su verdad. [30]

---

[29] *Circunstancia y vocación,* p. 377.
[30] *Circunstancia y vocación,* p. 404.

Thus, reality has meaning only in the context of individual perspective, which is linked from the beginning with individual circumstances.

> Los dos conceptos que hemos analizado, circunstancia y perspectiva, son inseparables en la mente de Ortega, y en ello reside su fecundidad. ... Ambos son *aspectos* o ingredientes, acaso dimensiones, de una *realidad* superior desde la cual han de ser entendidos. ... Esa realidad es la *vida humana*. [31]

This seems to be very close to existentialist thought, and the comparison must certainly have come to Marías's mind, for a few lines later he hastens to add:

> Esto haría pensar que el pensamiento de Ortega es una forma de lo que se ha llamado "filosofía de la vida" o *Lebensphilosophie*. En la Introducción de este libro y en otros lugares me he referido con detalle a esta tendencia filosófica. Hay que advertir que Ortega nunca se ha vinculado a ella ni ha invocado su pertenencia, y más bien la ha nombrado en ocasiones como algo enteramente ajeno. Y, en efecto, la conexión de la filosofía orteguiana con la *Lebensphilosophie* es mínima; empezando porque lo que Ortega entiende por "vida" apenas tiene que ver con la "vida" o *Leben* de la *Lebensphilosophie*. [32]

Marías says that it would be a "methodological error" to talk further about this idea at present, and while there is some implication that he intends to do so at some more appropriate time, he does not return to the subject in the remainder of the volume. It should be noted also that his treatment of "life philosophy" in the Introduction is limited to a few lines, consisting largely in the reference to Kierkegaard already quoted. He continues:

> Quiero advertir ... para no perder de vista hacia dónde vamos, que la distancia entre la "vida" en Ortega y en la *Lebensphilosophie* es tal, que no se trata sólo de que tengan distintas ideas o interpretaciones de una realidad,

---

[31] *Circunstancia y vocación,* p. 405.
[32] *Circunstancia y vocación,* p. 406.

sino que designan realidades distintas; es decir, que no es que piensen cosas diferentes de la misma vida, sino que llaman así a realidades diversas. ... [33]

It is important to observe here, however, that Marías makes no comparison between what Ortega means by "vida" and what the so-called life philosophers mean by "existence," nor does he inquire whether they may be talking of the same reality under different names; he simply contends (with no proof) that they are not using a given word in the same sense:

> si se me apura, diría que la *Lebensphilosophie* no llama así a una *realidad* en sentido riguroso, sino a ciertas "interpretaciones" de las que parte, y que lo son, claro está, de algo que bajo ellas late y a lo cual indirectamente apuntan; ese algo es, efectivamente, la vida, pero ésta sólo se manifestará cuando se llegue a ella con un *método* adecuado, que estos pensadores no poseyeron nunca, por lo cual, cuando se dice que fueron los autores del "descubrimiento" de la vida, hay que hacer constar que, como las carabelas de Colón en su primer viaje, sólo descubrieron islas, indicios de un continente, pero no consiguieron poner pie en la *tierra firme.* Y vale la pena anticipar que la filosofía europea más reciente, por haberse originado en la tradición de esa "filosofía de la vida" y no haber llegado nunca al método adecuado, sigue sin haber trascendido esas interpretaciones para descubrir la vida humana en lo que tiene de realidad, en lo que Ortega llamará *realidad radical.* [34]

This is perhaps the weakest point of an otherwise excellent book, and contains several implicit contradictions of earlier ideas, both of Ortega and Marías. For example, in the section dealing with metaphor, Marías quoted Ortega's idea that metaphors are *interpretations* of reality, and that all words were originally metaphors. Therefore, if the "life philosophers" mean by "life," as Marías says, "certain interpretations of life" this is entirely consistent with Ortega's ideas. And Marías has explained only a few paragraphs earlier that perspective is one aspect or dimension of life. Perspective is inconceivable without interpretation. Granted that there may be

---

[33] *Circunstancia y vocación,* p. 406.
[34] *Circunstancia y vocación,* pp. 407-408.

some difference in meaning, but it is only a minor inflection; it does not add up to separate and distinct realities.

In his remarks on "method" Marías says that the "life philosophers" and their successors in the most recent European philosophy stopped short of real discovery because their methods were inadequate. Yet he himself has said that Ortega's method was phenomenological; and of the critics surveyed in Chapter I, those who wrote of methodology were unanimous in calling phenomenology the method of existentialism.

Marías at his best is a critic *par excellence,* and when he fails to make his case, it is a strong indication that the case is untenable in itself. Actually, even if his point were better taken, and the difference between Ortega's concept of "radical reality" and that of the other life philosophers were clearly shown, this would hardly be conclusive. The several existentialists have been most vocal in their insistence on their various differences, and critics as well have noted as much their differences as their similarities. But this does not alter the fact that there is an intellectual and philosophical reality designated by "existentialism." That there are different interpretations is by no means proof that nothing exists; it is simply proof that the reality in question has more than one side.

Marías obviously deplores the association with existentialism. A point in evidence is his scrupulous avoidance of even a single use of the word or its derivatives. Without inquiring into the reasons behind them, his motives are clear: he wants to separate Ortega as far as possible from any imputation of existentialist influence.

> Una prueba de lo que acabo de decir —la independencia entre la idea de la vida en Ortega y la *Lebensphilosophie—* y totalmente pertinente, porque se refiere precisamente a los comienzos, es el hecho decisivo de que Ortega *no llama al principio "vida" a la realidad que ha descubierto.* Si hubiese "partido" de la "filosofía de la vida," habría utilizado desde luego ese término. [35]

This proves only that in the beginning, Ortega was not using existentialism as a point of departure. It proves nothing about later

---

[35] *Circunstancia y vocación,* p. 407.

influences, and in fact strongly suggests the possibility that during the course of Ortega's search for a name for the "reality he had discovered," he was influenced by the same forces that influenced the existentialists.

In subsequent sections Marías discusses the meaning of "yo soy yo y mi circunstancia" and the use of phenomenological method (as well as various other theories of knowledge) in Ortega's early philosophy. Much is epistemological explanation, concerning the ideas of concept, recognition, intuition, and phenomenon. After considerable elaboration of the significance of the first part of the formula, "yo soy yo y mi circunstancia" in which he discusses the psychological reality of the ego, Marías returns to the idea of circumstances:

> Ortega insiste en que hemos de buscar para nuestra circunstancia, justamente en lo que tiene de limitada y peculiar, de concreta, individual e inmediata, "el lugar acertado en la inmensa perspectiva del mundo"; y en que, en lugar de extasiarnos ante valores hieráticos, conquistemos a nuestra *vida individual* su puesto oportuno —es decir, circunstancial— entre ellos. [36]

In this description of circumstance as limited, concrete, and individual, there is a striking resemblance to the existentialist concept of the individual's "historicity."

The ethical aspects of the philosophy emerge in a section entitled "Heroísmo y tragedia":

> El tema del heroísmo cruza persistente las *Meditaciones del Quijote*. Cuando Ortega habla de "el héroe" que avanza raudo y recto hacia una meta, no hay en ello narcisismo ni mera literatura, sino la insinuación de un tema intelectual de primer orden. "Todos, en varia medida, somos héroes" —agrega—; y en otro lugar: Nada impide el heroísmo —que es la actividad del espíritu— como considerarlo adscrito a ciertos contenidos específicos de la vida." Si esto es así, si todos somos héroes y el heroísmo no se limita a contenidos particulares de la vida, quiere decirse que

[36] *Circunstancia y vocación,* p. 431.

> Ortega llama heroísmo a una dimensión o carácter de toda
> vida humana. [37]

Being a hero, according to Ortega, consists in being oneself. This
being oneself consists in action, in projects—in becoming what one
is not, in contradistinction to what one is (in terms of custom, tradition, nature, society, history).

> Los muchos proyectos posbiles dependen de uno originario
> y radical; el de uno mismo. Es a sí mismo a quien proyecta
> el héroe; y ese proyecto implica los demás. Frente a las
> presiones exteriores de *lo otro,* la *mismidad* del héroe que
> quiere ser *él mismo* y hacer que de él emerjan sus actos.
> Es decir, el héroe es el hombre auténtico. Bajo la especie
> heroicidad introduce Ortega la idea de *autenticidad,* que
> acaba de definir con rigor; a ella se opone el abandono
> a la inercia y a las presiones colectivas, las diferentes
> formas de "socialización." [38]

These words could have been written by Heidegger himself. It is
possible that the similarity also struck Marías, for a few lines later,
in writing of the difficulties of living "authentically," he says:

> Resistencia e invención constituyen, pues, la autenticidad;
> son las dos caras de la vida auténtica, que para reivindicar
> su originalidad, el que los actos emerjan de su *mismidad,*
> necesita previamente librarse de las presiones y tentaciones
> del contorno social, de la costumbre, del hábito, de lo
> que hacen los demás, esto es, cualquiera (piénsese en lo que
> Heidegger llamará el *Man*). [39]

Clearly, Marías intends his comparison to apply only to the social
"other," which Ortega later calls the "hombre masa."

Since the hero is the person who wants to be himself, heroism
consists in an act of will, a decision. Ortega says the hero is "tragic"
in proportion to the extent he wishes to be himself, the extent to
which he resists giving up an "ideal part," or the "rôle" in life which
he has imagined for himself. "Ese yo auténtico consiste, pues, en

---

[37] *Circunstancia y vocación,* pp. 434-435.

[38] *Circunstancia y vocación,* p. 435.

[39] *Circunstancia y vocación,* p. 436.

ser proyecto, pretensión, programa vital, personaje novelesco, papel o *rôle*. Y todavía hay más; es esencial al héroe *querer* su trágico *destino*." [40] Marías explains that man does not choose his destiny, which is why it is destiny, but he has to decide whether or not he will accept it: "Tiene que elegir *serle o no fiel,* es decir, con las palabras mismas de Ortega, *quererlo o no*; y la consecuencia que extrae es que *es auténtico el que quiere su destino,* el que adhiere a sí mismo, el héroe." [41]

Again, Marías alludes indirectly to the resemblance between these ideas and the tenets of existentialism, without, however, ever naming that school of thought:

> Ortega llega a mayores precisiones, que anticipan —y salvando ciertos errores— la filosofía europea de los dos últimos decenios. El carácter de lo heroico "estriba en la *voluntad de ser lo que aún no se es*".... El héroe "anticipa el porvenir y a él apela".... A la vida humana en lo que tiene de más propio y auténtico, —que Ortega llama aquí heroísmo— pertenecen la *futurición* y el *utopismo*. ... [42]

In his summary, Marías obsessively returns to the idea that Ortega's ideas as first presented in *Meditaciones del Quijote* are not related to the "philosophy of life":

> Lo úncio que falta —y esto prueba que Ortega no partió de lo que entonces se llamaba "filosofía de vida" y que, como vemos, apenas nada tenía que ver con la suya— es este nombre, porque Ortega no había llegado aún a esa sencillez última que tanto se le ha reprochado y en que estriba su mayor profundidad. El modo de ser de la vida humana le resulta visible a Ortega en ciertas formas extremas de ella. ... Se le revela la estructura de la vida bajo la especie de la heroicidad o la tragedia. Realidad e irrealidad, modo de ser lo que todavía no es, vivir con medio cuerpo fuera de la realidad, pretender realizar un proyecto, querer ser *sí mismo,* ser auténticamente aquel que se ha de ser, porque libremente se ha elegido así, originalidad "práctica," "papel" o *rôle* en que el sujeto consiste, reabsorción

---

[40] *Circunstancia y vocación,* p. 437.
[41] *Circunstancia y vocación,* p. 437.
[42] *Circunstancia y vocación,* p. 438.

> de la circunstancia, realidad material e inerte y realidad
> ficticia de la voluntad proyectiva, destino libremente queri-
> do. Todo ello aparece en las *Meditaciones del Quijote*
> como teoría del héroe o del personaje trágico, no —todavía
> no— como *teoría de la vida humana.* [43]

This "filosofía de vida" had hardly anything to do with Ortega's,
says Marías—yet in his summary of themes in Ortega's philosophy,
even in its embryonic stage, almost everything mentioned is thoroughly existential.

The final chapter, entitled "Teoría de la realidad" has as its first
subdivision "El bosque como realidad vital." Marías begins with the
"Meditación preliminar" of *Meditaciones del Quijote,* which, while
appearing to be literary criticism, is actually a philosophic investigation, the description of a forest, "La Herrería" in the Escorial, well
known to Ortega. It is not a mere object, but a concrete reality
rooted in my life, says Ortega, so that I necessarily enter into the
description of the forest. Without me, there is no forest; even though
it is perfectly real and objective. Nor am I an ingredient or element
of the forest. But the forest needs me to be itself; to be the particular
forest it is.

"Los árboles no dejan ver el bosque" appears to be a joke, says
Marías, but it is the starting point. The few dozen trees immediately
around one are not the true forest; the real forest is composed of
invisible trees, "es una naturaleza invisible." [44] The adage is used
to illustrate Ortega's concept of reality, an objective reality which
nevertheless depends upon the subjective ego for its existence as
it is (an interpretation of reality). However, one is tempted to
question whether Marías also cannot see the forest for the trees, or
has not reached a total "circunstantial" perspective of Ortega's
thought due to his extreme familiarity with its individual components.

Continuing with the analysis of Ortega's theory of reality, Marías
states:

> No hay interpretación sin visión, ni visión sin interpretación.
> *La percepción es interpretativa y la interpretación es per-
> ceptiva.* Por eso lo que llamamos "cosas" son *interpreta-*

---

[43] *Circunstancia y vocación,* pp. 438-439.
[44] *Circunstancia y vocación,* p. 445.

ciones —se entiende, de la realidad. ... Recordemos que para Ortega "el ser definitivo del mundo no es materia ni es alma, no es cosa alguna determinada, sino una perspectiva." [45]

Marías continues for some forty more pages, analyzing Ortega's use of "verdad y razón," and the meaning of "culture": *"La vida es el texto eterno. ... La cultura* —arte o ciencia o política— *es el comentario."* [46] These ideas are preliminary to the articulation of Ortega's much mentioned theory of "vital reason." A large part of Marías's interpretive work has been devoted to showing how this theory evolved from its earlier "anticipations" in Ortega's writing. He concludes:

> *Ortega ha puesto en marcha la razón vital* en la investigación sobre la vida humana y la realidad en general que hemos examinado paso a paso. La teoría es intrínsecamente *dramática,* según vimos al considerar sus requisitos. Tiene que ser *circunstancial,* entendida esta noción en un sentido *biográfico,* por una parte, y por otra *real* y no meramente intencional, lejos, pues, de todo pensar utópico y abstracto. Esa teoría sólo se constituye en una *perspectiva,* frente a la imagen vigente de ella. ... En Ortega toda visión es perspectiva y ésta se justifica por ser la condición misma de la realidad, pues la *realidad sólo existe como tal perspectivamente.* El destino concreto del hombre, la condición, por tanto, de la vida, es la *reabsorción de la circunstancia,* su humanización mediante un proyecto, su *aprehensión* mediante un sistema de *conexiones,* gracias al instrumento del *concepto,* dentro del *sistema de las realidades.* Pero esto es *razón,* y esa razón no es cosa distinta de la vida, es la vida misma en la función de aprehender la realidad ligando "cosa a cosa y todo a nosotros." Esto es lo que quiere decir *razón vital,* al menos en el momento de su descubrimiento y puesta en ejercicio. [47]

Thus what Marías conceives as the meaning of "razón vital" comes close to embracing all of the concepts of Ortega's philosophy

---

[45] *Circunstancia y vocación,* pp. 450-451.
[46] *Circunstancia y vocación,* p. 482.
[47] *Circunstancia y vocación,* p. 496.

at the time of its "discovery," and the concepts with which it is elaborated read like a glossary of existentialist terms.

Filosofía actual y existencialismo en España (published originally as two separate volumes) contains two chapters which refer to Ortega: "Vida y razón en la filosofía de Ortega" and "La génesis de la razón vital." He also writes on Unamuno, Zubiri, and García Morente, among others, the latter two being mentioned by some critics as disciples of Ortega. Most of what Marías has to say of these is pure exposition and must be omitted here in the interests of coherence.

Marías protests what he considers an indiscriminate use of the existentialist label:

> Desde 1900, aproximadamente, con antecedentes en el siglo pasado, la filosofía está alterando sus supuestos, sus temas e incluso su propio sentido. Esta mudanza tiene tan gran volumen, que su evidencia se impone aun a los menos perspicaces; pero cuando se trata de precisar lo que realmente sucede, y desde cuándo y dónde está sucediendo, la claridad suele ser menor. Se aplican promiscuamente los nombres de *filosofía existencial,* o *filosofía de la vida* a movimientos intelectuales absolutamente dispares y que apenas tienen puntos de contacto; se suele agregar que se trata de "irracionalismo," se la considera con frecuencia como antropología y se llega a afirmar que su objeto único es el hombre existente, a pesar de que el propio Heidegger advierte al comienzo de su libro capital que el tema de su investigación es el problema del sentido del ser. ... [48]

In the first part of this double volume, *Filosofía actual,* Marías makes it clear that he wishes to deal with Ortega's philosophy as separate and apart from the problem of existentialism: "No es de este lugar ni de esta hora entrar en el tema. Me interesa sólo precisar la génesis de algunas ideas de Ortega, capitales dentro de su filosofía." [49] Here again he wants to show how Ortega's mature ideas are anticipated in his earlier work, with the object of establishing

---

[48] Julián Marías, *Filosofía actual y existencialismo en España* (Madrid, 1955), pp. 257-258. Hereafter referred to as *Filosofía actual.*
[49] *Filosofía actual,* p. 258.

the priority of "discovery" by Ortega of certain ideas claimed by the existentialists, and particularly credited to Heidegger:

> Porque la prioridad de los descubrimientos orteguianos sobre los espléndidos desarrollos posteriores de esos mismos hallazgos o de otros simplemente afines es indudable y de fácil comprobación, aunque se dé el caso peregrino de que, precisamente entre los círculos más hostiles a Heidegger, en nuestro país, se procure desvirtuar esa prioridad para atribuirla a ese filósofo. [50]

As examples of such "prior discoveries" Marías mentions Ortega's "soy yo y mi circunstancia" which he says "puede valer como mínima expresión del núcleo de la filosofía de Ortega" and refers to "Adán en el Paraíso" as containing an earlier expression of the idea of "la vida como un 'hacerse.'" [51] It should be noted here that while Marías is concerned with demostrating Ortega's originality (or that he was not "influenced," especially by Heidegger, in the inception of these ideas) he is inadvertently emphasizing the similarity between Ortega's ideas and those of the existentialists.

Perhaps he is not unaware of this tendency of his argument, for later on he remarks: "La filosofía de Heidegger y la de Ortega son coetáneas y las dos están, por supuesto, a la *altura de los tiempos*. Esto basta para explicar su afinidad, que, por cierto, no pasa de afinidad." [52]

The prologue to *El existencialismo en España* may give some clue to how Marías uses the word "existencialismo" — on the limited number of occasions he uses it and its derivatives: "el mundo se ha llenado de novelas que *ahora* se llaman existenciales, y que responden en una u otra medida a los caracteres que descubrí en las de Unamuno en el nuevo género que bauticé, en 1938, con el nombre de novela existencial o personal." [53] Marías elsewhere refers to the "novela existencial o personal de Unamuno" so that it appears that the two terms are equivalent.

---

[50] *Filosofía actual,* p. 258.
[51] *Filosofía actual,* p. 258.
[52] *Filosofía actual,* p. 276.
[53] *Filosofía actual,* p. 20.

With regard to existentialism as such, Marías has this to say: "En cuanto al existencialismo, de linaje kierkegaardiano, desarrollado sobre todo durante el último cuarto de siglo, parece la filosofía del futuro, en todo caso la del presente." [54] However, he does not believe that this is true of Spain: "En España hay ciertamente neo-tomismo... Pero no hay existencialismo. ¿Cuales pueden ser las razones de esta ausencia?" [55] In an apparent effort to answer this question, Marías shows the acquaintance of Unamuno, Ortega, Zubiri, and Gaos with Kierkegaard, Heidegger and Dilthey, but particularly emphasizes the differences between them. These differences lead him to observe:

> Existencialismo es una palabra bastante equívoca; algunos de sus representantes más inteligentes y más responsables —Gabriel Marcel, por ejemplo— no la encuentran ya cómoda y prefieren evitarla. Tal vez su significación va a restringirse y se va a designar con ese nombre la posición filosófica que plantea el problema fundamental como una cuestión de prioridad de la existencia sobre la esencia —es decir, en términos demasiado escolásticos y que renuncian a renovar realmente la metafísica, a ir al fondo del problema; con demasiada frecuencia, las actitudes de mayores pretensiones revolucionarias, al aceptar el planteamiento de la cuestión y, simplemente, darle la vuelta, se convierten en lo que llamé una vez *ontologie traditionnelle à rebours,* ontología tradicional —escolástica o fenomenológica— a contrapelo. [56]

This is as close as Marías ever comes to dealing directly with the question of existentialism. Even in this book whose title indicates the likelihood of more extensive analysis. Marías limits himself to his oft-repeated criticism of the ambiguity of the term. In his speculation about the possible future restriction in the use of "existentialism" Marías maneuvers to give the word a definition which makes it feasible for him to show the absence of this type of existentialism in Spain.

---

[54] *Filosofía actual,* p. 26.
[55] *Filosofía actual,* p. 26.
[56] *Filosofía actual,* p. 45.

Returning to the issue of differences between contemporary existentialists, Marías searches for a common denominator: "En todo caso hay algunos rasgos comunes a la mayoría de las tendencias, y sobre todo el carácter descriptivo y puramente fenomenológico, cuyo aspecto negativo es cierto irracionalismo." [57] This, he feels, is sufficient to distinguish the Spanish philosophers as distinct and separate: "Frente a esto, la metafísica de Ortega, y toda corriente de pensamiento que la toma como punto de partido, se define esencialmente por el uso del método de la razón vital." [58] The long chapter which follows, "Ortega y la idea de la razón vital," was published separately as a book under the same name, and will be treated later. For Marías, the area of greatest emphasis in Ortega's philosophy is "la razón vital."

Ensayos de teoría [59] is a collection of essays, most of which contain some reference to Ortega but Ortega is not the principal subject. "Los géneros literarios en la filosofía" clearly shows the influence of Ortega's ideas and could be considered ancillary to some of Ortega's studies of aesthetics. "La razón en la filosofía actual" champions Ortega's "razón vital" against other current thinking.

In *Sur* Marías protests the many misinterpretations of Ortega.

> ¿Cuántos han dedicado a la lectura, relectura y meditación de los escritos de Ortega la cuarta parte de la atención, tiempo y agudeza que parece normal invertir en el estudio de Hegel, Dilthey, Bergson, Husserl o Heidegger? ¿Cuántos de los que *escriben* sobre Ortega y lo "superan" se atreverían a afrontar un examen sobre el contenido efectivo de la doctrina orteguiana? [60]

Almost everything one reads *about* Ortega, says Marías, is perfectly useless if not misleading, and suggests a complete lack of acquaintance with the subject. Most of the article is dedicated to an investigation of the reasons for these misinterpretations of Ortega. Paradoxically, the first reason is that Ortega *wanted* to be undertood,

---

[57] *Filosofía actual,* p. 46.
[58] *Filosofía actual,* p. 46.
[59] Julián Marías, *Ensayos de teoría* (Barcelona, 1954).
[60] Julián Marías, "El futuro de Ortega", *Sur,* No. 241 (July-August, 1956), 16-17.

and hence did not write in cryptic formulas or neologisms. Because of his extreme accessibility he has been read only superficially instead of receiving the study due. Second, Marías blames the lack of any "technical" philosophic tradition in Spain, which would provide a critical background for understanding and appreciating the philosopher. However, the most important explanation of the widespread failure to understand Ortega is his uniqueness:

> Pero hay otra razón, y ésta es la decisiva, que explica la posición singular del fenómeno histórico de Ortega. Y es que en él han hecho nuestros pueblos y nuestra lengua la *experiencia plena* de la filosofía... una interpretación *filosófica española* del mundo, no la ha habido hasta Ortega. ... Ortega ha iniciado una esencial posibilidad hispánica: nuestro ingreso *histórico* en la filosofía. [61]

In an article written in *Insula* entitled "Realidad y ser en la filosofía española," Marías discusses the relationship between Unamuno and Ortega. His consideration is limited to the former's *Del sentimiento trágico de la vida* and the latter's *Meditaciones del Quijote*. He sees the first as "forcing" the second. "Ortega no puede esperar más para *llegar* a su descubrimiento de la razón vital, provocando, alumbrado por la exasperante iluminación de las chispas que Unamuno arrancaba." [62]

Writing for the *Revista de ciencias sociales* Marías envisions *El hombre y la gente* as a second part of *La rebelión de las masas*. He says that sociology for Ortega is a theory of society, of collective life, but cannot be understood if we do not understand clearly what "life" means:

> La teoría de la "vida" colectiva no es sino un capítulo de la teoría general de la vida humana, la cual es la mía, es decir, vida individual o personal, hasta el punto de que es problemático en qué sentido puede llamarse vida a la que no sea —como la colectiva o la histórica—. Si queremos hacer sociología, si pretendemos saber *qué es* la sociedad, tenemos que preguntarnos por la "vida" colectiva

---

[61] Marías, "El futuro de Ortega," pp. 18-19.
[62] Julián Marías, "Realidad y ser en la filosofía española," *Insula,* X (Sept. 1955), 1.

y social, y esto nos remite a la teoría de la vida humana —a esa doctrina sobre la vida humana nombrada al final de *La rebelión de las masas*— la cual es ni más ni menos que la metafísica. [63]

The above passage is of considerable theoretical importance since it relates *La rebelión de las masas* to Ortega's metaphysics, even though Marías does not show here in what way it is related. In the following pages we have an indication that Marías is using "metaphysics" in a peculiar sense. Referring to *El hombre y la gente,* he says: "Toda la primera parte de este libro es metafísica estricta, teoría de la vida humana." [64]

Lest this "theory of human life" be interpreted as existentialism, however, Marías hastens to add:

> El lector atento podrá ver con claridad total lo que Ortega con frecuencia insinuó y otros hemos dicho taxativamente muchas veces —que se trata de algo bien distinto del existencialismo, en ocasiones opuesto. Para Ortega, por cierto, "existir" significa asomar, brotar, surgir; sugiere que sea originariamente un vocablo de lucha y beligerancia que designa "la situación vital en que súbitamente aparece, se muestra o hace aparente, entre nosotros ... un enemigo que nos cierra el paso con energía, esto es, nos resiste y se afirma o hace firme a sí mismo ante y contra nosotros. En el existir va incluido el resistir, y por tanto, el afirmarse el existente si nosotros pretendemos suprimirlo, anularlo, o tomarlo como irreal. Por eso lo existente o surgente es realidad, ya que realidad es todo aquello con que ... tenemos que contar. ... [65]

The "attentive reader" will also see clearly that Marías has not made his case. Whether or not "existir" was used by Ortega with the connotations Marías suggests in no way proves that his "teoría de la vida humana" is completely distinct from existentialism. Marías is playing with semantics, and has implicitly disproved his point

---

[63] Julián Marías, "*El hombre y la gente*: el lugar de la teoría de la vida social en la filosofía de Ortega," *Revista de ciencias sociales,* I (March 1957), 414.

[64] Marías, "*El hombre y la gente...*," p. 416.

[65] Marías, "*El hombre y la gente...*," p. 416.

when he says "the existent is reality" for he has stated in many places that for Ortega life is the "radical reality." For example: "La realidad radical es aquélla en que radican los demás... era muy dudoso que en la mente de Ortega pudiera haber realidad superior a la vida humana, tal vez ni siquiera *otra* que ella." [66] Logically, therefore, the three terms, "life," "radical reality," and "existent" or its derivatives must have been used in an equivalent sense by Ortega, at least occasionally.

Marías next tries to show that there is no affinity between Ortega and Jean-Paul Sartre:

> Según Ortega, importa más que la filosofía nuestra sensa-
> ción cósmica. Al acabar la primera meditación de sus *Me-*
> *ditaciones del Quijote,* hablaba Ortega de una "emoción
> telúrica que se filtraba" en su ánimo; su corazón estaba
> "lleno de asombro y de ternura por lo maravilloso que es
> el mundo." De esta "sensación cósmica" ha nacido la filo-
> sofía de Ortega. ¿No podía preverse que ésta tendría poco
> que ver con aquella otra nacida de un temple para el cual
> todo lo real "está de más" ("de trop") y suscita la náusea? [67]

While no names are mentioned, the reference to Sartre is obvious. It is made in a general way, however, so that it may be taken to apply to all of existentialism, particularly by an uninitiated reader. It may be granted that there are points of divergence, and even opposition, between Ortega and individual existentialists, but also among the existentialists themselves.

If Marías really wants to prove that Ortega's philosophy "has little to do" with "that other" philosophy, he should consider each in its totality, rather than emphasizing semantic differences, or differences in personality between the various writers.

This article does not follow Ortega's "teoría metafísica" as set forth in *El hombre y la gente*; rather Marías wishes to indicate only the "localización o radicación de la sociedad en la realidad, y por tanto de la sociedad en el sistema de Ortega." [68] The concepts of "truth," "loneliness," "circumstance" or "world," "doing," "choice,"

---

[66] Marías, "*El hombre y la gente...*," p. 415.
[67] Marías, "*El hombre y la gente...*," p. 416.
[68] Marías, "*El hombre y la gente...*," p. 417.

"freedom," "responsibility" are most relevant in the first chapters. Life is a dialogue between Man and World, a dramatic event in which both elements are equally primary and necessary. In this perspective Ortega makes a theoretical attempt to derive from human life (radical loneliness) the Other. Marías makes no mention of it, but the similarity between these ideas and the major themes of existentialism is most striking.

> La vida humana, por ser intransferible, esencialmente es soledad, *radical soledad*.
> Quedarse solo es quedarse solo de los demás. Y lo más humano, lo propiamente humano, es *esa* radical soledad. El tema de la soledad domina todo este libro en que se pone —por fin— en claro qué es la sociedad y qué es la gente. "Sólo en nuestra soledad somos nuestra verdad" dice Ortega.
> ... ...
> Desde ese fondo de soledad constante que es nuestra vida, emergemos constantemente en un ansia, no menos radical, de compañía. [69]

The theme of the book is a demonstration of what happens to man in and with *social* reality. Life is "pseudo-hacer" because we are in a world of irresponsible interpretation of others, people, and can only have an authentic life in our own life as "radical soledad." The retirement to this "radical loneliness" is known as philosophy.

María next analyzes Ortega's idea of *vida personal*. We do not give it to ourselves, but find it when we find ourselves. We have to choose *within* our circumstances, but we do not choose our world. Here, too, the affinity with existentialism is plain even in Marías's interpretation—and there is no reason to suppose that he wishes to give an existentialist flavor to Ortega's words.

"Al partir, dice Ortega, de la vida como realidad radical, saltamos más allá de la milenaria disputa entre idealistas y realistas. Hombre y mundo son igualmente reales, no menos primariamente uno que otro." [70] It will be remembered that in the conclusion to Chapter I it was mentioned that all of the existentialists considered used

---

[69] Marías, "*El hombre y la gente...*," pp. 417-418.
[70] Marías, "*El hombre y la gente...*," p. 419.

individual existence as their point of departure, and all of them found traditional idealism and realism equally untenable.

> Partiendo de la corporeidad del hombre muestra que es nuestro cuerpo quien hace que sean cuerpos todos los demás y que lo sea el mundo. El hombre es "alguien que está en un cuerpo." ... Por eso el hombre es espacial, está en un sitio, consignado a un *aquí*. Esto lleva Ortega a la teoría de la general "localización." [71]

Although Marías does not mention it, this is also the logical origin of Ortega's perspectivism. Here he is concerned particularly with existence and co-existence. Man is spatial, and the world is spatial; however, "nuestra relación pragmática con las cosas, aun siendo corporal, no es material, sino dinámica." [72] "El Otro" is one who co-exists, for whom I exist and co-exist, and who responds reciprocally. As Ortega would say, it is not that there is a certain "tú" who is an alter ego, but rather I am an "alter tú." .

Marías points out that Ortega makes an important distinction between the ideas of "inter-individual" and "social":

> Ortega descubre lo social en el fenómeno de los *usos*. El uso es lo que *se* hace, *se* dice, *se* piensa, etcétera. El sujeto de lo que *se* hace es la *gente*. La sociedad, la gente, son *desalmadas*, lo humano sin el hombre, lo humano sin espíritu, sin alma, deshumanizado. [73]

Marías does not deal with the second half of *El hombre y la gente* in the above article.

Another volume by Marías, *La escuela de Madrid*, contains little that has not been published in other places. It is a reprinting of all the material in *Filosofía actual y existencialismo en España*, plus several articles published shortly after Ortega's death in various periodicals which printed *homenajes*, and the article just considered above. "Ortega: historia de una amistad," "Ortega, amigo de mirar," and "El hombre Ortega" are tributes to Marías's teacher and friend,

---

71 Marías, "*El hombre y la gente*...," p. 420.
72 Marías, "*El hombre y la gente*...," p. 420.
73 Marías, "*El hombre y la gente*...," p. 421.

and were never intended as literary or philosophical criticism. "La metafísica de Ortega" begins with a distinction between *realidad radical* and *realidades radicales,* but soon turns (as Marías seems almost inevitably to do) to *la razón vital.* [74] Detailed examination of this can be omitted here, because Marías has written on this theme at greater length in many other places.

"Vieja y nueva política: el origen de la sociología de Ortega" has an almost self-explanatory title. Written while *El hombre y la gente* was in press, its chief importance is as another example of Marías's systematizing of Ortega's writings. It shows the origin of Ortega's ideas of *generaciones, usos, masas,* and *minorías* in *Vieja y nueva política* (1914) and ties them to *La Rebelión de las Masas* (1930), theorizing that *El hombre y la gente* is the "second part" of *La Rebelión de las Masas* which Ortega planned for many years to write. [75]

"Conciencia y realidad ejecutiva: La primera superación orteguiana de la fenomenología" is the only portion of *La escuela de Madrid* theoretically relevant to the problem at hand. Marías shows that in the same year in which Husserl's major work of phenomenological theory was published, Ortega wrote three articles explaining and discussing it. He quotes at great length from Ortega's early exposition of Husserl's idea, paying particular attention to the words used by Ortega. The following paragraph summarizes both Marías's intent and his conclusions:

> De toda esta cita sólo me interesa aquí subrayar que Ortega emplea en ella cuatro veces la palabra *ejecutivo,* precisamente como lo opuesto a lo meramente "espectacular," a lo "puesto entre paréntesis," es decir, a lo fenomenológicamente reducido. Sólo sobre este telón de fondo se entiende plenamente un texto orteguiano que, hasta donde llegan mis noticias, no ha sido nunca interpretado desde este punto de vista, y que contiene, a mi modo de ver, la primera superación de la fenomenología y de la idea de conciencia. [76]

Ortega y tres antípodas, subtitled "Un ejemplo de intriga intelectual," is primarily polemical in nature. It is Marias's "answer"

---

[74] Julián Marías, *La escuela de Madrid* (Buenos Aries, 1959), pp. 237-245.
[75] Marías, *La escuela de Madrid,* pp. 265-272.
[76] Marías, *La escuela de Madrid,* p. 259.

to the following books: Joaquín Iriarte, *Ortega y Gasset. Su persona y su doctrina* (Madrid, 1942), José Sánchez Villaseñor, *José Ortega y Gasset. Pensamiento y trayectoria* (México, 1943), and by the same author, *La crisis del historicismo y otros ensayos* (México, 1945), Juan Roig Gironella, *Filosofía y vida. Cuatro ensayos sobre actitudes* (Barcelona, 1946), Joaquín Iriarte, *La ruta mental de Ortega* (Madrid, 1949). The first of the two books by Sánchez Villaseñor has been translated to English with the title *Ortega y Gasset. Existentialist. A Critical Study of His Thought and its Sources.* (This was the only example found of a title linking Ortega's name with existentialism.) This book (available only in translation) will be dealt with apart from the study of Marías because of its treatment of existentialism, but Marías's rebuttal of Sánchez Villaseñor is entirely adequate. Of the other books, all except Roig Gironella's were inspected, and it has been decided, in view of our complete agreement with Marías's remarks, to omit them from any specific examination in this study.

Marías notes that the above books are all dedicated, "exclusiva o principalmente a intentar explicar que Ortega no es un filósofo." [77] He finds this very strange, noting: "Pasan de dos mil millones los hombres que no son filósofos —contando sólo los vivientes— y no parece menester insistir especialmente sobre ello..." [78]

The books in question are all written by clerics, and their bias is easily demonstrable. Marías calls it the "will to misunderstand." His major case in point is the practice followed by all three of quoting out of context. He writes a short, tongue-in-cheek theoretical treatise called "El arte de citar" pointing out that it has always been the practice in critical writing to consider the context of a quotation, or the definition of a concept. Most of the volume is devoted to a book-by-book examination of the writings of Ortega's "antípodas" and a demonstration that they are based on misquoting, quoting out of context, or a complete lack of first-hand acquaintance with Ortega's works. Marías's tone is less academic than in some of his later writing, but his work is no less scholarly. It is an admirable piece of criticism, and further examination of it is here omitted only

---

[77] Julián Marías, *Ortega y tres antípodas* (Madrid, 1951), p. 13.
[78] Marías, *Ortega y tres antípodas,* p. 13.

because it deals primarily with misunderstandings of Ortega rather than with Ortega himself.

El método histórico de las generaciones (Madrid, 1949) is a collection of twelve lectures in which Marías attempts to put Ortega's theory of generations in its "just perspective." The first several deal with the theme of generations in literature (beginning with the Bible) and in the 19th century, and Ortega is not even mentioned. Another major portion of the book deals with the vicissitudes of the idea of generations in our century, in which connection Marías summarizes the use of the concept by at least eight historical and sociological theorists. Thus very little of the book is actually devoted to Ortega, although the title suggests that his philosophy is the major object of discussion. Of the portion strictly concerned with this part of Ortega's work, much is simply a chronological listing of the places where the idea of generations is mentioned, while much more consists of lengthy quotations in accordance with the chronology so established. Probably the principal worth of the book lies in the comparative survey of various theories of generations, rather than in its utility as an instrument for understanding Ortega. Ortega's own exposition of his theory is briefer and at least as simple as Marías's explanation of it.

Ortega y la idea de la razón vital is probably the work which its author would consider his single most important critical contribution to the understanding of Ortega. It has been published several times subsequently as part of other volumes, and has come to form the core of Marías's interpretation of Ortega's thought. As is clear in *Ortega, I, Circunstancia y vocación,* and a number of other writings, Marías believes "vital reason" is Ortega's greatest and most personal "discovery."

The first third of the book is introductory in nature and treats Ortega's biography and intellectual formation. Marías then gives some background for the long-standing philosophic conflict between realism and idealism, in order to emphasize the relevance of Ortega's contribution, of which he remarks:

> La filosofía de Ortega se presenta, en una de sus dimensiones, como una superación del realismo y del idealismo. Como deseo, la cosa es relativamente antigua, e incluso se ha intentado algunas veces; pero, en general, no se ha

abandonado el idealismo sino para recaer en el realismo, agregando a éste ciertas restricciones cautelosas, o bien se ha tratado de recuperar la objetividad sin salir de la tesis idealista. En rigor, realismo e idealismo no han llegado a ser ideas de la realidad, sino sólo ideas distintas acerca de la primacía de unas realidades respecto de otras. [79]

Ortega's revolutionary discovery is not of ego or circumstances, or a third thing combining them, says Marías, but a completely new concept of reality:

Ortega no se limita a mostrar que la realidad primaria no es ni las cosas ni el yo, sino que aquello que descubre como realidad radical no es una tercera cosa, sino algo que no es *cosa*; esto es, la innovación de Ortega es esencialmente una nueva idea de la realidad, desde la cual resulta visible la porción de error y de verdad del realismo y del idealismo, y la constitutiva limitación e insuficiencia de ambos. [80]

Both realism and idealism are seen as *partial* perspectives, representing truth insofar as it is visbile to their limited vision. But errors have been made by both because of this limitation, and the situation can only be resolved from a "more radical" point of view which shows the truth and error of each.

"Y esto conduce, por último, a una nueva concepción de la filosofía y aun del conocimiento en todas sus formas, definida por su función y su justificación en la vida humana." [81] This new conception of philosophy, which is also a new method, is "vital reason." Philosophy does not have a method, says Marías, but *is* a method, a way to reality. Thus, he refers to both "la teoría de la razón vital" and "el método de la razón vital" in much the same sense.

The critic states that he does not plan to attempt any exposition of Ortega's metaphysics for the simple reason that at the time of his writing, the books which contain the "systematic elaboration"

---

[79] Julián Marías, *Ortega y la idea de la razón vital* (Madrid, 1948), p. 29. Hereafter referred to as *Razón vital*.

[80] *Razón vital*, p. 30.

[81] *Razón vital*, p. 31.

of Ortega's metaphysical ideas have not yet been published. (Apparently Marías believed that the books had been written already in 1948; some still remain unpublished.)

Marías limits himself to explaining the "nucleus" of the idea of vital reason, therefore, and does so in terms that are strikingly similar to those of existentialism. "La vida es —dice Ortega— 'lo que hacemos y lo que nos pasa'; se entiende, lo que hacemos y los que nos pasa a cada uno de nosotros; la vida es *mía*, es siempre la de cada cual, y ésta, mi vida, es la realidad radical." [82] Life is given, not finished and complete but as a task or problem; "la vida no son las cosas, no es cosa alguna, sino lo que yo hago con las cosas." [83]

Not every activity is "un *hacer*"; it must be done because of something and for some purpose. Life is *drama,* for each man has to decide each instant what he is going to do, what he is going to be in the following.

> ¿Qué es lo que decide, lo decisivo? Una pre-tensión, un proyecto vital de cada uno de nosotros, previo a nuestra vida. La vida es, suele repetir Ortega, faena poética. Yo tengo que inventar o imaginar antes el que voy a ser; se entiende, el que voy a intentar ser en vista de esa circunstancia en que me ha tocado vivir. [84]

Marías explains what is meant by "circumstance" but since his ideas on this have already been examined in considerable detail in connection with *Circunstancia y vocación,* they need not be repeated.

Having explained what Ortega means by reality or "vida" Marías turns to his concept of reason. After purpusing the question for a time, he concludes that what Ortega means by reason is not "pure reason."

> Esto implica una nueva idea de la razón, conexa con la nueva idea de la realidad. Visto desde la vida, el racionalismo resultaba insostenible; la filosofía optó, en consecuencia, por el irracionalismo; pero esa disyuntiva no es

---

[82] *Razón vital,* p. 35.
[83] *Razón vital,* p. 36.
[84] *Razón vital,* p. 37.

inevitable. La razón pura era la razón abstracta, es decir, la razón que abstrae de la concreción circunstancial de la vida y piensa las cosas como absolutas y *sub specie aeterni*; pero si la realidad radical es la vida, toda visión real de las cosas es desde ella, en su perspectiva concreta. [85]

Perspective is one of the components of reality; everything must be seen from some specific point of view. The world is not an abstract world, and no perspective of it is an abstract perspective.

La razón no es una consideración abstracta de las cosas *sub specie aeterni,* sino su aprehensión conceptual dentro de mi vida, en la perspectiva concreta en que se constituyen como realidades; es una forma y función de la vida, y *el tema de nuestro tiempo* consiste en someter la razón a la vitalidad. En suma "la razón pura tiene que ser sustituida por una razón vital." [86]

Marías gives many examples of the function of perspective, and further illustrates what is meant by vital reason, but does not substantially alter the interpretation of the idea as presented above. One of the more important points relates vital reason to "historical reason," which might equally well be called "circumstantial reason." It is used in much the same sense as vital reason (although some critics have thought the concepts were separate and distinct); however, historical reason may be more specifically concrete with reference to particular individual circumstances, while vital reason includes the possibility of generalization of the same principle.

The last section of *Ortega y la idea de la razón vital* is entitled "Los problemas de la vida colectiva" and is in large measure devoted to an explanation of Ortega's use of mass and minority or elite, the distinction between *inter-individual* and *social, hombre* and *gente* and what is meant by *usos.* This has all been covered earlier in connection with other of Marías's writings. Its relevance in this context is summed up in the phrase "Vivir es convivir" which implicitly suggests the ethical ramification of *la razón vital* although no detailed investigation is made.

---

[85] *Razón vital,* p. 43.
[86] *Razón vital,* p. 44.

Structurally a part of the book, but intrinsically a postcript is a short section subtitled "La razón vital como posibilidad" in which Marías speculates about the philosophic future of vital reason. This is the only part of the book in which he refers to existentialism, and it is to voice his usual lament that the word is inexact, misleading, and covers a multitude of evils:

> En efecto, la casi totalidad de lo que hoy se hace en filosofía bajo la rúbrica de lo que se suele llamar "existencialismo." Es claro que esta palabra, que un día tuvo algún sentido, si bien nunca muy preciso, apenas quiere decir ya nada, y una elemental higiene mental aconseja evitarla. [87]

Marías concedes that the thought of Europe which is opposed to existentialism is "formalmente arcaico," listing the Neo-Kantian, Neo-Hegelian, and Neo-Thomist schools among several examples. However, he feels that existentialism is also a declining movement: "el 'existencialismo' se mueve en un horizonte cerrado, hasta agotar y, en definitiva, desvirtuar el magnífico impulso inicial que recibió de Heidegger..." [88] Marías points out that the method of existentialism, phenomenology, is "pure description," and "la descripción, absolutamente necesaria, no es suficiente, y nos remite a una forma superior de conocimiento, que sea *teoría* o *razón*. Ahora bien, en Heidegger y, en general, en el 'existencialismo' no hay nada que sea equivalente de la idea de la razón vital, y por ello es cada vez más notoria su propensión irracionalista, con la última esterilidad que ello implica." [89] Thus he concludes that in this intellectual horizon, the idea of vital reason represents "una vía abierta hacia el futuro." The only flaw in his argument is the matter of internal inconsistency. He has earlier, in Ortega's case, made the point that philosophy does not *have* a method but *is* a method, and has frequently used "teoría de razón vital" and "método de razón vital" interchangeably, so that logically phenomenologic method would also have to be phenomenologic theory. Granted that existentialism may lack an equivalent of "vital reason," this does not mean that it lacks all theory of knowledge beyond pure and simple description of phenomena.

---

[87] *Razón vital*, pp. 82-83.
[88] *Razón vital*, p. 84.
[89] *Razón vital*, p. 86.

Insofar as application in the individual existence is concerned, existentialist theory (whatever it may be) has much the same effect in the ethical sphere as "vital reason." It may well be true, as Marías feels, that Ortega has surpassed the existentialists in his development of this theory, but it is not necessary to ignore certain applications of existentialism in order to make his point. It should be possible to show that Ortega has made a more complete and comprehensible statement of the idea, particularly with regard to ethical or practical aspects, while acknowledging that similar suggestions are to be found in existentialism.

José Ferrater Mora and José Gaos

Although Marías is unrivaled as the foremost specialist in the philosophy of Ortega, he is worthily seconded by two very able critics who are only slightly less specialized, José Ferrater Mora, and José Gaos. The latter is considered a "disciple" of Ortega.

Although Ferrater Mora usually writes in Spanish, his most important work on Ortega to date was written in English: *Ortega y Gasset: An Outline of his Philosophy*. A Spanish translation was published the following year under the title *La filosofía de Ortega y Gasset* (Buenos Aires, 1958). Since the Spanish version is the work of a translator, the English original may render more faithfully the author's intent.

Ferrater Mora agrees with Marías that there is consistency and organization in Ortega's thought, despite the great variety of topics. He observes, however: "This does not mean that Ortega is a systematic philosopher. Nor does he, we hope, pretend to be one. The emphasis that has been placed by both his followers and opponents on his 'system' or on his 'lack of system' is false." [90] He notes that if Ortega is said to have a system, it must be an "open" rather than a "closed" one, but prefers not to lose the flavor of variety in Ortega's thought by insisting too much upon its unity. He considers Ortega's thought in the framework of three fundamental

---

[90] José Ferrater Mora, *Ortega y Gasset: An Outline of his Philosophy* (New Haven, 1957), p. 9. Hereafter referred to as *Ortega*.

stages or phases of intellectual development, "objectivism," "per-spectivism," and "ratio-vitalism." The first phase extends from 1902 to 1914, including juvenilia and a number of early essays and ending with *Meditaciones del Quijote*. For the second phase (1914-1923) Ferrater Mora takes his label from *El Espectador*. The closing year of this period, 1923, marked the publication of *El tema de nuestro tiempo*, which the critic calls a major work containing ratio-vitalistic assumptions. In this book, however, Ferrater feels that

> Ortega emphasized the theme of life far more than his own doctrine of vital reason would permit. We shall consequent-ly rule this work out of the third period and study it instead as the crowning point of the second. Needless to say, the third period will provide us with most of the themes that have come to be viewed as characteristically Ortegean. [91]

Ferrater Mora believes the third phase is most important. It is the longest and the most philosophical, or most concerned with technical aspects of philosophy. He devotes relatively more space to this final period, and interprets the first two in the light of the third. His treatment of Ortega's two earlier "periods" can be omitted in the interests of brevity, since we have seen enough to indicate the direction of his thought. He divides the third period into a number of themes: (1) the concept of vital reason; (2) the doctrine of man; (3) the doctrine of society, and (4) the idea of philosophy.

This critic by implication refers to existentialism when he states that he will not be concerned with the "problem of whether Ortega's claims of having long since foreshadowed many later philosophical developments in contemporary thought can be substantiated." [92] He feels that the truth about Ortega's originality lies somewhere between the detractions of his adversaries and the enthusiastic claims of his adherents, but "the achievements of a philosopher must be measured in terms of truth rather than originality." [93] Ferrater Mora avoids nearly all of the points of critical controversy, deliberately placing his study above and beyond them. He is scrupulous in staying within

---

[91] *Ortega*, p. 13.
[92] *Ortega*, p. 13.
[93] *Ortega*, p. 13.

the limits defined for himself, and consequently his work may be considered the most objective produced to date on this subject.

Ferrater Mora examines a number of philosophic definitions of vitalism. Ortega's own philosophical position is a vitalism which "claims to be a philosophy asserting that knowledge is, and must necessarily be, of a rational character, except for the fact that as life remains the central philosophical issue, reason must try above all to probe its significance." [94] He points out that, according to Ortega, man is continually casting doubts upon his own life, or that "man's existence is deeply problematic." This he identifies as a major issue in Ortega's "philosophy of human existence," a term perhaps dictated by the critic's wish to avoid controversial labels. Ferrater Mora uses many labels of his own devising, but basically discusses the same major themes in Ortega's work as did Marías. For example, he uses "historical sense" to describe "the feeling that man is not an immutable creature living in a historical setting but an entity whose reality is decisively shaped by his own history." [95] He observes that Ortega in his third phase made many remarks on this issue. In singling out "historical sense" as an important theme, Ferrater Mora is clearly referring to Ortega's idea that man has no nature but instead has history, and to the importance of circumstances in the definition of the ego. It could be demonstrated through other reference to Ferrater Mora's definition of his terms that he emphasizes much the same central issues in Ortega's philosophy as did Marías. In order to avoid a lengthy and largely tangential disquisition, it seems preferable to omit Ferrater Mora's labels where possible.

> The doctrine of human life is a central issue —or rather *the* central issue— in Ortega's philosophy. Let us hasten to assure the reader that no idealism and, of course, no anthropocentrism are involved in this position. Human life is certainly not the sole reality in the universe. It can hardly be said to be the most important reality. But it is, as Ortega puts it, the *basic* reality, since all the other realities appear within it. [96]

---

[94] *Ortega,* p. 38.
[95] *Ortega,* p. 45.
[96] *Ortega,* pp. 46-47.

Ferrater takes up the question of the nature of human life, pointing out that it would be an error to suppose that it is a "thing":

> [It is] neither body nor mind, neither a thing like matter nor a thing like spirit. ... It is not even a "being." It has no fixed status; it has no nature. Life *happens* to each one of us. It is a pure "happening" or, as Ortega puts it, a gerundive, a *faciendum,* and not a participle, a *factum.* Instead of being something ready-made, we have to make it unceasingly. Life, in short, is a "being" that makes itself, or rather "something" consisting in making itself. [97]

The existentialist tones of this concept of life which Ferrater Mora has gleaned from Ortega's philosophy need not be overemphasized. Nevertheless it should be pointed out that this critic, who (like Marías) deliberately avoids mention of existentialism, cannot describe Ortega's philosophy other than in terms of existentialist themes. This is further evinced in the following excerpt:

> What does vital reason discover in its description of human life? ... Human life is, properly speaking, neither mind nor body. Mind and body are realities we have to live and contend with, in exactly the same sense as we have to live and contend with our physical and social environment. We find ourselves in a world which has not been chosen by us. We live in constant intercourse with our circumstances. We are not a "thing" but *the* person *who* lives a *particular* and *concrete* life with things and among things. There is no abstract and generic living. Ortega's old principle, "I am myself and my own circumstances," therefore plays a fundamental role in the descriptive ontology of human life. Against realists, Ortega claims that our life is the basic reality and the point of departure for any sound philosophical system. Against idealists, he holds that life can only be understood as an entity fully immersed in the world. Ortega's statements in this respect are numerous. Life exists as "a perpetual migration of the vital Ego in the direction of the Not-self." To live is "to hold a dialogue with the environment," namely, "to deal with the world, to turn to it, to act on it." To live is to be outside oneself, to

---

[97] *Ortega,* pp. 47-48.

> contend with something, with the world and with oneself.
> In short, to live is always to *live with*. [98]

The first of Ferrater Mora's renderings of Ortega's statements sounds like Sartre and Heidegger; the others bear marked resemblance to ideas of Jaspers.

Ferrater Mora points out the ethical implications of this definition of life:

> Confronted with all these circumstances, man is forced
> to make his own life and to make it, whenever possible,
> in an authentic fashion. This is, incidentally, the main rea-
> son why what we do in our life is *not* immaterial. In his
> essay on Goethe, Ortega has pointed out that Goethe's
> celebrated sentence, "My actions are merely symbolic,"
> was but a way of concealing from himself the *decisive*
> character of his behavior. [99]

To summarize, Ferrater Mora recognizes that this is a philosophy of action, a philosophy to live by as well as a philosophy *about* living. The emphasis on the decisive nature of Ortega's thought is even more strongly stated in the following passage:

> In fact, human life has not only to cause itself; it has also
> to determine the self it is going to cause. We have *always* to
> decide what we are going to do with our lives. Not for
> a single moment is our activity of decision allowed to rest.
> ... We are free beings in a most radical sense, because we
> feel ourselves *fatally* compelled to exercise our freedom.
> Man is free by compulsion, for even when he forsakes his
> liberty he has to decide it beforehand. We must therefore
> commit ourselves perpetually ... because we cannot escape
> this inexorable condition of our existence. Freedom is so
> absolute in human life that we can even choose not to be
> "ourselves." [100]

These words could almost have been written by Sartre, and while Ferrater Mora avoids the comparison, it must have been in

---

[98] *Ortega*, p. 49.
[99] *Ortega*, pp. 50-51.
[100] *Ortega*, pp. 52-53.

the critic's mind, for a few lines later he observes: "Ultimate decisions are always a purely personal affair. Inasmuch as solitude —'existential' and not merely 'physical' solitude— is an outstanding feature of human life, only decisions made in complete solitude will really be authentic." [101] It is probably significant that Ferrater Mora refers to existential solitude in order to explain Ortega's position; apparently he found no other description quite so apt. He points out that life is seen as a vital design, or vital program, and that these expressions are, to some extent, synonymous with vocation and destiny. This does not imply any "leaving it to fate," however, or a resignation to what the future may bring. Life is also a struggle: "Ortega's metaphysics of human life implies insecurity as one of its outstanding features. The opinion that life is in itself a problem, the comparison of life with a shipwreck, are quite common in Ortega's works." [102]

144268

The foregoing pages suffice to give the flavor of Ferrater Mora's book. His approach is primarily expository or descriptive, and secondarily interpretative. As does Marías, he singles out *la razón vital* as the aspect of Ortega's philosophy to be most emphasized. Lest there be any misunderstanding, his intent apparently is not to present Ortega as an existentialist, but he cannot avoid existentialist echoes in his description of Ortega's philosophy.

Two of the articles by Ferrater Mora on Ortega, "Una fase en el pensamiento de Ortega, el objetivismo" [103] and "Ortega y la idea de la sociedad," [104] are in essence repeated in the book just considered. In an article entitled "De la filosofía a la 'filosofía'" [105] Ferrater Mora contends that there are two groups of philosophers, those for whom philosophic truth is analysis or science, and those for whom it is the ultimate in human life, vital function, activity. Ortega is of the latter group. The rest of the article considers "sources," remote and recent.

---

[101] *Ortega*, p. 53.

[102] *Ortega*, pp. 53-54.

[103] *Clavileño*, VII (1956), 11-15; also published in *La Torre*, XV-XVI (July-Dec. 1956).

[104] *Humanitas*, III (1956-57), 13-20; also published in *Insula*, X (Nov. 15, 1955).

[105] *Sur*, No. 241 (July-August 1956), 21-24.

Ferrater Mora is also the author of *La filosofía en el mundo de hoy,* in which he distinguishes what he terms extreme-right, right, center-right, center, center-left, left, and extreme-left wings of existentialism—atheist, almost-atheist, somewhat-less-atheist, more-or-less-theist, outright-theist, Christian Catholic, and various denominational brands. He also remarks: Hay una forma de existencialismo académica y otra bohemia.

> Ciertos existencialistas contribuyen a la confusión pretendiendo que no son existencialistas. Otros pregonan que el existencialismo es, de hecho, la forma auténtica, o la más plausible, del marxismo, o inclusive del tomismo. Hay un existencialismo de la angustia, otro de la esperanza, otro de lo absurdo; hay uno de la plenitud del Ser y otro de la vacuidad de la nada. [106]

This has a purely negative relevance in that nowhere in the book does he mention Ortega as falling into any of the above categories of existentialism. But existentialism is not the major topic of the book.

Ferrater Mora has also reviewed two of the posthumously published works of Ortega, *Idea del teatro,* and *La idea de principio en Leibniz y la evolución de la teoría deductiva.* Only the latter is really relevant here. Of this work, Ferrater Mora says it is "incomplete" although it is over four hundred pages. It is an investigation of several different philosophies, a study of Leibniz and the things which made possible his philosophy. Ferrater Mora observes:

> Para quien, como Ortega, se interesa en este libro por una serie de "modos de pensar" —el euclidiano, el euclidiano-aristotélico, el aristotélico, el aristotélico-escolástico, el estoico, el cartesiano, el existencialista y, desde luego, el leibniziano— es justificado preguntarse ¿cuál es su propio modo de pensar? [107]

Of Ortega's work on Leibniz, Ferrater Mora notes that it is not merely a study of essential moments in the history of philosophy; it

---

[106] José Ferrater Mora, *La filosofía en el mundo de hoy* (Madrid, 1959), p. 32.
[107] *Cuadernos del Congreso por la libertad de la cultura,* XLII (May-June 1960), 49.

is not an "historical" work. "Es un ataque en regla a la cuestión de la filosofía misma en cuanto se plantea dentro de nuestra situación o 'nivel' y *como consecuencia de ello.*" [108] In this work more than any other may be found Ortega's thought regarding the fundamental philosophical problem, that of philosophy in itself as a way of thinking, states the reviewer. In it, Ortega rejects, in one way or another, all prior philosophy, insofar as it is "accepted." He explains that a philosophy is not "accepted" so long as it is possible to raise its veils to see what is behind them, or in other words, to examine its presuppositions. What one usually finds, he observes, is the level which the other philosopers together have reached, which is the only method of finding the current level of philosophy itself.

> Algunos han creído que este nivel actual era el existen-
> cialismo —como otros creyeron antaño que era el neokan-
> tismo. Filósofos de toda laya se han "gargarrizado," como
> dice Ortega, con ideas harto cuestionables, por ejemplo, la
> idea de que el hombre es, en último término, Nada, o que
> consiste en preguntarse por el Ser. Han actuado, sin saberlo,
> como meros receptores— a veces, según ocurre con Hei-
> degger, como "receptores geniales." [109]

It is not immediately clear whether the critic is expressing his own ideas, or those of Ortega; however, it later emerges that the above position is his own interpretation.

The final reference by Ferrater Mora to Ortega was found in his *Diccionario de Filosofía,* which nicely summarizes, but adds nothing to, the ideas in his book.

José Gaos's articles have been conveniently collected and published in a volume entitled *Sobre Ortega y Gasset.* Many of the essays represented were published earlier in various periodicals, but the book also contains a certain amount of material before unpublished. There are also a number of essays dealing with the history of ideas in Spain and Latin America which have no direct relevance to Ortega.

---

[108] *Cuadernos del Congreso...,* p. 49.
[109] *Cuadernos del Congreso...,* p. 51.

The first essay, entitled "La profecía en Ortega" [110] is an extremely detailed and erudite tracing of the idea of prophecy in Ortega's writings, a careful compilation of the occasions where predictions occur in his works. In a second section, Gaos considers in turn each of a vast number of Ortega's "prophecies" to determine how many have been fulfilled and how many have proved erroneous, finding a high degree of success or accuracy in prediction.

"La Salvación de Ortega" [111] was first published in *Cuadernos Americanos* as part of the *homenaje* by that review, and is not primarily critical. It contains several anecdotes and biographical references, and a too-brief attempt to give an overall view of Ortega's thought as divided into stages of *raciopurismo, raciovitalismo, raciohistoricismo,* and a return to *raciovitalismo.* Gaos presents Ortega as one who passionately wanted to be a philosopher, and who in a life pervaded by *amor intellectualis* fulfilled a personal imperative. This can be compared with Marías's treatment which showed the philosopher living *necessarily* as he did, in terms of his own individual authenticity.

"Los dos Ortegas" [112] distinguishes a joyous, optimistic Ortega (a period of twenty years, beginning with the earliest writings and including the first four volumes of *El Espectador,* 1902 to 1923), and the second, a restless, bitter, preoccupied, doubting, if not pessimistic, Ortega. Gaos explains the differences largely in terms of changed national and international circunstances.

"Ortega y España" [113] surveys several of Ortega's writings on Spain, especially *Meditaciones del Quijote, España invertebrada,* and portions of *El Espectador,* demonstrating Ortega's continuing preoccupation with his country and summarizing Ortega's political activity. This might well be read as a corollary to Marías's defense of Ortega against the charges of Germanophilia and the imputations of lack of patriotism.

---

[110] José Gaos, *Sobre Ortega y Gasset* (México, 1957), pp. 9-72. Hereafter referred to as *Sobre Ortega.*
[111] *Sobre Ortega,* pp. 73-86.
[112] *Sobre Ortega,* pp. 87-97.
[113] *Sobre Ortega,* pp. 99-115.

"Ortega en política" [114] is intrinsically a continuation of the preceding article, and its title is self-explanatory. It is biographical as well as being an analysis of some of Ortega's political pronouncements, concentrating on his association with the Reublic.

The most relevant section of Gaos's book consists of two closely related articles. The first is a review of a book by Eduardo Nicol, entitled *Historicismo y existencialismo,* and the second is a point by point airing of Gaos's disagreements with Nicol's thesis and interpretations. The articles are, respectively, "De paso por el *Historicismo y existencialismo*" and "De paso por el *Historicismo y existencialismo*: Parerga y paralipomena." [115] Nicol's book, notes the reviewer, is a sort of history of historicism and existentialism. The book is conceived as a phase in the transcendence of both philosophies through a new one:

> los filósofos a quienes Nicol dedica sendos capítulos son únicamente aquellos que representan para él las principales articulaciones del desarrollo de la filosofía historicista y existencialista, mas uno del que trata por muy otros motivos: aquéllos son... Leibniz y Hegel, Marx, Kierkegaard, Nietzsche, Bergson, Dilthey, Heidegger; el uno es Ortega y Gasset. [116]

Implicit in Gaos's distinction above is his exclusion of Ortega from the categories represented by the other philosophers mentioned above.

Nicol treats Ortega in the same chapter with Nietzsche. Gaos lists these elements as outstanding:

> Una nueva y sugestiva historia del tema del héroe en Nietzsche, Kierkegaard... Heidegger y Ortega, quien da origen a un examen del problema de la profecía en historia y de la teoría de las generaciones; la exposición y crítica del vitalismo biológico de Ortega... y el final del capítulo, una explicación del existencialismo por la personalidad de los existencialistas. [117]

---

[114] *Sobre Ortega,* pp. 117-137.
[115] *Sobre Ortega,* pp. 181-192, 193-246.
[116] *Sobre Ortega,* p. 181.
[117] *Sobre Ortega,* pp. 182-183.

Hegel, notes Gaos, is Nicol's "classic," to whom he returns repeatedly as an authority with whom to confront the later philosophers, most of whom fare rather poorly at his hands:

> Con todo y las reservas o las discrepancias de Nicol ante Marx, Nietzsche y Bergson, la apreciación que éstos le merecen resulta más calurosa que la obtenida en definitiva por Dilthey y Heidegger, fría a pesar de cuanto Nicol reconoce que se les debe, sin excluirse a sí mismo de los deudores. De franca antipatía es su actitud frente a Kierkegaard. Pero el peor papel en el reparto le toca a Ortega. [118]

Nicol repeats all the old criticisms of Ortega, and in particular those of lack of system and method and originality. Gaos adds this observation: "Nicol no aplica a Ortega los mismos patrones de medida que a los demás." Gaos himself obviously feels insulted by the slighting references to Ortega's adherents: "insinúa Nicol la incompetencia filosófica de los devotos de Ortega y el final del capítulo sobre éste lo inicia refiriéndose a las 'reiteradas frustraciones que producen los escritos de Ortega a quien acude a ellos con ánimo de estudio.'" [119] Apparently this last remark stung Gaos to write his refutation of Nicol.

Much of the article is irrelevant, referring to personal exchanges between the two critics, and to their correspondence. Further, Gaos undertakes to defend all the philosophers whom he feels were slighted by Nicol, and thus it is a relatively small portion which has to do with Ortega.

Of Nicol's chapter entitled "La crítica de la razón histórica, Ortega y Gasset," Gaos observes:

> En este capítulo es un gran acierto el haber aplicado a Ortega el "método historicista" de seguir y trazar la evolución cronológico-ideológica de un pensador, atendiendo a las influencias ejercidas sobre él en la fundamentalidad que les corresponde. Es una manera prácticamente insólita aún de tratar a Ortega, a pesar de ser la única de que es posible hacerle justicia —aunque Nicol la emplee para no hacérsela, según expongo en parágrafo posterior de este trabajo. [120]

---

[118] *Sobre Ortega,* p. 183.
[119] *Sobre Ortega,* p. 184.
[120] *Sobre Ortega,* p. 219.

After this initial rendering of justice to his adversary, however, Gaos removes the velvet gloves: "Puede afirmarse que la apreciación que hace Nicol de Ortega es, a pesar de concesiones incidentales, de menosprecio o desprecio global y constante." [121] He particularly objects to Nicol's tendency to find influences or sources for all of Ortega's philosophy: Nietzsche and Bergson for *la razón vital* and Dilthey and Heidegger for *la razón histórica.* Gaos devotes considerable space to countering this imputation, and then turns to Nicol's allegations of lack of coherency or consistency in Ortega's work. He questions whether there is more consistency in Nicol's own book than in any given book of Ortega's, or between any two of Ortega's works. He observes that considerable philosophic differences do not prevent the grouping together of various thinkers into a single stream of thought:

> Y a tres gigantes como Fichte, Schelling y Hegel, a pesar de cuanto hicieron por distinguirse entre sí, los alineamos en lo que llamamos el idealismo alemán, como hemos empezado a alinear a Heidegger y Jaspers, Marcel y Sartre, Chéstof y Berdiáef, Unamuno, Ortega y Caso en lo que llamamos existencialismo. [122]

Gaos does not follow up this tantalizing reference, nor does he elucidate in any way. It is not clear who he means by "we" but he apparently refers more to what he considers convention than to personal conviction. The excerpt is especially interesting, nonetheless, since it is the only case where a "disciple" of Ortega's groups him with the existentialists.

THE LESSER CRITICS: BOOKS

In the pages which follow, thirteen minor critics are studied. Seven of them are definitely antagonistic; two (Salmerón and Borel) are definitely sympathetic and can be considered as Ortega's "disciples" because of their association with Gaos and Marías, respectively. The four remaining critics are relatively objective.

---

[121] *Sobre Ortega,* p. 232.
[122] *Sobre Ortega,* p. 239.

One rather startling generalization can be made about these minor critics. Those favorable to Ortega (and this applies equally to Marías, Ferrater Mora, and Gaos) have seen him as the embodiment of an ideal life in the existentialist sense, but have scrupulously avoided using the word in connection with Ortega's name. On the other hand, the antagonistic critics (most of whom write from an orthodox Catholic point of view) have used "existentialist" (in those cases where it was mentioned) in an almost exclusively condemnatory sense. There may well be a meaningful connection between this and the avoidance of the existentialist label by Ortega's adherents. None of them would want to seem to be agreeing with their antagonists.

The arrangement of authors in these pages is neither chronological nor by camps; it is rather a mixing together which hopefully affords better comparison and contrast of critical points of view.

El caso Ortega y Gasset by Patricio Canto is a book of little critical value, taking the well-worn standpoint that Ortega has no system, and attempting to counter what Canto calls a prejudice in favor of Ortega based on a voluntary lack of acquaintance. This author's very obvious bias against Ortega is based on an equal lack of acquaintance, as evinced by this characterization and dismissal of Ortega as the chosen mouthpiece of the colonial aristocracy of South America, interested in a show of pride to conceal their true debasement. He asserts that "No es necesario matar lo que el tiempo —muy poco tiempo— ha matado ya. La realidad misma se encargó de desmentir cualquier semejanza ocasional que hubiera habido entre literatura, política o religión y lo que Ortega nos decía de ellos." [123] Despite his stand that Ortega is being quickly swallowed by well-deserved oblivion, Canto blames Ortega's "attitudes" for what he considers the moral abdication of Spanish writers during the last thirty years. He therefore devotes nearly two hundred pages to Ortega's pernicious influence.

Ortega y Gasset ante la crítica [124] has been quite adequately criticized by Julián Marías, and little need be added. The work is that of a cleric and a strong Catholic bias is evident throughout.

---

[123] Patricio Canto, *El caso Ortega y Gasset* (Buenos Aires, 1958), p. 10.
[124] Juan Ruiz Barberá (Madrid, 1950).

The author has not yet forgiven Ortega for an article written in 1910 supporting lay education. The book is subtitled "El idealismo en *El Espectador* de Ortega y Gasset" and it would be unfair to say that this is not investigated, but the author's major preoccupation is the religious orthodoxy or "apostasy" of Ortega's works. Saiz Barberá provides a vague, rather too general history of idealism, which is not directly related to Ortega, but introduced for the purpose of demonstrating in a later chapter that Ortega was "idealistic" or divorced from reality, reality as represented by the Church. The author shows great concern with philosophic sources, his most extensive comparison being drawn between Ortega and Husserl, with a section on Ortega and Rousseau which he relates to Ortega's "vitalistic pantheism" and "spiritualistic pantheism." There is an attempt made to show the evolution of Ortega's philosophy from perspectivism (which Saiz Barberá uses in the sense of extreme relativism) to idealism (which he uses in the sense of a philosophy consisting of ideas existing only in the mind of the philosopher).

The Historical Thought of José Ortega y Gasset is also the work of a cleric, but religious bias is kept very much in the background. There is a long introductory section on Ortega's life and works, which is undoubtedly the best biographical treatment available in English. The author notes:

> Ortega was a seedbed of ideas, anticipating or perhaps simply accompanying the thought of such men as Spengler, Dilthey, Jaspers, Heidegger and Toynbee. These startling similarities may perhaps be best explained by Ortega's concept of the "generation," wherein all the members partake of the same intellectual climate and inheritance. ... [125]

This excerpt is indicative of the procedure of Ceplecha, in that he attempts to relate Ortega's concepts to reality for illustrative purposes, rather than taking them out of context to find inconsistencies. In a section entitled "Notes on the Philosophy of Ortega" he aligns himself with the critics who contend that Ortega had no system: "Unfortunately, Ortega never systematized his philosophical ideas and

---

[125] Christian Ceplecha, *The Historical Thought of José Ortega y Gasset* (Washington, D. C., 1958), pp. 31-32.

suggestions. They are to be found scattered throughout his voluminous writings. This lamentable fact has induced Julián Marías, one of his immediate disciples, to attempt a systematization of the master's thought." [126] Ceplecha reviews the main themes of Ortega's philosophy, mentioning opposition to both realism and idealism; the interdependency of subject and object ("yo soy yo y mi circunstancia"); perspectivism; Ortega's definition of life and of reality (for which he quotes Ortega); and the concepts of vital reason and historical reason. The major section of his work is devoted to Ortega's concept of history, which includes his ideas of mass and minority, generation, society, and the process of historical change. Ceplecha concludes with Ortega's explanation of one of the great historical crises, that of the fifteenth and sixteenth centuries when the effective beliefs of European man changed from Christianity to Rationalism. Ceplecha feels that the study of Ortega's historical thought leaves expectations unfulfilled, or that his work comes to a sudden halt. (This may be explained by the fact that he did not have all of Ortega's works available, as many posthumous volumes have been published since, or are still in process of publication.)

Ceplecha detects strong influences of idealism and perspectivism in Ortega's thought, with a development into historicism, and remarks: "The existentialist approach is seen in Ortega's extreme idea of human liberty." [127] There is no other reference to existentialism. The author's religious orientation emerges clearly only on the last page:

> The Spanish philosopher took a line from Don Quijote that says the road is better than the inn. This phrase sums up his whole attitude. At first hearing it sounds adventurous. But it hides the sadness of Ortega's life. His longing for a kind of absolute could not be fulfilled by his philosophy of becoming. Yet he almost instinctively recoiled from probing the ultimate questions. His common sense observations and "old-fashioned" moral statements regarding the present situation alike have their roots in that Christian past from which he has so consciously departed. What Ortega insinuated and covered with glittering phrases his disciple

---

[126] Ceplecha, p. 34.
[127] Ceplecha, p. 163.

Gaos has openly proclaimed: anti-intellectualism, skepticism and atheism. [128]

Mocedades de Ortega y Gasset [129] is dedicated to Gaos. The author is one of his pupils. It is, as the title indicates, concerned with Ortega's earliest works, and in fact is even more limited in scope than Julián Marías's *Circunstancia y vocación* which also deals with juvenilia. Salmerón treats only works prior to the publication of *Meditaciones del Quijote*. He observes that one may, without irony, divide the studies of Ortega into two groups, those which attack and those that defend, and alleges that his book is less the result of desire to join in the dispute than of conviction that the dispute is based on misunderstanding, random quoting, and a superficial study of Ortega's works. Salmerón believes that Ortega's thought is clearly "evolutionary" or that it develops logically through several stages, and that it can be apprehended only in this constant fluidity. Salmerón's expressed intent is to follow Ortega's fundamental concepts, clarifying each in its context, "un intento de explicar a Ortega por sí mismo." [130] His study (which antedates Marías's *Circunstancia y vocación*) is marked by a similar attempt to relate Ortega's work to his historical, and particularly national, circumstances. It is a thoroughly creditable critical effort, and the two books taken together represent a more than adequate coverage of this period of Ortega's life and works.

Raison et vie chez Ortega y Gasset is dedicated to Julián Marías, and like the book of Salmerón just considered, approaches Ortega in an effort to understand him in the light of his Spanish "circumstance": "une des caractéristiques du philosophe est d'avoir décidé d'accepter et d'assumer le plus intégralement possible son 'destin' espagnol." [131] That this is not a casual theme with Borel is indicated by his assertion a few pages later: "C'est par sa formation kantienne et hégélienne qu'Ortega aboutit à la nécessité de partir de

---

[128] Ceplecha, p. 166.

[129] Fernando Salmerón (México, 1959). This author has an article by the same title in *La Torre*, XV-XVI (July-Dec. 1956) which anticipates certain material in his book.

[130] Salmerón, p. 21.

[131] Jean-Paul Borel, *Raison et vie chez Ortega y Gasset* (Neuchâtel, 1959), p. 14.

l'unité de l'homme avec sa circonstance—c'est-à-dire de l'unité de lui, Ortega, avec son destin espagnol." [132] He notes that various critics have contended that Ortega had no real system, and announces his own intention of a systematic exposition of Ortega's thought, following the "stages" of his formation, which he divides according to the following table:

I	1902-1913:	Apparition des thèmes; la philosophie surgit du heurt de l'homme avec sa circonstance.
II	1914:	Première étape; la philosophie surmonte les premières contradictions nées de la confrontation de la conscience avec le monde.
III	1915-1922:	Epoque de transition; malgré le conflit qui les oppose, la raison et la vie apparaissent comme inséparables.
IV	1923:	Deuxième étape (moins fortement marquée); la collaboration entre la vie et la raison aboutit à la notion de "raison vitale."
V	1924-1932:	Epoque de transition; la raison vitale s'essaie, et s'affirme comme méthode.
VI	1933-1935:	Troisième étape, très importante; la raison vitale, s'enrichissant d'une dimension *historique,* fonde un système.
VII	1939-1940:	Quatrième étape; la raison historique exprime la totalité de la circonstance humaine.
VIII	1941-1942:	Dernière étape; l'histoire apparaît comme un progrès, mais aussi comme une possible falsification. [133]

Both Borel's orientation and his method are clear from this topical outline, which is consistently followed throughout. Borel is frequently reminiscent of Marías, and the general level of his exposition and commentary is high. It should be noted that the appendices contain a very useful chronology and an excellent bibliography.

---

[132] Borel, p. 25.
[133] Borel, p. 33.

Al margen de Ortega y Gasset bears the subtitle "Crítica a *El tema de nuestro tiempo.*" The criticism is largely adverse, with the critic utilizing the guise of exposition to introduce his disagreements. He begins, for example, with Ortega's idea of generations, and after an investigation which is neither extensive nor intensive, concludes on the second page: "Nuestro filósofo no precisa su concepto ni prueba su existencia. Da a ésta por aceptada, y afirma que en ella está el fenómeno 'primario de la historia.' Va, pues, de fantasía en fantasía." [134] Jiménez Grullón's one reference to Ortega and existentialism leaves one very much in doubt as to how he feels Ortega's thought is related to existentialism:

> Por último, unas palabras sobre el existencialismo y el intuicionismo. Pese a que no niegan la razón, la subordinan a la vida, o a la intuición. Son, pues, irracionalistas. No me propongo —el tema ahora no lo requiere— hacer su exégesis. Pero sí debo apuntar que se trata de corrientes que sólo cubren zonas burguesas. Ello explica que sea casi exclusivamente en esta clase social donde ha logrado alcanzar difusión la filosofía de Ortega. [135]

The critic is in favor of scientific exactness in philosophy, rather than poetic vagueness. On these grounds he begins a point-by-point disagreement with Ortega, finding fault particularly with his metaphors and other instances of inexact expression. He feels that Ortega slights culture in favor of life. While he frequently mentions the second half of Ortega's "La vida tiene que ser culta, pero la cultura tiene que ser vital," the first half is not quoted in the entire book. On various other occasions Jiménez Grullón appears to distort Ortega's meaning, taking words out of context in order to arrive at an opposite interpretation for the sake of disagreeing. A case in point is his persistent construction of Ortega's concept of "masa" in the sense of "proletariat," despite the fact that numerous statements that this is not the meaning can be found in Ortega's writings. The criticism is purely destructive and lacks even the merit of being well done.

---

[134] Juan Isidro Jiménez Grullón, *Al margen de Ortega y Gasset* (Havana, 1957), p. 7.

[135] Jiménez Grullón, p. 37.

El pensamiento social de Ortega y Gasset deals mostly with the theory of the *hombre-masa,* his origin and character, the *pueblos-masa,* mass and minority in history, and what Ortega means by "revolt" of the masses. Lagos Matus sees the *hombre-masa* in very existential terms:

> Masa es el hombre vaciado de su propia historia, sin entrañas de pasado y por lo mismo dócil a todas las disciplinas internacionales por la simple razón de que el pasado nacional y la tradición nacional no han entrado dentro de su patrimonio espiritual. ... Más que un hombre es sólo un caparazón de hombre, carece de un yo que no se puede revolcar. Está vacío de destino propio, de intimidad, de secreto personal. [136]

He observes that the mass man consequently does not choose between the possibilities which his circumstances offer, but has abdicated his own ego in favor of action "en masa," dictated by his instinctive reactions. He is not exercising his liberty, not living in the existential sense. Although the book does not consider strictly philosophical aspects of Ortega's thought, it is permeated by an apparently unself-conscious existentialist tone in the exposition of concepts treated as primarily political. It seems logical to conclude that this reflects the tone of the original source.

El Centauro is a collection of three essays. Two of these are not directly relevant to the problem at hand. "Contorno del 'Centauro'" deals with the formative circumstances of Ortega, and "El Centauro ante el Altar" with religious themes in Ortega's work. The first of the three essays, entitled "Ortega, o el Centauro," begins with the observation that many Spaniards and Latin Americans read with profound admiration in Scheler, Jaspers, or Heidegger concepts which first appeared in Ortega's *Meditations.* Marrero notes that the philosophic rejection of both idealism and realism is a theme which Ortega shares with several existentialists:

> Hacía años que el catedrático español planteaba en sus cursos el problema de la superación, por un lado, del idea-

---

[136] Gustavo Lagos Matus, *El pensamiento social de Ortega y Gasset* (Santiago de Chile, 1956), p. 12.

lismo, y por otro, del realismo, a través de una meditación del cambio y de la identidad, que era toda una crítica del substancialismo clásico desde Parménides a nuestros días, y proponía, a través de un análisis estructural de la vida del hombre, las bases de una nueva antropología filosófica. Esta tarea la comenzó un danés genial de la primera mitad del siglo pasado, Soren Kierkegaard, y la han continuado con seriedad en nuestro siglo Heidegger, Jaspers, Scheler y Sartre. [137]

Shortly afterward, however, Marrero changes the subject without having further clarified what he means by philosophical anthropology, or stating grounds for comparing Ortega with the other philosophers mentioned. He turns to Ortega's social and political writings, and like many other critics misinterprets the *hombre-masa*. He asks: "¿Es su concepto de *hombre-masa* de carácter ético o de orden social? ¿O es acaso un concepto de valoración intelectual? Esto no lo aclara la tesis de Ortega." [138] Actually, Ortega states clearly that the *hombre-masa* occurs in all social classes, and his examples make it clear that the concept is psychological and ethical. Marrero, however, assumes that it is social: "Ortega ve las masas con aire aprehensivo y resentido, temeroso de un desplazamiento. ... Su análisis es injusto con el proletariado. ..." [139] Much of the remainder of the essay concerns Ortega's aristocratic scorn for the masses, and Marrero relates anecdotes of Ortega's relationship with students intended to illustrate his pride. He proceeds to characterize Ortega as an apologist of the will to power and an inspiration of contemporary Fascism, an imputation certainly unjustified in view of Ortega's devotion to the Spanish Republic.

Turning to *El tema de nuestro tiempo,* Marrero remarks: "Tan pronto sale Ortega de la atmósfera idealista de Marburgo, va elaborando una posición que él denominará el tema de nuestro tiempo, que no es otro que el tema de Nietzsche, Dilthey y ... Soren Kierkegaard." [140] He finds fault with Ortega's own interpretation of his early works, the idea being that while Ortega tries to prove the

---

[137] Domingo Marrero, *El centauro* (Puerto Rico, 1951), pp. 18-19.
[138] Marrero, p., 30.
[139] Marrero, p. 31.
[140] Marrero, p. 56.

"priority" of his own works, he is simply taking a better idea and saying, "That's what I said."

> ¿Cuáles son esos conceptos de Heidegger que preexisten trece años antes en Ortega? Él se encarga de decírnoslo. La idea de la vida como inquietud, preocupación e inseguridad, y preocupación por la seguridad. El concepto de la vida como "enfronte del yo y su circunstancia."
> ¿Qué otros conceptos de Heidegger anticipó Ortega? Él los enumera: la liberación del substancialismo, el concepto de la vida como futurición, la teoría del "fondo insobornable" que más luego ha llamado Ortega "del yo auténtico," y el concepto de verdad como *aletheia* —desvelación— que según Ortega, aparece en las *Meditaciones del Quijote* bajo el nombre —tan hiperactual— de *luz y claridad,* y el concepto de la vida como habérselas con el mundo. [141]

Marrero doubts that many of these are true correlates, and attempts to show distinctions between Ortega's concepts and those of Heidegger. His treatment is too brief to be conclusive, and it is never quite clear why he refuses to accept Ortega's own definition of his terms.

B. Ventura Chumillas is the author of two books, both negative criticism of Ortega. ¿*Es Don José Ortega y Gasset un filósofo propiamente dicho*? (*Buenos Aires,* 1940) answers the question in the negative, asserting that Ortega is merely an essayist. Ventura Chumillas points out what he calls the great problems of philosophy on which Ortega has written nothing, since his essays deal only with "secondary themes." *Filósofos y literatos* purports to be a critique of Ortega's recently published *Ideas y creencias,* which he calls "una colección de ensayos, de cinco ensayos, de índole diversa, sin ninguna unidad entre ellos." [142] Although the book ostensibly deals with *Ideas y creencias* and particularly with unity or system in Ortega's thought, it is actually little more than a rephrasing and extensive citing of an earlier book by this same critic, who is continually pointing out that he has already handled each successive

---

[141] Marrero, p. 79.
[142] B. Ventura Chumillas, *Filósofos y literatos* (Buenos Aires, 1941), p. 14.

point in his other book. It might be noted that Ventura Chumillas is also a cleric.

Miguel de Unamuno y José Ortega y Gasset has a prologue by José Vasconcelos who remarks "siempre ví en Ortega un divulgador del idealismo alemán. ..." [143] The first fourteen chapters deal with Unamuno, and can be dismissed with the note that he is not interpreted primarily as an existentialist. The section on Ortega contains chapters on the appropriateness of the title, "El Espectador," and on Ortega's versatility, with the only relevant section being four pages subtitled "Existencialismo y perspectivismo orteguianos": "Altivo, elegante y aristocrático, el pensamiento de Ortega y Gasset ancla en el existencialismo de nuestro tiempo, sólo que su hermetismo celoso de intimidad, apenas si deja traslucir el mismo escepticismo, la misma tragedia que anidó en Kierkegaard, Heidegger y Unamuno." [144] Most of the rest of the section is devoted to Nietzsche as a source of inspiration, and to Ortega's relativism which this critic considers disastrous, remarking: "Sin hacer ninguna discriminación de los desencadenados instintos vitales, José Ortega y Gasset considera la vida ética por sí misma. ¡Auténticamente esto se llama: inmoralismo!" [145] The remainder of the section on Ortega is a tirade against the immorality of his relativistic ethics, against his negative criticism of Spain and Latin America, his "germanismo hasta el descastamento." The third part of the book compares Unamuno and Ortega with regard to their personality differences (on a very superficial level) and on the points of *españolismo* and *europeización*. Chapter XXV is entitled "Existencialismo acéfalo y metafísica existencial ascendente" and expresses a purely arbitrary preference for Unamuno because of his preoccupation with eternity, from the standpoint of orthodox Catholicism. "Ortega y Gasset en su estructura de la vida desemboca en un quehacer sin brújula, en un existencialismo acéfalo. Miguel de Unamuno, en cambio, con metafísica existencial ascendente, desembocó —como San Agustín— en el ser y se acogió al misericordioso corazón de Dios." [146]

---

[143] *Miguel de Unamuno y José Ortega y Gasset,* by Agustín Basave Fernández del Valle (Madrid, 1950), p. 9.
[144] Basave Fernnádez del Valle, p. 84.
[145] Basave Fernández del Valle, pp. 87-88.
[146] Basave Fernández del Valle, p. 169.

Filosofía de la existencia, subtitled "Notas sobre Ortega y Gasset," also touches on the point of Ortega's "authentic existential" life: "Leyéndole, percibimos lo que es vivir en la autenticidad de nuestra persona y lo que es inteligir filosóficamente la cultura en forma de ideaciones existenciales." [147] Moreno defines the authentic man as one who serves nothing which is not his own life, and observes that this means finding oneself. He digresses at length on the nature of the ego and consciousness, and includes chapters on ethnic groups (vaguely related to different points of view or perception) and "Biología y Pedagogía," which have little relevance to Ortega and none to existentialism. Moreno's exposition of Ortega's social theories is somewhat garbled, but leads to this observation:

> La prolongación perversiva e innoble de aquella actitud ("piensa mal y acertarás") interpersonal expresa el imperio de la falsía en la esfera de las relaciones sociales. Para la filosofía existencial de Ortega y Gasset el correlato psicólogo de una conducta semejante será éste: que suplantamos o fingimos el goce de la función comunicativa con prácticas y convencionalismos de sociedad que no dejan sino interior desazón. [148]

This is followed by an essay on "Kantismo y darwinismo" which is a reproach to Ortega for lack of clarity in *la razón vital* (without explanation of vital reason or its place in the philosophy of existence). The book concludes with an exposition (far from the best) of "yo soy yo y mi circunstancia" and chapters on "Vocación y profesión" and "Actitudes vitales," neither of which are clearly related to existentialism or to Ortega's total philosophy.

José Ortega y Gasset [149] begins with a chapter on the principal themes of the generation of '98, and a personality sketch of Ortega as an undidactic professor of Philosophy. Chapter III, "Visión de España" (Ortega's concept of Spain) is undoubtedly the best part of the book. "Cultura y vida" deals mostly with the theme of culture (especially Greek) in Ortega, while "Posición filosófica" notes the importance of the individual and "soy yo y mi circunstancia."

---

[147] Julio Moreno, *Filosofía de la existencia* (Quito, Ecuador, 1940), pp. 8-9.
[148] Moreno, pp. 44-45.
[149] Medardo Vitier (Havana, 1936).

Chapter VI on Ortega's themes notes three principal directions in his books: philosophical, historical, and aesthetic, the second and third being primarily interpretative. The concluding chapters deal with Ortega as a writer, and with his influence, still at an early stage.

José Sánchez Villaseñor's book, *Pensamiento y trayectoria de José Ortega y Gasset* (México, 1943) was available only in its English translation, *Ortega y Gasset, Existentialist*. A preliminary perusal indicates that Julián Marías has dealt with the book quite adequately in *Ortega y tres antípodas*. After the introduction which gives a sketchy biography, Sánchez Villaseñor rarely returns to Ortega. Both the Spanish and the English titles are misleading in this sense, although the subtitle of the latter, "A Critical Study of His Thought and Its Sources," is not an unreasonable description so long as one realizes that the emphasis is on sources. The critic is inclined to give Ortega little credit for originality, and most of the material which is not devoted to exposition of the philosophy of various others (Heidegger, Kant, Renan, Dilthey, and pantheism) is an attempt to show Ortega as an imitator, or to censure him for his lack of ethics. The theological bias of the author is evident throughout, and while this need not invalidate a critic's observations, in this case it has so colored them that it is difficult to recognize Ortega in the picture painted by Sánchez Villaseñor. One is inclined to agree with Marías's judgment that the book is based on a willful lack of acquaintance with Ortega's original works; substantiating this is the fact that while there are many supposed paraphrases and indirect quotes of the philosopher, his works are almost never quoted directly. A few excerpts will serve to give the flavor of this critic's work:

> Ortega agrees with the Heideggerian tradition in admitting the primacy of human life and the utilitarian character of the intellect. But faithful to his positivistic ideology, he rejects the possibility of reaching reality, even through emotions. In the Ortegan concept of life we can distinguish three periods. In the first, life is considered as the highest value. In the second, it is established as the fundamental reality, thanks to the existentialist influence. Finally, in *Ideas y creencias* all reality is declared unknowable and human life becomes an insoluble enigma. [150]

---

[150] Sánchez Villaseñor, pp. 172-173.

Sánchez Villaseñor never reconciles his reasons for placing Ortega in the "Heideggerian tradition" with the philosopher's claims to have anticipated numerous of Heidegger's ideas by some thirteen years. He speaks of "Ortega's existentialist writings" but nowhere relates Ortega to Kierkegaard, Jaspers, or Sartre. (No mention of any of the three is made, other than a remark that Ortega read Kierkegaard.) He concludes:

> In the sinister light of the world conflagration which we have experienced with horror, the Ortegan message contains unusual tragic significance. Unnoticed aspects of his thought receive unexpected emphasis.
> Not with impunity are imagination and instinct enthroned in society at the expense of intelligence. Whoever defends relativistic dilettantism in metaphysics can do no less than profess immorality in ethics. . . .
> It is painful to see a philosopher of Ortega's stature seriously trying to legitimize with Nietzsche's criterion the immorality of great statesmen in whom one sees the brutal profiles of the superman. . . . Ortega's is a frightening responsibility before history for having exchanged philosophy's noble mission for acrobatic sport. [151]

There are a number of other books which contain chapters on Ortega, but since none of them are directly relevant to the problem of existentialism, it has been decided for the sake of brevity and coherency to treat them in the appendix.

THE LESSER CRITICS: ARTICLES

The following pages study a number of articles which appeared in various reviews during the past several years. The vast majority of such articles will be treated in the appendix, according to the arrangement outlined in the opening pages of this chapter. The articles here included are those which have some direct relevance, positive or negative, to the question of Ortega as an existentialist. The order of arrangement is chronological. An alternative arrangement,

---

[151] Sánchez Villaseñor, pp. 232-233.

by implicit and explicit recognition of existentialist traits was considered and discarded, since it seemed to give an excessive impression of repetition. It is hoped that this arrangement will convey the maximum variety (not a great variety) available in the relevant critical articles.

Alberto del Campo deals primarily with the idea of reason in Ortega's philosophy, but also with the themes of life and circumstances, particularly insofar as they can be conceived as generating thought:

> *Pienso* por tanto, a causa de un sentimiento de angustia y de naufragio. *Pienso por una razón sentimental y vital.* ... En otros términos: el conocimiento no se explica por sí solo, sino como miembro de la conciencia humana total. ... como gusta decir Ortega, el hombre es un náufrago que piensa por motivos extraintelectuales: para mantenerse a flote... para salvar su vida. [152]

Franz Niedermayer relates Ortega to Heidegger and Jaspers in a number of passages:

> El rival de Ortega era y sigue siendo, en varios aspectos actuales, Heidegger; en cambio, el hermano de Ortega es Jaspers, que comparte con él muchos y profundos elementos intelectuales.
> Ortega junto a Heidegger y Jaspers: Esto equivale a nombrar a los tres más famosos pensadores europeos de hoy en día. [153]

He remarks that Ortega is better translated (and more widely) than Heidegger, and therefore better known. In his opinion, Ortega is closer to Jaspers than to Heidegger. Heidegger is more systematic, while "Jaspers y Ortega están unidos también por el perspectivismo relativista frente a la verdad en la ciencia y la moral en la religión, la apasionada intensidad del filosofar existencial, el método abierto del pensar... los mismos anhelos por la comunicación." [154]

---

[152] Alberto del Campo, "Crítica y rehacimiento de la razón en la filosofía de Ortega y Gasset," *Escritura,* III (June 1949), 60-61.

[153] Franz Niedermayer, Ortega y Gasset y su relación con Alemania," *Clavileño,* IV (Nov.-Dec. 1953), 71.

[154] Niedermayer, p. 74.

Eduardo Sarmiento makes the following observation:

> La filosofía de Ortega tiene esto en común con el existencialismo, que busca dar el primer paso filosófico desde dentro de la experiencia humana y no comenzar desde lo abstracto, que es querer colocarse el hombre en un plano que no le corresponde. . . . [155]

The *Revista Cubana de Filosofía* dedicated its January-June, 1956 number (Vol. IV) to Ortega. Of all the commemorative issues, this is the most philosophically oriented. Several of its articles are concerned with the "system" controversy, and others are devoted to material of little relevance, such as exposition of Ortega's aesthetics. These will be treated in the appendix, along with others similarly oriented.

"Valor de la circunstancia en la filosofía de Ortega y Gasset," by Mercedes García Tudurí contains much historical background, or exposition of the philosophical situation in the time of Aristotle and the Middle Ages —the background of the being-becoming, rationalism-vitalism dichotomies. The stated object of the article is to present the concept of circumstance as the axis of Ortega's entire philosophy, and the author is careful to point out that the idea is originally Ortega's alone, since it appeared in *Meditaciones del Quijote* in 1914, "es decir, trece años antes que *Sein und Zeit,* debe estimársele auténticamente orteguiano, porque él implica una concepción superadora del conflicto vida-razón que no fue considerada nunca por Heidegger." [156] This author also asserts Ortega's priority in the enunciation of the "existentialist" idea of personal liberty:

> Aquí también innova Ortega, planteando de un modo personal el problema de la libertad: mucho antes de que Sartre dijera que el hombre estaba condenado a ser libre, el filósofo español afirma que no es que el hombre pueda ser libre, sino que tiene que serlo, pues, paradójicamente, para lo único que el hombre no es libre es para no serlo. [157]

---

[155] Eduardo Sarmiento, "Orteguianismo y Cristianismo," *Atlante,* III (1955), 167.

[156] Mercedes García Tudurí, "Valor de la circunstancia en la filosofía de Ortega y Gasset," *Revista Cubana de Filosofía,* IV (Jan-June 1956), 10.

[157] García Tudurí, p. 11.

"Ortega y Gasset y la idea de la vida," by Humberto Piñera Llera, places Ortega among philosophers distinguished by having life as the focal point of their thought:

> Desde 1850 se puede reducir la filosofía a muy pocas cabezas pensantes, tan pocas como éstas: Dilthey, Nietzsche, Husserl, Bergson, Heidegger y Ortega. Lo demás es paisaje. ... Y el pensamiento de los seis gira en torno a una idea fundamental, es a saber: la *idea* de la *Vida*. [158]

The purpose of his article, states Piñera Llera, is to answer this question: Is Ortega a *filósofo de la vida*? His method is quantitative; the critic notes that the idea of *la Vida* appears 162 times in Ortega's *Obras Completas,* and from its earliest appearance in 1908, figures as the theme of forty-six of Ortega's works. He surveys the various forms in which life appears, analyzing Ortega's many descriptions and metaphors:

> vemos que la Vida es para Ortega esencialmente una "estructura," así que, o se da esa estructura en la cual consiste la vida antes de que pueda ser otra cosa, o la vida propiamente tal es imposbile. Pero, por otra parte, la vida es "brinco e innovación," "duración y mudanza," la "ocasión de someterse a la necesidad," y una vez dominada ésta, el ejercicio del "lujo vital de la libertad." Pero, además, la vida es "flujo," el "hecho cósmico del altruismo," "diálogo con el contorno," "ocupación con las cosas en torno," "proyecto," "dinamismo," "drama," "brevedad," "elección," "esfuerzo de cada ser viviente por ser sí mismo," "hacer algo determinado," "porvenir," "selva," "biografía," "invento." La vida es "sumersión de cada cual en un absoluto problema," "faena hacia adelante," "naufragio," "reacción a la inseguridad radical que constituye su sustancia," "elegir y acertar," "intimidad," "libertad," "un conjunto de problemas esenciales a que el hombre responde con un conjunto de soluciones: la cultura". ... [159]

The resemblance between many of these descriptions of life and the metaphors used to explain existence by various existentialists is too

---

[158] Humberto Piñera Llera, "Ortega y Gasset y la idea de la vida," *Revista Cubana de Filosofía,* IV (Jan-June 1956), 15.

[159] Piñera Llera, p. 18.

obvious to be overly stressed; however, the lengthy quotation may serve the reader as a convenient summary to which to return during the later consideration of primary sources.

After further investigation of Ortega's idea of life in which he particularly stresses its problematical aspects ("problematicidad"), Piñera Llera concludes that Ortega's idea of life is not one idea but many, or that Ortega gives us a varied and multiple version of the appearance which life has for him on different occasions. He examines the place of reason in life and concludes:

> Pues Ortega nos dice una y otra vez, hasta el cansancio, que la razón es un aspecto de la Vida, pero su *razón vital* se presenta como un despliegue de racionalidad que impresiona. Por esto es que se niega resueltamente a dejarse filiar como *existencialista,* aun cuando lo es en las consecuencias y en la terminología. Pues *naufragio, drama, elección* y *decisión, peligro, azar, invención, proyecto, soledad radical, programa, compromiso, circunstancia, relativismo,* y otras muchas, ¿qué otra cosa pueden ser sino parte efectiva y destacada del repertorio conceptual del existencialismo? [160]

"Imagen de Ortega y Gasset," by Jorge Mañach, subtitled "Impresión total del hombre y de la obra", attempts to find a perspective from which to view the philosopher and his work. It also purports to demonstrate the extent to which Ortega has achieved a unity of thought, and thus enters that controversy in support of Ortega. Mañach quickly disposes of another point of conflict, the question of whether Ortega is *filósofo* or *literato* by referring to "la doble condición de filósofo y escritor." [161]

Regarding Ortega's life, Mañach takes a position very similar to that of Marías and Salmerón:

> A la mentalidad periodística suele hacérsele no poca injusticia, pues se la juzga comunmente por sus medidas más íntimas. Pero esa mentalidad es la forma más solita

---

[160] Piñera Llera, p. 24.

[161] Jorge Mañach, "Imagen de Ortega y Gasset," *Revista Cubana de Filosofía,* IV (Jan-June, 1956), 104. This was also published in monograph with same title (Havana, 1957).

de la que hoy día los existencialistas llaman *engagée,* es decir, comprometida con lo vital. [162]

Mañach gives rather lengthy consideration to epistemological aspects of Ortega's thought, and concludes: "Ortega hace de la relación la categoría básica, primero [sic] del conocer; después del ser mismo, del ser que existe, que está en la realidad, y no sólo en nuestra mente." [163] He cites Ortega's definitions "cada cosa es una relación entre varias" and "La esencia de cada cosa se resuelve en relaciones." This implies a sort of "co-existentialism," in that no existence is complete in itself:

> Vivir no es sólo *ser,* como son, por ejemplo, los contenidos de la conciencia—; ni siquiera existir con existencia aislada y autónoma. Vida es *coexistencia*; es "convivir, vivir una cosa de otra, apoyarse mutuamente, conllevarse, alimentarse y potenciarse." [164]

Ortega's ethic of excellence (as in *Rebelión de las masas*) also presupposes others, although Mañach sees Ortega's ethics as more of a moral relativity.

> [Ortega] postuló siempre una correspondencia entre la conducta y el ser "auténtico" de cada cual —el que resulta de las intimaciones más profundas del yo. "Veo la característica del acto moral en la plenitud con que es querido. Cuando todo nuestro ser quiere algo —sin reservas, sin temores, integralmente— cumplimos con nuestro deber, porque es el mayor deber la fidelidad consigo mismos." "No se ha de considerar la moral como un sistema de prohibiciones y deberes genéricos, el mismo para todos los individuos. Eso es una abstracción." [165]

Thus for Ortega right exists only in the context of concrete circumstances, and while this seems dangerous to Mañach, he is not unconscious of the fact that abstract moral standards can often produce a purely negative morality. Nevertheless, his final interpretation is

---

[162] Mañach, p. 105.
[163] Mañach, p. 111.
[164] Mañach, p. 112.
[165] Mañach, p. 119.

unfavorable: "Resulta en verdad difícil no ver en esta doctrina, según la cual el único pecado es la falsificación, la hipocresía, un peligroso relativismo ético." [166] It should be remembered that other critics, particularly Marías, have pointed out that for Ortega the individual has a responsibility not only to himself, but to society, history, the world, and his destiny. We will examine more closely the nature of this responsibility in the chapter which deals with Ortega himself. Mañach observes that although Ortega was rich in ideas, he lacked moral ideals and *dimensión humana,* but his concluding remarks are nonetheless of praise and appreciation for Ortega's philosophic contribution. He sees him as a synthesist:

> En el orden filosófico, aún están por precisar los linderos de su originalidad respecto del pensamiento europeo. Es probable que cuando esto se haga, quepa reconocerle al filósofo español el intento más deliberado de resolver ciertas antimonías que aquel pensamiento no había logrado superar —la oposición entre subjetivismo y objetivismo, idealismo y realismo, absolutismo y relativismo—; que se pueda ver en él, al mismo tiempo, al salvador de la razón frente a las demasías irracionalistas y, con Bergson, de la intuición frente al racionalismo excesivo... que se le acredite, en fin, frente a las oscuridades existencialistas, el planteamiento más luminoso de la filosofía de la vida después de Dilthey. ... [167]

A number of other commemorative articles have a philosophical orientation. Vicente Mengod emphasizes the importance of circumstance in Ortega's philosophy. [168] Most of the article deals with his definitions of life. Eleazar Huerta takes a position similar to that of Marías and other critics regarding Ortega's life in relation to his own individual circumstances. [169] He envisions Ortega as forced to his particular media and form of expression, and with references to his life and political activities, sees Ortega as *engagé.*

---

[166] Mañach, p. 119.

[167] Mañach, pp. 124-125.

[168] Vicente Mengod, "El tema de las ideas en Ortega," *Atenea,* CXXIV (1956), 34-43.

[169] Eleazar Huerta, "La prosa de Ortega," *Atenea,* CXXIV (1956), 48-72.

One of the strongest cases for considering Ortega an existentialist is made by Alfredo Stern, who intended to demonstrate something quite different. His article is entitled "¿Ortega existencialista o esencialista?" and begins with the observation that he believes certain parts of Ortega's work show decidedly existentialist traits, while others belong to the essentialist school of philosophy. The article is an attempt to prove this, and its author feels he has done so successfully:

> Creemos haber demostrado nuestra tesis de que en la obra filosófica de Ortega rige un dualismo. En la teoría de la vida y de la razón vital como funciones del tiempo histórico hemos encontrado un *existencialismo antifenomenológico*. La Estimativa de Ortega, por el contrario, constituye un *esencialismo fenomenológico*. [170]

Stern observes that there are numerous concepts of a marked similarity in the work of Ortega and Heidegger, and strongly defends Ortega's priority:

> Y es uno de los errores más trágicos que hasta en España la relación entre Ortega y Heidegger haya sido, tan frecuentemente, concebida de tal manera que el pensador español apareció como un simple propagador de la filosofía heideggeriana. Un examen de las obras de los dos filósofos demuestra, sin embargo, la absoluta prioridad de Ortega en todo lo esencial. [171]

Among Ortega's concepts which were rediscovered by Heidegger he mentions the idea of life as a dialogue between the individual and his circumstances, and the interpretation of truth as *aletheia*, in the etymological sense of discovery. He feels that the two philosophers make the same differentiation between being and existence, although Ortega substitutes life for the latter term. Stern's conclusion from the foregoing almost makes Ortega the father of existentialism:

> Son éstas las tesis básicas del existencialismo moderno, delineadas por Heidegger en 1927, en su famoso libro *Sein*

---

[170] Alfredo Stern, "¿Ortega existencialista o esencialista?," *La Torre*, XV (July-Dec. 1956), p. 398.

[171] Stern, p. 386.

und Zeit. Si, trece años antes, Ortega escribió en sus *Meditaciones del Quijote*: "Yo soy yo y mi circunstancia," si, diecisiete años antes, calificó en su *Adán en el paraíso* nuestra existencia como un "convivir" o "coexistir," es evidente que es él quien dio la descripción básica de la existencia humana y así proclamó los principios del existencialismo moderno. [172]

The concepts of man as a vital project, of the future as possibility, of the individual as necessarily free are, says Stern, purely existentialist. He cites as the best proof of this the fact that Sartre adopted them in detail in *L'Etre et le Néant,* eight years after they were enunciated by Ortega in *Historia como sistema.* "Es superfluo mencionar que Sartre no se refiere a su ilustre predecessor." [173] Stern's treatment of Sartre and Ortega consists of a point by point comparison of several ideas held in common, and the indication that in each case, Ortega was first to publish by a number of years. These ideas include that of man as *what he does,* the idea that human nature is a false concept, the idea that an individual *is* his past.

En su librito *L'Existentialisme est un Humanisme,* publicado en 1946, Sartre escribió: "L'homme n'est rien d'autre que ce qu'il se fait. Tel est le premier principe de l'existentialisme." Si es así, entonces no cabe duda de que Ortega debe ser considerado como existencialista. Porque ya once años antes de Sartre el pensador español había escrito: "El hombre es el ente que se hace a sí mismo," se hace en vista de la circunstancia y, así, es un "Dios de ocasión" o "el novelista de sí mismo, original o plagiario." Con esta idea Ortega sigue una tradición existencialista que va de Kierkegaard a través de Heidegger hasta Sartre. [174]

This writer feels, however, that there are numerous existentialist ideas not present in Ortega's works. He mentions in particular the ideas of anguish and despair. He does not conceive existentialism as a philosophy which is concerned to any significant extent with ethics, and therefore feels that Ortega's concern with ethics distinguishes him further from the rest of existentialism.

---

[172] Stern, p. 388.
[173] Stern, p. 389.
[174] Stern, p. 389.

The remainder of Stern's article is devoted to showing that Ortega is equally an essentialist, and as such is much less successful. His argument is based on one point, Ortega's idea of *valores*. This the critic considers to be an objective, and therefore essentialist, category. Stern feels that Ortega was strongly influenced by Scheler's theory of values, and much of the article deals with their similarities.

Paulino Garagorri relates Camus to Ortega in a rather surprising fashion: "Como discípulo de Ortega—porque también lo reconoció paladinamente con ocasión del premio (Nobel)—tenía del hecho generacional no un incontrolable sentimiento, sino conceptos bastante precisos." [175]

Writing on "Ortega y Gasset and Goethe," Kassel Schwartz notes Ortega's intellectual debt to Germany, and his lifelong interest in Goethe. Goethe was preoccupied ceaselessly with his life because life is preoccupation with self. Therefore he was the first contemporary or Romantic who saw that life is not a reality which confronts problems, but that it consists of the problem of itself exclusively. Goethe, says Ortega, spent his life looking for his self, or fleeing it, "que es todo lo contrario que cuidando la exacta realización de sí mismo." [176] "The existential implications of Ortega's theories are obvious," remarks Schwartz, and mentions Ortega's claim to thirteen years of published priority on certain of Heidegger's ideas. He also compares Ortega's and Sartre's ideas on the nature of man as action, but does not follow up with a demonstration of the relation of existentialism to Ortega's interest in Goethe, a point which might well have been made.

A final article relevant to the question of Ortega's relationship to existentialism is entitled "Existencia y destino del hombre según Ortega y Gasset y Jean-Paul Sartre." [177]

This author begins with a definition of life according to Ortega, and then observes:

> Como el hombre orteguiano, el hombre sartreano es
> *d'abord un projet.* Como no hay naturaleza humana ni

---

[175] Paulino Garagorri, "Albert Camus y su generación," *Cuadernos del Congreso por la libertad de la Cultura*, XLIII (July-August 1960), 83.

[176] Kessel Schwartz, "Ortega y Gasset and Goethe," *Hispania*, XLIII (Sept. 1960), 324.

[177] Hugo Rodríguez Alcalá, *Cuadernos Americanos*, CX (May-June 1960).

dada ni fija, no hay determinismo, y por tanto el hombre es libre, "el hombre es libertad." Solo, abandonado a su libertad, lanzado a su tembladal ontológico, sin ningún ser superior a quien recurrir, el hombre está condenado a ser libre.

...en ambos escritores, la existencia precede a la esencia y el viejo problema de la libertad y del determinismo se resuelve de idéntica manera: soy libre porque no teniendo una naturaleza fija, debo hacerme a mí mismo y elegir lo que he de ser. [178]

Rodríguez-Alcalá notes that the concepts of *circunstancia* and *situation* would need special study before any comparison could be made, although the notions are similar:

Según Ortega, mi deber para con mi circunstancia es reabsorberla. Es decir, debo asumir todas las responsabilidades impuestas por mi circunstancia intransferible y cumplir mi destino en una lucha constante con aquello que no soy yo, pero sin lo cual yo no sería ni tendría ser. Parejamente, Sartre afirma que mi deber en mi personal *situation* es *m'engager,* comprometerme, asumir las responsabilidades que me impone mi situación personal en las circunstancias que afectan mi vida y la del prójimo. [179]

He states that Sartre has attempted a reconciliation of realism and idealism very similar in form to Ortega's idea of *razón vital,* in his declaration of the interdependence of things and conscience. He distinguishes these points of difference between the two: "En Ortega, las tesis existencialistas tienen una dimensión historicista y vitalista... En punto al meditar histórico, no hay similitud entre Ortega y Sartre. En las obras del primero, la historia tiene un lugar e importancia que no tiene en las del segundo." [180] Further, destiny is more complex for Ortega than for Sartre, and carries a moral imperative lacking for the latter:

Sartre no plantea el problema de la vocación en su investigación del sentido del destino; hace hincapié en el

---

[178] Rodríguez-Alcalá, p. 96.
[179] Rodríguez-Alcalá, p. 98.
[180] Rodríguez-Alcalá, p. 100.

hecho de la libertad humana. Tanto que, si voy contra mi vocación, si la contrario hasta el punto de obliterarla solamente porque tal es mi voluntad, yo cumplo un destino, es decir, *mi* destino. Para Ortega, por el contrario, el concepto del destino es inseparable de un *deber ser* moral, de un imperativo que demanda un austero respeto a la voz de mi vocación. Destino es vocación oída y obedecida. Destino auténtico, se entiende. [181]

The handful of articles just reviewed exemplifies the critical treatment of existentialism in Ortega's work. The fact that all the articles are covered together may give the impression that existentialism has been a more important theme with critics than is actually the case. Well over one hundred articles listed in the appendix did not touch on the subject.

To resume, the articles most pertinent to the present study have made these points:

1) Franz Niedermayer related Ortega to Jaspers and Heidegger.

2) Humberto Piñera Llera studied the theme of life in Ortega's works and related several of his terms to the existentialist repertory.

3) Jorge Mañach questioned whether Ortega was a philosopher of life, and concluded that he was, although he separated this idea from existentialism in his conclusion.

4) Kessel Schwartz felt that there were obvious existentialist implications in Ortega's work, though he did not elaborate. He briefly compared Ortega and Sartre.

5) Hugo Rodríguez-Alcalá compared Ortega's and Sartre's concepts of man and destiny.

6) Alfredo Stern argued that Ortega's philosophy is both existentialist and essentialist, and yet made by far the strongest case for considering Ortega an existentialist. He stressed the priority of Ortega to both Heidegger and Sartre and made extensive comparisons between several concepts held by both Ortega and Sartre, strongly suggesting the possibility that an unacknowledged indebtedness exists on the part of the latter.

---

[181] Rodríguez-Alcalá, p. 106.

This is, of course, far from constituting a critical consensus but it is more than enough to suggest that there is *something* in Ortega's philosophy which has been overlooked or ignored by the major critics. As was pointed out earlier, Ferrater Mora, Gaos and Marías do not broach the subject of existentialism, although the latter two and several of the lesser critics favorable to Ortega have made much of his living in accord with his principles — which are precisely the ideas in his philosophy which other critics have cited as existentialist. When raised by the Catholic critics, the issue of existentialism has been equated with moral relativism, atheism, or heresy. Most of their works deal with philosophic sources and influences, at times to the near exclusion of Ortega himself. The tone of these writings is usually condemnatory.

It is quite possible that the avoidance of the issue of existentialism by Ortega's adherents is one aspect of their conflict with his detractors who have used existentialism as an epithet, or a verdict of guilty, although much of their criticism has been extremely flimsy.

CHAPTER III

THE MAJOR THEMES OF ORTEGA

Among the thousands of pages of Ortega's works appears this line: "Todo escritor tiene derecho a que busquemos en su obra lo que en ella ha querido poner." [1] In the Prologue to the 1932 Espasa-Calpe edition of his *Obras,* Ortega remarked:

> No hay grandes probabilidades de que una obra como la mía, que, aunque de escaso valor, es muy compleja, muy llena de secretos, alusiones y elisiones, muy entretejida con toda una trayectoria vital, encuentre el ánimo generoso que se afane, de verdad, en entenderla. Obras más abstractas, desligadas por su propósito y estilo de la vida personal en que surgieron, pueden ser más fácilmente asimiladas, porque requieren menos faena interpretativa. Pero cada una de las páginas aquí reunidas resumió mi existencia entera a la hora en que fue escrita y, yuxtapuestas, representan la melodía de mi destino personal.

Marías quotes the above passage on the frontispiece of *Circunstancia y vocación,* and the differences between his interpretation and the one which follows would seem to demonstrate the truth of Ortega's feeling for interpretations of his work. My interpretation is frankly subjective, a response to the promptings of intuition. It is at the same time that attempt to find the writer's meaning which Ortega says is the right of every author. Perhaps the ultimate truths of the philosopher's intent will forever elude us, but the relating of his works to

---

[1] José Ortega y Gasset, *Obras Completas,* II (Madrid, 1946), 73. Hereafter referred to as *Obras Completas.*

the themes of existentialism should provide, at least, much food for thought.

From the work of the critics cited in the preceding chapter, there can be no doubt that human life, or existence, is a central theme in Ortega's work. Human nature, defined in terms of the ego and its biological, social and historical surroundings ("yo soy yo y mi circunstancia") also emerges as one of the pivotal points of Ortegan philosophy. Mentioned less frequently, but nonetheless repeatedly, are the concepts of authenticity, of "mass man" and elite, and Ortega's ideas of the nature of knowledge and of the relationship of individual and society. While some idea of Ortega's definition and use of these and other elements of his philosophy may have been gleaned from the various critical interpretations, undoubtedly the best understanding can be reached through an analytical look at Ortega's own words.

Ortega's earliest works or *mocedades* have been very thoroughly studied by Marías and Salmerón, to mention only the most extensive analyses to date, and while both aimed to show the internal cohesiveness of Ortega's system by indicating anticipatory ideas, they have at the same time pointed out and interpreted major themes in the works prior to 1914. Therefore, our consideration of this period may be brief, inasmuch as some ninety percent of Ortega's work remains virtually unexamined. The reader particularly interested in Ortega's earliest period is referred to the previously cited books by Marías and Salmerón.

In Ortega's first published essay (1902), he speaks out in favor of a personal or individual standard of literary criticism rather than the impartial or objective norm. The critic must take a stand, must commit himself, for this is the nature of life: "¿Creen ustedes que la vida se deja taladrar y arrastrar sin lucha? El crítico ha de luchar. La crítica es una lucha... ¿es posible salirse de la vida?" [2] "El poeta del misterio" which ostensibly deals with Maeterlinck, at the same times serves Ortega as a vehicle for the expression of his idea of the unknowable, the realm beyond the senses, which can never be adequately expressed.

---

[2] *Obras Completas*, I, 14.

El individuo no ha existido nunca: es una abstracción. La humanidad no existe todavía: es un ideal. En tanto que vamos y venimos, la única realidad es la nación, nuestra nación; lo que hoy constituye nuestros quehaceres diarios, es la flor de lo que soñaron nuestros abuelos. ... Tenemos, pues, un terrible deber con el porvenir. [3]

The article in which the foregoing remarks appear deals ostensibly with a linguistic work by Julio Cejador, *Diccionario del Quijote*. It was written in 1904. Even in these early works, one may distinguish Ortega's preoccupation with the nature of the individual and his relation to society, with the nature of reality, and with the ethical imperative thereby imposed.

It might be well to reiterate here that it is not our purpose to enter the fray over whether or not Ortega has a system, or even to study the evolution of his ideas as such. However, some personal conclusions on these issues will be well-nigh unavoidable in the course of a search for Ortega's major themes, and such conclusions are not entirely unrelated to the ultimate resolution of the problem of this study.

Concerning Ortega's early works (roughly the period up to 1930) the procedure is rather more expository than otherwise. It is during these years that the evolution of Ortega's thought, if we may use the term without inviting controversy, is most apparent. Numerous citations relating to Ortega's philosophy of existence (particularly with reference to life and to human nature) are adduced, but little effort is made to show them in an existentialist context. During the later years, however (that is, from *La rebelión de las masas* on), there is a greater attempt to show individual works as susceptible of placement in the overall framework of a philosophy of existence. This is first done in the case of *La deshumanización del arte e ideas sobre la novela*. While it becomes clear that this latter work can be fitted into an existentialist outlook, it is not one of the most important of Ortega's philosophical doctrines, and thus it is that the serious interrelating begins with *La rebelión de las masas*.

Ortega's early articles seem at first glance to range over a wide and diverse body of subjects, but common attitudes and

---

[3] *Obras Completas*, I, 39.

preoccupations emerge, the central concern with "life." Thus, in an article which compares ancient and modern poetry, Ortega observes: "El arte es una subrogación de la vida." "No creo que puede haber arte en su noble acepción que no radique en esas realidades perennes." [4]

Of the articles cited thus far, the apparent subject of each is a specific case of literary criticism; however, in each there are portions which are less literary than philosophical, echoing the question Ortega posed in his first essay: "¿Es posible salirse de la vida?"

Ortega's philosophical criticisms are equally personal. Although he may present an exposition of another's philosophy, Ortega is soon inserting ideas of his own. In an article entitled "El sobrehombre," inspired by a book of Goerge Simmel about Nietzsche, Ortega observes that its major problem is the definition of man, adding: "Las revoluciones políticas, la del 89 patentemente, son también luchas por la definición del hombre. ...La definición del hombre, verdadero y único problema de la Ética, es el motor de las variaciones históricas." [5]

Turning back to Nietzsche, Ortega speaks of the latter's ideas on life and ethics. Without attempting to decide whether Ortega's presentation has been colored by his own latent ideas or whether his later ideas result from Nietzsche's influence, let us note in passing a similarity between the two philosophers' ideas of life: "Para Nietzsche vivir es *más vivir,* o de otro modo, vida es el nombre que damos a una serie de cualidades progresivas, al instinto de crecimiento, de perduración, de capitalización de fuerzas, de poder." [6] Ortega concludes the article with a strong emphasis on the moral aspects of Nietzsche's philosophy, pointing out that he does not preach the breaking of all moral laws. The words with which he demonstrates this indicate that Ortega's *minorías selectas* are similar, at least on the ethical plane, to the "superman": "El hombre distinguido honra en sí mismo al potente, al que tiene poder sobre sí mismo, al que sabe hablar y callar, que ejercita placentera rigidez

---

[4] *Obras Completas,* I, 51-52.
[5] *Obras Completas,* I, 92-93.
[6] *Obras Completas,* I, 94.

y dureza consigo mismo y siente veneración hacia todo lo rígido y duro." [7]

A series of subsequent articles continues the effort to define man: "El hombre primitivo," "El hombre clásico," "El hombre oriental," "El hombre mediterráneo," "El hombre gótico." [8] The theme of "Alemán, latín y griego" is culture, culture as an orientation to life: "queremos vivir, vivir la vida elemental, respirar aire, andar, ver, oír, comer, amar y odiar. Necesitamos todo lo contrario de lo que Francia puede ofrecernos: cultura de pasiones y de ideas, no de formas... Necesitamos una introducción a la vida esencial." [9] A long study of Freud, "Psicoanálisis, ciencia problemática" [10] is basically philosophical in its attempt to define the effective limits of science. Ortega's interest in psychoanalysis is part of his attempt to define the nature of man, and to understand the nature of knowledge.

The first important political pronouncement which Ortega made, the lecture "Vieja y nueva política" (1914) is imbued with an idea of action which is strikingly existential:

> En épocas críticas puede una generación condenarse a histórica esterilidad por no haber tenido el valor de licenciar las palabras recibidas, los credos agónicos, y hacer en su lugar la enérgica afirmación de sus propios, nuevos sentimientos. Como cada individuo, cada generación, si quiere ser útil a la humanidad, ha de comenzar por ser fiel a sí misma. [11]

It would be inaccurate to represent this lecture as other than primarily political in nature and intent. The excerpt serves to indicate the consistency with which Ortega's political ideas fit into the larger structure of his ethics and philosophy of life.

In his foreword to the reader, which accompanies the *Meditaciones del Quijote,* Ortega points out the ethical weight of his nascent philosophy:

---

[7] *Obras Completas,* I, 95.
[8] *Obras Completas,* I, 195-205.
[9] *Obras Completas,* I, 209.
[10] *Obras Completas,* I, 216-238.
[11] *Obras Completas,* I, 270.

> Espero que al leer esto nadie derivará la consecuencia de serme indiferente el ideal moral. Yo no desdeño la moralidad en beneficio de un frívolo jugar con las ideas. Las doctrinas inmoralistas que hasta ahora han llegado a mi conocimiento carecen de sentido común. Y a decir verdad, yo no dedico mis esfuerzos a otra cosa que a ver si logro poseer un poco de sentido común.
>
> Pero, en reverencia del ideal moral, es preciso que combatamos sus mayores enemigos, que son las moralidades perversas. Y en mi entender —y no sólo en el mío—, lo son todas las morales utilitarias. [12]

His meditations are motivated by what the philosopher calls an imperative of understanding, and he states: "Van empujadas por filosóficos deseos." [13]

It is in the introduction to *Meditaciones del Quijote* that the concept of circumstance first is explained:

> El hombre rinde el máximum de su capacidad cuando adquiere la plena conciencia de sus circunstancias. Por ellas comunica con el universo.
> ¡La circunstancia! ¡*Circum-stantia*! ¡Las cosas mudas que están en nuestro próximo derredor! Muy cerca, muy cerca de nosotros levantan sus tácitas fisonomías con un gesto de humildad y de anhelo, como menesterosas de que aceptemos su ofrenda y a la par avergonzadas por la simplicidad aparente de su donativo. [14]

The idea of the individual existence as the philosophic point of departure also appears: "Debiéramos considerar que así la vida social como las demás formas de la cultura, se nos dan bajo la especie de vida individual, de lo inmediato." [15]

Ortega relates this to his idea of perspective, or individual point of view (which appears as a major doctrine in later works): "¿Cuándo nos abriremos a la convicción de que el ser definitivo del mundo no es materia ni es alma, no es cosa alguna determinada, sino una perspectiva? Dios es la perspectiva y la jerarquía: el pecado de

---

[12] *Obras Completas*, I, 315.
[13] *Obras Completas*, I, 318.
[14] *Obras Completas*, I, 319.
[15] *Obras Completas*, I, 321.

Satán fue un error de perspectiva." [16] In finding for our individual perspective its place in the world perspective, or relating our individual circumstance to what Ortega might call cosmic circumstances, the philosopher sees man's destiny:

> Hemos de buscar para nuestra circunstancia, tal y como ella es, precisamente en lo que tiene de limitación, de peculiaridad, el lugar acertado en la inmensa perspectiva del mundo. No detenernos perpetuamente en éxtasis ante los valores hieráticos, sino conquistar a nuestra vida individual el puesto oportuno entre ellos. En suma: la reabsorción de la circunstancia es el destino concreto del hombre. [17]

The idea of action is predominant in the above passage: not contemplation, but conquest.

As Ortega's first book, *Meditaciones del Quijote* has an undeniable importance; however, Marías has analyzed and interpreted the book with great thoroughness, showing quite conclusively that all of the significant philosophical ideas therein are repeated in later works, or are anticipatory of later concepts. Any summary of its principal themes, therefore, would be repetitious, both with regard to our consideration of Ortega's mature works, and the previous detailed examination of Marías's study. Since such repetition would add little, it seems better to go immediately to those of Ortega's writings which have not been so carefully studied.

Several articles have been written recently which compare Unamuno and Machado; Sánchez Barbudo is the author of a book entitled *Estudios sobre Unamuno y Machado* (Madrid, 1959), which relates the two Spaniards to contemporary existentialism, comparing Machado with Jaspers, Scheler and Husserl. Marías himself wrote un article "Machado y Heidegger" (*Insula*, VIII). It is interesting, therefore, to find an article written by Ortega in 1912 which compares Unamuno and Machado:

> El alma del verso es el alma del hombre que lo va componiendo. Y este alma no puede a su vez consistir en una estratificación de palabras, de metáforas, de ritmos.

---

[16] *Obras Completas,* I, 321
[17] *Obras Completas,* I, 322.

> Tiene que ser un lugar por donde dé su aliento el universo,
> respiradero de la vida esencial, *spiriculum vitae,* como de-
> cían los místicos alemanes.
>
> Yo encuentro en Machado un comienzo de esta noví-
> sima poesía, cuyo más fuerte representante sería Unamuno
> si no despreciara los sentidos tanto. [18]

This is strong evidence of Ortega's competence as a critic. It may
be more, however; Ortega's early recognition of the two poets'
relatedness to the philosophy of life may have been the result of a
realization of the similarity of some of their ideas to his own.

In his introduction to *El Espectador,* Ortega reflects upon the
relation between contemplation and action, or between philosophy
and life, life in a very utilitarian sense:

> la vida española nos obliga, queramos o no, a la acción
> política. El inmediato porvenir, tiempo de sociales hervores,
> nos forzará a ella con mayor violencia. Precisamente por
> eso yo necesito acotar una parte de mí mismo para la con-
> templación. Y esto que me acontece, acontece a todos.
> Desde hace medio siglo, en España y fuera de España, la
> política —es decir, la supeditación de la teoría a la utili-
> dad— ha invadido por completo el espíritu. [19]

The germs of many of the ideas in *La rebelión de las masas* can
be seen in the above quotation. The passage is an excellent example,
also, of Ortega's tendency to use common words in a particular,
restricted sense peculiar to himself. After the introduction given in
the last sentence of the passage quoted, Ortega uses *política* repeatedly in the sense of utilitarianism. Since he also uses it in the
conventional sense, it is not difficult to see how many misunderstandings of Ortega have arisen, particularly in the cases of those
whose acquaintance embraces only a small portion of his works,
or whose acquaintance is second-hand.

El Espectador has usually been considered a miscellaneous
collection of newspaper articles, some on issues of the day, others
on literary criticism, philosophy, travel and lighter themes. Its author

---

[18] *Obras Completas,* I, 564-565.
[19] *Obras Completas,* II, 15.

indicates that it is more than mere observation; its intent is to provoke contemplation:

> El escritor, para condensar su esfuerzo, necesita de un público, como el licor de la copa en que se vierte. Por esto es *El Espectador* la conmovida apelación a un público de *amigos de mirar,* de lectores a quienes interesen las cosas aparte de sus consecuencias, cualesquiera que ellas sean, morales inclusive. Lectores meditabundos, que se complazcan en perseguir la fisonomía de los objetos en toda su delicada, compleja estructura. ... [20]

El Espectador, the book of "the spectator" is of course clearly related to Ortega's perspectivism. *El Espectador is* his perspective. Perhaps one of the best theoretical statements of the doctrine of point of view is found in the introduction to *El Espectador*:

> La verdad, lo real, el universo, la vida —como queráis llamarlo—, se quiebra en facetas innumerables, en vertientes sin cuento, cada una de las cuales da hacia un individuo. Si éste ha sabido ser fiel a su punto de vista, si ha resistido a la eterna seducción de cambiar su retina por otra imaginaria, lo que ve será un aspecto real del mundo.
>
> Y viceversa: cada hombre tiene una misión de verdad. Donde está mi pupila no está otra: lo que de la realidad ve mi pupila no lo ve otra. Somos insustituibles, somos necesarios. ... La realidad, pues, se ofrece en perspectivas individuales. [21]

In the uniqueness of each individual perspective, in the importance of each observation as *part* of reality, one can discern the foreshadowing of the imperative of authenticity, and only a little more remotely, of the individual existence as basic reality.

"Cuando no hay alegría" is a rather enigmatic little essay, almost lyric. Reading it carefully, one discovers the idea of the radical solitude of the individual existence, and, in the closing line, a note very like the existentialist concept of anguish:

---

[20] *Obras Completas,* II, 17.
[21] *Obras Completas,* II, 19.

Cuando no hay alegría, el alma se retira a un rincón de nuestro cuerpo y hace de él su cubil. De cuando en cuando da un aullido lastimero o enseña los dientes a las cosas que pasan. ... Y como la gracia y la alegría y el lujo de las cosas consisten en los reflejos innumerables que las unas lanzan sobre las otras y de ellas reciben —la sardana que bailan cogidas todas de la mano—, la sospecha de su soledad radical parece rebajar el pulso del mundo. ... Y presentimos que hay dondequiera oculto un nervio que alguien se entretiene en punzar rítmicamente. En la estrella, en la ola marina, en el corazón del hombre, da su latido a compás el dolor inagotable. ... [22]

In the series of essays grouped under the title "Ideas sobre Pío Baroja," appears a philosophic justification of Ortega's interest in literary criticism, which directly relates it to the philosophy of life:

Cuando hemos leído ya mucha literatura y algunas heridas en el corazón nos han hecho incompatibles con la retórica, empezamos a no interesarnos más que en aquellas obras donde llega a nosotros gemebunda o riente la emoción que en el autor suscita la existencia. Y llamamos retórico, en el mal sentido de la palabra, a todo libro en cuyo fondo no resuene ese trémolo metafísico. [23]

An essay entitled "Teoría de la felicidad" presents the idea of happiness as all-absorbing activity, dependent upon having a goal toward which to struggle:

Cuando pedimos a la existencia cuentas claras de su sentido, no hacemos sino que nos presente alguna cosa capaz de *absorber nuestra actividad*. Si notásemos que algo en el mundo bastaba a henchir el volumen de nuestra energía vital, nos sentiríamos felices y el universo nos parecería justificado. ¿Puede hacer esto la ciencia o el arte o el placer? Todo depende de que esas cosas dejen o no en nosotros porciones de vitalidad vacantes, inejercidas y como en bostezo.

---

[22] *Obras Completas,* II, 31.
[23] *Obras Completas,* II, 72.

> Aquí está, aquí está el origen de la infelicidad. ¿Quién, que se halle totalmente absorbido por una ocupación, se siente infeliz? [24]

The critics who recoiled in horror from Ortega's "dangerous moral relativism" might do well to ponder passages such as the one above. The overall tendency of his philosophy is toward an ethic, although the ethic be subjective. But objective standards, being abstractions or generalizations, are limited. Cases can always be found where they do not apply. The subjective norms of conduct, consistently applied, should have no exceptions, precisely because they are adjustable for each individual instance. In this connection, the first imperative for Ortega is sincerity: "No hay valores absolutos ni absolutas realidades. Todo puede valer absolutamente, ser absolutamente real si es sinceramente sentido. Ser y ser sincero valgan como sinónimos." [25]

Ortega returns to the ideal of action in an essay with the title "La acción como ideal," in which he observes: "La aventura de una ficción de sentido a la vida, la hace interesante, pone en ella claroscuro, matiz, peripecia." [26] Action is related again to philosophy, and to circumstance:

> Todos nuestros actos, y un acto es el pensar, van como preguntas o como respuestas referidos siempre a aquella porción del mundo que en cada instante existe para nosotros. Nuestra vida es un diálogo, donde es el individuo sólo un interlocutor: el otro es el paisaje, lo circunstante. ¿Cómo entender al uno sin el otro? [27]

In an essay on Azorín, Ortega introduces some of his ideas on history, first in the conventional sense of the word. He inquires if progress, in fact, exists, and answers his own question as follows:

> La progresión es siempre relativa a la meta que hayamos predeterminado. El progreso de la vida humana será real si las metas ideales a que la referimos satisfacen

---

[24] *Obras Completas,* II, 79.
[25] *Obras Completas,* II, 83.
[26] *Obras Completas,* II, 90-91.
[27] *Obras Completas,* II, 145.

> plenamente. Si el ideal cuya aproximación mide y prueba
> nuestro avance es ficticio o insuficiente, no podemos decir
> que la vida humana progrese. [28]

History is important as part of one's philosophical orientation, an
art of the necessary knowledge of one's circumstances or reality:

> Decía yo antes que debemos retener nuestro pasado y
> fijar bien nuestra aspiración hacia mañana, para que una
> y otra, convergiendo en nuestro presente, den a éste
> plenitud, triple dimensión, grosor, volumen. Cuantas más
> porciones de nosotros se hallen presentes en nuestro pre-
> sente, mayor será su realidad. Una decisión tomada en el
> momento, sin consultar a nuestro yo de ayer y al de mañana,
> tendrá mucha menos densidad personal, será mucho menos
> *nuestra* decisión que la formada con la asistencia y cola-
> boración del resto de nuestra vida. [29]

It is in the same series of essays on Azorín that Ortega's concept
of mass and minority, used in the context of intellectual elite and
masses, rather than politically, appears. This was written in 1916,
almost twenty years before the publication of *La rebelión de las
masas,* and while the concept was more fully elaborated later, it is
indisputably the same:

> Los espíritus selectos tienen la clara intuición de que eter-
> namente formarán una minoría —tolerada a veces, casi
> siempre aplastada por la muchedumbre inferior, jamás
> comprendida y nunca amada. Cuando la muchedumbre ha
> pulido un poco más sus apetitos y ha ampliado su percep-
> ción, la minoría excelente ha avanzado también en su
> propio perfeccionamiento. El abismo perdura siempre entre
> los menos y los más, y no será nunca allanado. Siempre
> habrá dos tablas contrapuestas de valoración: la de los
> mejores y la de los muchos —en moral, en costumbres, en
> gestos, en arte. [30]

It is interesting to note that at this early date, Ortega sees the
minority and mass as an ethical concept as well. He also relates it

---

28 *Obras Completas,* II, 158-159.
29 *Obras Completas,* II, 159-160.
30 *Obras Completas,* II, 165.

to society at large, in much the same fashion as Kierkegaard in his writing on the individual and society: "El hombre trivial tiene la ventaja de coincidir siempre con su derredor; a cada palabra suya parece aguardar en el aire un hueco recortado a la medida. Lo que piensa y dice es lo que los demás acaban de pensar y decir, o se disponen a pensar y decir." [31]

Another instance of Ortega's application of his philosophical attitudes in specific literary criticisms occurs in an article on Anatole France. Ortega observes that France has not changed; he has exactly the same ideas, the same emotions, the same technique as he has had for forty years, which to Ortega is a fault, since it indicates a lack of vitality:

> Su obra, exenta de ocaso, no ha gozado, en cambio, de un alba invasora que alancea a la noche y, aún balbuciente, pregona ya el mediodía. A esta belleza, que aspira sobre todo a ser incorruptible y sin edad, confieso preferir un arte más saturado de vida que se sabe hijo de un tiempo y con él destinado a transcurrir. [32]

Continuing the same line of thought, Ortega reflects that life is flux with the threat of death:

> La vida es duración y mudanza: nace, florece, muere y deja tras sí la ocasión para otras vidas sucesivas y distintas. ... Todas las formas vivientes, inclusive las artísticas son perecederas. La vida misma es un frenético escultor, que, incesantemente afanado en producir nuevas apariencias, necesita de la muerte, como de un fámulo, para que desaloje del taller los modelos concluidos. ... ¡O, sí, la mayor sabiduría es secundar esta misteriosa universal voluntad de la vida! Aprendamos a preferir lo corruptible a lo inmutable. [33]

In *Vieja y nueva política,* Ortega stated that a primary function of politics should be increasing the national vitality. In the third book of *El Espectador,* some seven years later, he attributes a related function to pedagogy:

---

[31] *Obras Completas,* II, 165.
[32] *Obras Completas,* II, 225.
[33] *Obras Completas,* II, 225.

> Por lo pronto, tenemos que asegurar la salud vital, su-
> puesto de toda otra salud. Y el sentido de este ensayo no
> es otro que inducir a la pedagogía para que someta toda
> la primera etapa de la educación al imperio de la vitalidad.
> La enseñanza elemental debe ir gobernada por el propósito
> último de producir el mayor número de hombres vitalmente
> perfectos. Lo demás, la bondad moral, la destreza técnica,
> el sabio y el "buen ciudadano," serán atendidos después. [34]

In a footnote, Ortega observes that none of these (morality, technical accomplishment, etc.) are possible except as the "emanation of a healthy vitality." *Vitalidad* is not the exact equivalent of Ortega's later use of *vida,* but there can be no doubt that the two are closely related.

The tendency to relate everything to life appears in Ortega's "Notas de viaje" when he compares the Castilian countryside with that of France: "Goce de vivir, desdén de vivir; estos dos modos últimos y opuestos de sentir la existencia palpitan en los paisajes de dos naciones tan próximas, y a la vez tan distantes, como Francia y España." [35]

Ortega's attempt to define the ego appears again in a linguistic meditation:

> El hombre empieza a conocerse por las cosas que le perte-
> necen. El pronombre posesivo precede al personal. La idea
> de "lo mío" es anterior a la del "yo." Más tarde, el acento
> se transfiere de "nuestras" cosas a nuestra persona social.
> La figura que hacemos en la sociedad, que es lo más ex-
> terno de nuestra personalidad, toma la representación de
> nuestro verdadero ser. [36]

He sees the inner self as an abstraction from the concrete, outer self. The inner self, consciousness, is present in everything else:

> No podemos hablar de cosa alguna que no se halle en
> relación con nosotros, y esta su relación mínima con nos-
> otros es la relación consciente. Los dos objetos más dis-
> tintos que quepa imaginar tienen, no obstante, la nota co-

---

[34] *Obras Completas,* II, 285.
[35] *Obras Completas,* II, 367.
[36] *Obras Completas,* II, 387.

mún de ser objeto para nuestra mente, de ser objetos para un sujeto. [37]

Because consciousness is a universal, omnipresent phenomenon, Ortega considers it the most difficult of all to conceive, perceive, describe and define: "Este fenómeno universal de la relación entre el sujeto y el objeto, que es el darse cuenta, sólo podrá concebirse comparándolo con alguna forma particular de las relaciones entre objetos. El resultado será una metáfora." [38] Ortega notes the danger of identifying the metaphor with the reality it represents, and them proceeds to a consideration of realism and idealism, which he will later describe as *las dos grandes metáforas*.

The theme of death is less prominent in Ortega's writings than is the case with the usual existentialist writer. Perhaps this is partly a result of the Spanish circumstance: because the theme of death is so important in Spanish literature, it seems by comparison more slighted in Ortega's writings than it really is. We have already seen at least one example of Ortega's treatment of the theme of death. He returns to it in an essay subtitled "La muerte como creación":

> Ni en ética ni en biología se ha atendido aún suficiente-
> mente al hecho capital de la inevitabilidad de la muerte.
> Hace poco un gran fisiólogo (Ehrenberg) ha mostrado cómo
> no puede definirse la vida sin la muerte. Es aquélla un
> proceso químico en cadena, cada una de cuyas reacciones
> dispara inevitablemente la sucesiva hasta recorrer la serie
> predeterminada y fatal. Desde el primer momento, como
> un móvil en su trayectoria, va la vida lanzada a su consu-
> mación: tanto vale decir que se vive como que se desvive.
> El fenómeno del morir se va produciendo desde la concep-
> ción. [39]

In spite of the importance of life in Ortega's thought, he does not define it as the highest value, nor is its simple preservation or pro-longation good in itself:

> Esta es la manera de sentir propia del espíritu indus-
> trial, del ánimo burgués. Quiere a toda costa vivir, y no se

---

[37] *Obras Completas,* II, 388.
[38] *Obras Completas,* II, 388.
[39] *Obras Completas,* II, 423.

resigna a conocer en la muerte el atributo más esencial de
la vida. ... ¿Por qué ha de triunfar la moral de la vida
larga sobre la moral de la vida alta? [40]

Certain existentialists have interpreted the individual's power to
choose (if he so desires) the time and manner of his death as the
ultimate freedom (perhaps the only one which remains in certain
extreme cases). Ortega's position as represented in the following
paragraph seems highly compatible:

No se comprende por qué el imperativo que nos ordena
tomar la vida bajo nuestra voluntad y gobernarla empleán-
dola en levantados destinos, no ha de extenderse a la
muerte. Si es ella de tal modo un ingrediente, un factor
de la vida, lo mismo que debemos usar deliberadamente de
ésta, debiéramos también usar de la muerte, aprovecharla,
emplearla. [41]

As Ortega sees it, an advanced morality would not accept the principle of avoiding risk for the simple end of surviving to a natural
death. This is necessary, involuntary, chemical death like that of
animal or plant. He believes it would be more dignified to take advantage of the fact of death, subject it to one's will, and give it
meaning thereby. After centuries of fleeing death, he says, it would
be well to give some attention to the art of dying:

La muerte química es infrahumana. La inmortalidad es
sobrehumana. La humanización de la muerte sólo puede
consistir en usar de ella con libertad, con generosidad y
con gracia. Seamos poetas de la existencia que saben hallar
a su vida la rima exacta en una muerte inspirada. [42]

Lest this seem in any way morbid, it should be remembered
that death, as "the most essential fact of life" is used in this context
as almost synonymous with the goal of life, or some similar concept.

Ortega returns once more to the problem of human nature, or
the nature of the ego:

---

[40] *Obras Completas,* II, 423.
[41] *Obras Completas,* II, 424.
[42] *Obras Completas,* II, 425.

Sólo el hombre en quien el alma se ha formado plenamente posee un centro aparte y suyo, desde el cual vive sin coincidir con el cosmos. ¡Dualidad terrible, antagonismo delicioso! Ahí, el mundo que existe y opera desde su centro metafísico. Aquí, yo, encerrado en el reducto de mi alma, "fuera del Universo," manando sentires y anhelos desde un centro que soy yo y no es del Universo. Nos sentimos individuales merced a esta misteriosa excentricidad de nuestra alma. [43]

Man, however, is the "prisoner" of his soul. Whether he wishes it or not, he has to be himself and only himself. He thus feels a separation from the rest of his circumstances, "una trágica secesión de la existencia unánime del Universo." The terms in which Ortega describes this are not those of "nausea," but a certain kinship (the comparison with an unpleasant physical state) is noticeable:

Todo hombre o mujer que llega a madurez sintió en una hora ese gigante cansancio de vivir sobre sí mismo, de mantenerse a pulso sobre la existencia, parecido al *odium professionis* que acomete a los monjes en los cenobios. Es como si al alma se le fatigasen los propios músculos y ambicionase reposar sobre algo que no sea ella misma, abandonarse, como una carga penosa al borde del camino. No hay remedio, hay que seguir ruta adelante, hay que seguir siendo el que se es. ... [44]

There is one escape from this, and here Ortega is strongly reminiscent of Jaspers:

Pero sí, un remedio existe, sólo uno, para que el alma descanse: un amor ferviente a otra alma... el alma enamorada realiza la mágica empresa de transferir a otra alma su centro de gravedad, y esto, sin dejar de ser alma. Entonces reposa. La excentricidad esencial queda en un punto corregida: hay, por lo menos, otro ser con cuyo centro coincide el nuestro. Pues, ¿qué es amor, sino hacer de otro nuestro centro y fundir nuestra perspectiva con la suya? [45]

---

[43] *Obras Completas,* II, 461.
[44] *Obras Completas,* II, 462.
[45] *Obras Completas,* II, 462.

Somewhat later, the idea of perspective is related to the problem of man's nature, and the nature of reality:

> Toda intimidad, pero, sobre todo, la intimidad humana —vida, alma, espíritu—, es inespacial. De aquí que le sea forzoso, para manifestarse, cabalgar la materia, trasponerse o traducirse en figuras de espacio. Todo fenómeno expresivo implica, pues, una trasposición; es decir: una metáfora esencial. El gesto, la forma de nuestro cuerpo, es la pantomima de nuestra alma. El hombre externo es el actor que representa al hombre interior. Ciertamente que en nuestra figura y gestos no se deja ver toda nuestra intimidad; pero ¿es que alguien ha visto todo un cuerpo? ¿Quién ha visto, por ejemplo, entera una naranja? [46]

No matter from what position we look at an object, we will see only that side which is toward us; its other side remains always beyond our vision. The best we can do is to walk around various corporal objects and add together the aspects successively presented. It is important to remember this, says Ortega, because it is usual to believe that the material world is completely visible or obvious, when actually it is completely (or as a whole) beyond our apprehension.

The point of view is much more than visual, as Ortega emphasizes in this passage:

> Cada cosa, para ser bien vista, nos impone una distancia determinada y muchas otras condiciones. Si queremos ver una catedral a la distancia a que vemos bien un ladrillo, acercándolo al ojo, percibiremos sólo los poros de una de sus piedras. La Pampa no puede ser vista sin ser vivida. No basta el aparato ocular con su función abstracta de ver. Todo el ser tiene que servir de órgano y colaborar en la percepción de este paisaje, que parece sin forma porque la tiene sutil. [47]

Thus the point of view or perspective begins to emerge not only as a philosophy, but a specific way of life.

---

[46] *Obras Completas*, II, 573.
[47] *Obras Completas*, II, 631.

In the closing pages of the eighth and last book of *El Especta-dor,* Ortega gives his philosophic motivation for the care devoted to the observation of many mundane, everyday events and things:

> La insistencia con que me he ocupado en filiar los rasgos de "nuestro tiempo" no es una manía, ni siquiera me es peculiar, sino que, a su vez, constituye uno de los rasgos esenciales de "nuestro tiempo." Porque vivimos en una co-yuntura tal vez sin ejemplo hasta ahora. Se ha producido en la humanidad un cambio radicalísimo de origen irra-cional, al mismo tiempo que goza el hombre de una gran clarividencia y aguda conciencia de sí mismo. Por vez pri-mera el hombre asiste a su propia mutación; cambia, y sabe que cambia. Antes, en cada cambio efectivo se creía eterno y no se veía a sí mismo —sus creencias y modos de vida— como algo transitorio, sino como algo definitivo. Por tanto, el cambio no era tal para el cambiante. [48]

Not only the concept of change or flux is important, but also man's consciousness of himself. And in connection with this aware-ness, Ortega points out the intellectual "closeness" of his generation, and recognizes that there is nothing unique about his point of view, seeing himself as part of a movement characteristic of the times.

This new closeness, and especially the awareness of change (of the fact of insecurity) necessitate a new point of view or philosophy:

> El hombre no tiene más remedio que aprender a vivir en esta forma dual y sentirse a la par mudable y eterno. Esto nos obliga a modificar profundamente la óptica de la vida. Antes se interesaba el hombre en una forma de arte, en una idea científica, en un principio político, porque le parecían definitivos. Cuando no se lo parecían, caía en escepticismo, que es la suspensión de la vida. Ahora nece-sitamos aprender que sólo somos definitivos cuando henchi-mos bien el perfil transitorio que nos corresponde; es decir, cuando aceptamos "nuestro tiempo" como nuestro destino, sin nostalgia ni utopismos. [49]

---

[48] *Obras Completas,* II, 722.
[49] *Obras Completas,* II, 722.

There are several strongly existentialist elements in this series of observations. A particular case in point is the paradox of man as changing and eternal. We can only be definitive (authentic?) when we accept our transitory role, and decide likewise to accept the destiny implied by our particular historical time and circumstances, accepting it fully and without longings for escape. One cannot hope for absolutes, yet Ortega does not believe in scepticism. His occasional closeness to a sceptical stance is evident, however, in certain remarks: "Me gustaría haber conocido a aquel hombre del siglo XV que escogió como divisa estas palabras: *Rien ne m'est sûr que la chose incertaine.*" [50] Ortega has not yet solved to his own satisfaction the epistemological dilemma, but he avoids, as it were instinctively, the pitfalls of scepticism, for his philosophy is intrinsically ethical, a philosophy of living, of action.

In volume III of Ortega's *Obras Completas* are collected, in addition to various articles, three of his most important works: *España invertebrada, El tema de nuestro tiempo,* and *La deshumanización del arte e ideas sobre la novela.*

In *España invertebrada,* Ortega analyzed the dearth of effective leadership in Spain and examined various historical theories in search of the reason for this lack. In a much-publicized chapter entitled "La ausencia de los mejores," he theorizes that Spain's never having had a true feudalism is a causal factor. Many of the ideas in this section are more fully developed in the later *Rebelión de las masas.*

El tema de nuestro tiempo contains ideas on a philosophy of history, on epistemology, and "life and culture," which give rise to the philosophical theory or method which Ortega called vital reason or ratiovitalism. Due perhaps to the work of Julián Marías, this last has been emphasized somewhat at the expense of other ideas in the work.

La deshumanización del arte e ideas sobre la novela contains, as its title suggests, themes which are primarily aesthetic. The ideas expressed are entirely compatible, however, with the central preoccupation in other works, and best understood in relation to an obsessive concern with man.

---

[50] *Obras Completas,* II, 729.

There have been many articles written pro and con on the questions whether Ortega's philosophy is a systematic one, whether his ideas are related, and whether his thought evolved logically. Therefore, the juxtaposition of the three works just mentioned is especially provocative. The thoughtful student is prompted to inquire just what, if any, is the theoretical relationship between a book which deals with the contemporary political situation (placing it in historical perspective), a book which introduces a philosophy called vital reason, and a book on art. Might all be parts of a larger scheme? Certainly only a framework as large as that of total consciousness or total existence would serve to hold them all. Perhaps he was not thoroughly aware of it himself, perhaps his theoretical justification was discovered only later, but in his ranging far and wide in thought and writing, Ortega was broadening his perspective, increasing his acquaintance with his circumstances, his knowledge of reality. In these three books, he has inquired into his socio-political circumstances, the importance of history and some important philosophical issues, and the contemporary intellectual or cultural scene.

Without denying that the ostensible themes of these books are those already summarized, it is nevertheless possible to find in them numerous passages which positively relate each work to a philosophy of life. First, Ortega relates the nation to the broader concept of existence in common: "En el capítulo anterior he sostenido que la incorporación nacional, la convivencia de pueblos y grupos sociales, exige alguna alta empresa de colaboración y un proyecto sugestivo de vida en común." [51] His interest in politics, in the national scene, is partially explained by these words:

> Para entender bien una cosa es preciso ponerse a su compás. De otra manera, la melodía de su existencia no logra articularse en nuestra percepción y se desgrana en una secuencia de sonidos inconexos que carecen de sentido. Si nos hablan demasiado de prisa o demasiado despacio, las sílabas no se traban en palabras ni las palabras en frases. ¿Cómo podrán entenderse dos almas de *tempo* melódico distinto? Si queremos intimar con algo o con alguien, tomemos primero el pulso de su vital melodía y,

---

[51] *Obras Completas,* III, 63.

> según él exija, galopemos un rato a su vera o pongamos
> al paso nuestro corazón. [52]

In order to understand a thing, says Ortega, one must be in time
with it. This is a new aspect of the relation between subject and
object (or ego and circumstance). Obviously the meaning is very
similar to that of his statement that man must absorb his circumstance. It is interesting to note that two of the metaphors used
above to illustrate his meaning are "the melody of existence" and
"vital melody."

Continuing with the same theme, Ortega uses another illustration,
that of the cinematographic technique where the growth of a plant
over a period of hours or weeks is telescoped into a matter of
minutes. He theorizes that this method could be applied to history,
giving an overall view not possible with more detailed approaches:

> Apretados unos contra otros los hechos innumerables, fun-
> didos en una curva sin poros ni discontinuidades, la historia
> de España adquiriría la claridad expresiva de un gesto, y
> los sucesos contemporáneos en que concluye el vasto ade-
> mán se explicarían por sí mismos como unas mejillas que
> la angustia contrae o una mano que desciende rendida. [53]

Although the present study deals with ideas rather than matters
of linguistics, it may be noted in passing that many of Ortega's
metaphors, illustrations, and various figures of speech are drawn
from individual existence, as in the case above, "unas mejillas que
la angustia contrae o una mano que desciende rendida."

As noted earlier, Ortega's opinion was that the essential task of
politics is to increase the national vitality; he now attributes a
similar function to those who exercise the power of government,
criticizing the Spanish regime for its failure in this respect:

> En vez de renovar periódicamente el tesoro de ideas
> vitales, de modos de coexistencia, de empresas unitivas, el
> Poder público ha ido triturando la convivencia española y
> ha usado de su fuerza nacional casi exclusivamente para
> fines privados.

---

[52] *Obras Completas,* III, 66.
[53] *Obras Completas,* III, 67.

¿Es extraño que, al cabo del tiempo, la mayor parte de los españoles, y desde luego la mejor, se pregunte: para qué vivimos juntos? *Porque vivir es algo que se hace hacia adelante, es una actividad que va de este segundo al inmediato futuro.* [54]

One of the most important distinctions which emerges in the survey of Ortega's political writings is the concept of existence as coexistence, of living as living together. In its consequences for the ethical part of Ortega's philosophy, this implies a generalization, from the subjective norm (for each) to society at large, a note of social consciousness which is usually lacking in Sartre and Heidegger, and finds a real parallel only in Jaspers. If, as Marías contends, Ortega has gone beyond existentialism, it may be in this respect even more than in his doctrine of vital reason. A second important element in the passage quoted above is the application of the concept of life as activity, meaningful, goal-directed activity, to the life of the nation.

The idea of the "other" as an important element in given individual existences is also applied to social groups: "Es preciso, pues, mantener vivaz en cada clase o profesión la conciencia de que existen en torno a ella otras muchas clases y profesiones, de cuya cooperación necesitan..." [55]

From here Ortega proceeds once more specifically to relate the national level of life to activity:

¿Cómo se mantiene despierta esta corriente profunda de solidaridad? Vuelvo una vez más al tema que es *leitmotiv* de este ensayo: la convivencia nacional es una realidad activa y dinámica, no una coexistencia pasiva y estática como el montón de piedras al borde de un camino. La nacionalización se produce en torno a fuertes empresas incitadoras que exigen de todos un máximum de rendimiento, y en consecuencia, de disciplina y mutuo aprovechamiento. [56]

In the last statement, Ortega should be understood to be referring to what is ideally the case, rather than what is actually true. And

---

[54] *Obras Completas,* III, 71.
[55] *Obras Completas,* III, 73.
[56] *Obras Completas,* III, 73.

ideally, national life demands a maximum of discipline, as Ortega applies his standard of individual excellence to the national existence.

Ortega recognizes that cooperation is not the only form of co-existence. His illustration of this calls to mind Sartre's view of interpersonal relatedness as conflict:

> Una nación es a la postre una ingente comunidad de individuos y grupos que cuentan los unos con los otros. Este contar con el prójimo no implica necesariamente simpatía hacia él. Luchar con alguien, ¿no es una de las más claras formas en que demostramos que existe para nosotros? Nada se parece tanto al abrazo como el combate cuerpo a cuerpo. [57]

The Spanish thinker sees in activity, even though it be conflict, a desirable evidence of vitality, of decision, of committedness. It is a meaningful form of association. But in the numerous cases of particularism, or separatist groups in Spain which he analyzes, even the willingness to fight for an ideal is lacking:

> Quedaría incompleto y aun tergiversado el análisis del estado presente de España que estas páginas ensayan si se entendiera que la inquietud particularista descrita en ellas ha engendrado un ambiente de feroz lucha entre unas clases y otras. ¡Ojalá que hubiese en España alguien con ansia de luchar! Por desgracia, acontece lo contrario. Hay disociación; pero lo que podía hacerla fecunda, de una impetuosa voluntad de combatir que pudiera llevar a una recomposición, falta por completo. [58]

Ortega considers the different attitudes of combatant and victor: the former is alert, watchful, with respect for the adversary; the latter is relaxed, lets down his guard, and prepares to enjoy his spoils. This is of particular relevance when related to Ortega's numerous comparisons of life to a battle or struggle; in the closing lines of Part I of *España invertebrada,* he diagnoses the national ills in these terms:

---

[57] *Obras Completas,* III, 79.
[58] *Obras Completas,* III, 83.

> Nos falta la cordial efusión del combatiente y nos sobra la arisca soberbia del triunfante. No queremos luchar: queremos simplemente vencer. Como esto no es posible, preferimos vivir de ilusiones y nos contentamos con proclamarnos ilusamente vencedores en el parvo recinto de nuestra tertulia de café, de nuestro casino, de nuestro cuarto de banderas o simplemente de nuestra imaginación. [59]

The philosopher further observes that in the Spanish situation of which he writes every one has a destructive ability, but no one has strength to be constructive. There are clear moral undertones here. Ortega dos not see the national life as mere vitality; is should be used constructively.

Much of what follows in the second part of *España invertebrada* is better presented in *La rebelión de las masas,* and for that reason can be omitted from detailed consideration here. Even were this not the case, sufficient evidence has been presented to demonstrate that *España invertebrada* fits into the framework of a philosophy of existence, and there is no need to labor the point.

With *El tema de nuestro tiempo,* Ortega has come to full philosophic stature. Ostensibly dealing with history, with epistemology, and with the working out of vital reason, he is throughout occupied with the theme of life—the life of the individual, of the nation, of the generation—and with the multiplicity of forms in which existence is manifested. The first task in this book is the definition of the concept of generation, which is done in vitalistic and naturalistic terms:

> Las variaciones de la sensibilidad vital que son decisivas en historia se presentan bajo la forma de generación. ... La generación, compromiso dinámico entre masa e individuo, es el concepto más importante de la historia, y, por decirlo así, el gozne sobre que ésta ejecuta sus movimientos.
> Una generación es una variedad humana, en el sentido riguroso que dan a este término los naturalistas. ...
> *Cada generación representa una cierta altitud vital,* desde la cual se siente la existencia de una manera determinada. [60]

---

[59] *Obras Completas,* III, 84.
[60] *Obras Completas,* III, 147-148.

Like the nation and the individual, the generation is subject to certain ethical imperatives:

> Si cada generación consiste en una peculiar sensibilidad, en un repertorio orgánico de íntimas propensiones, quiere decirse que cada generación tiene su vocación propia, su histórica misión. Se cierne sobre ella el severo imperativo de desarrollar esos gérmenes interiores, de informar la existencia en torno según el módulo de su espontaneidad. Pero acontece que las generaciones, como los individuos, faltan a veces a su vocación y dejan su misión incumplida. Hay, en efecto, generaciones infieles a sí mismas, que defraudan la intención histórica depositada en ellas. En lugar de acometer resueltamente la tarea que les ha sido prefijada... prefieren sestear alojadas en ideas, instituciones, placeres creados por las anteriores y que carecen de afinidad con su temperamento. Claro es que esta deserción del puesto histórico no se comete impunemente. La generación delincuente se arrastra por la existencia en perpetuo desacuerdo consigo misma, vitalmente fracasada. [61]

There are several important ideas in the above citation. The idea of authenticity has not yet been developed, but it is obviously present in the ideas of vocation and mission, and of infidelity in the generations who do not follow their vocation. Some idea of destiny is also present, in "la tarea que les ha sido prefijada." The life of the generation is seen in terms of its activity, and its success or failure in terms of its authenticity, or vocation, its originality and creativity.

Still further considerations are added to Ortega's definition of life:

> La vida no es un proceso extrínseco donde simplemente se adicionan contingencias. La vida es una serie de hechos regida por una ley. Cuando sembramos la simiente de un árbol prevemos todo el curso normal de su existencia. No podemos prever si el rayo vendrá o no a segarle con su alfanje de fuego colgado al flanco de la nube, pero sabemos que la simiente de cerezo no llevará follaje de chopo. Del mismo modo... la vida humana es un proceso interno en que los hechos esenciales no caen desde fuera sobre el

---

[61] *Obras Completas*, III, 151.

sujeto —individuo o pueblo—, sino que salen de éste, como de la semilla fruto y flor. [62]

It is precisely because of this element of predictability in life that history is possible: "Por ser la existencia humana propiamente vida, esto es, proceso interno en que se cumple una ley de desarrollo, es posible la ciencia histórica." [63] There are certain elements of necessity which must be considered when one attempts to understand any given fact. In some cases it is physical, mathematical, or logical; in human life, it is psychological. Ortega illustrates his point: when we hear that good citizen Pedro has killed his neighbor, we do not understand it until learning that the neighbor had dishonored Pedro's daughter. With this fact, theorizes Ortega, one might proceed inversely from the seduction of the girl to a prediction that Pedro would kill his neighbor. He believes that one can generalize this process, and with the proper knowledge of past and present circumstances foresee the future:

> En este caso se ve con toda claridad cómo al profetizar el futuro se hace uso de la misma operación intelectual que para comprender el pasado. En ambas direcciones, hacia atrás o hacia adelante, no hacemos sino reconocer una misma curva psicológica evidente, como al hallar un trozo de arco completamos sin vacilación su forma entera. [64]

Thus, Ortega would seem here to agree to some extent with deterministic theories, and in opposition to Sartre, he does not see life as entirely contingent:

> Es evidente que el próximo futuro nace de nosotros y consiste en la prolongación de lo que en nosotros es esencial y no contingente, normal y no aleatorio. En rigor bastaría, pues, con que descendiésemos al propio corazón y, eliminando cuanto sea afán individual, privada predilección, prejuicio o deseo, prolongásemos las líneas de nuestros apetitos y tendencias esenciales hasta verlas converger en un tipo de vida. [65]

---

[62] *Obras Completas,* III, 153.
[63] *Obras Completas,* III, 154.
[64] *Obras Completas,* III, 154.
[65] *Obras Completas,* III, 155.

The element of contingency appears from the above passage to be located in the individual himself, with determinism in the external circumstances.

From these reflections, Ortegas turns to a consideration of the place of the rational in life:

> En el puro pensamiento es, por consiguiente, donde imprime su primera huella sutilísima el tiempo emergente. Son los leves rizos que deja en la quieta piel del estanque el soplo primerizo. El pensamiento es lo más fluido que hay en el hombre; por eso se deja empujar fácilmente por las más ligeras variaciones de la sensibilidad vital. [66]

The ethical element enters the picture here; thought must not simply be left to drift:

> Nuestra generación, si no quiere quedar a espaldas de su propio destino, tiene que orientarse en los caracteres generales de la ciencia que hoy se hace. ... De lo que hoy se empieza a pensar depende lo que mañana se vivirá en las plazuelas. [67]

Ciencia is used in the sense of knowledge at the "height of the times."

The problem of the nature of truth next occupies the philosopher. In his reflections on this subject, he sounds a major existentialist note:

> Bajo el nombre "verdad" se oculta un problema sumamente dramático. La verdad, el reflejar adecuadamente lo que las cosas son, se obliga a ser una e invariable. Mas la vida humana, en su multiforme desarrollo, es decir, en la historia, ha cambiado constantemente de opinión, consagrando como "verdad" la que adoptaba en cada caso. ... Si queremos atenernos a la historia viva y perseguir sus sugestivas ondulaciones, tenemos que renunciar a la idea de que la verdad se deja captar por el hombre. Cada individuo posee sus propias convicciones, más o menos duraderas, que son "para" él la verdad. [68]

---

[66] *Obras Completas,* III, 156.
[67] *Obras Completas,* III, 156.
[68] *Obras Completas,* III, 157.

Ortega recognizes the relativism of such a stand and observes that if truth does not exist, relativism can hardly take itself seriously. Furthermore, "la fe en la verdad es un hecho radical de la vida humana: si la amputamos queda ésta convertida en algo ilusorio y absurdo. La amputación misma que ejecutamos carecerá de sentido y valor." [69] It is a pragmatic consideration which prevents an acceptance of epistemologic relativism and the scepticism to which it leads. The Spanish thinker considers the opposite position, rationalism, and finds pure reason even less acceptable, since it does not reflect the complexity of life and reality. As have other existentialists, Ortega finds himself unable to accept either of these doctrines:

> Hemos visto cómo el problema de la verdad dividía a los hombres de las generaciones anteriores a la nuestra en dos tendencias antagónicas: relativismo y racionalismo. Cada una de ellas renuncia a lo que la otra retiene. El racionalismo se queda con la verdad y abandona la vida. El relativismo prefiere la movilidad de la existencia a la quieta e inmutable verdad. Nosotros no podemos alojar nuestro espíritu en ninguna de las dos posiciones: cuando lo ensayamos, nos parece que sufrimos una mutilación. [70]

Even in such esoteric reflections, Ortega's point of reference is life or existence, and his underlying preoccupation is life, truth having importance not for itself but in its relation to existence.

During the next several chapters of *El tema de nuestro tiempo,* Ortega examines the dilemma of life and culture from various perspectives, those of Socrates and Don Juan, of Nietzsche and of Jesus, of Oriental philosophy and of positivism, and finds inadequacies in each:

> Hemos visto que en todas las culturas pretéritas, cuando se ha querido buscar el valor de la vida o, como suele decirse, su "sentido" y justificación, ha recurrido a cosas que están más allá de ella. Siempre el valor de la vida parecía consistir en algo trascendente de ésta, hacia lo cual la vida era sólo un camino o instrumento. Ella, por sí

---

[69] *Obras Completas,* III, 158.
[70] *Obras Completas,* III, 159.

> misma, en su inmanencia, se presentaba desnuda de calidades estimables, cuando no cargada exclusivamente de valores negativos. [71]

These attempts to find values or meaning in doctrines which transcend life Ortega blames on what he calls the incalculable error of the belief that life, abandoned to itself, tends to egoism, for it is essentially and inevitably altruistic: *"La vida es el hecho cósmico del altruismo, y existe sólo como perpetua emigración del Yo vital hacia lo Otro."* [72]

Ortega next turns to a purely biological point of view, the exaltation of animal values, and examines the stances of the utilitarian and the classic hedonist. While he finds these too zoological, he feels that they anticipate the future discoveries of the values immanent in life itself. He blames the intellectual disorientation of Europe on the failure of cultural or extra-vital standards of value and on the fear of taking an egoistic or immoral stance in place of the rejected cultural (Christian, rationalist, positivistic) norms. His attempt to resolve the dilemma here inherent leads to the doctrine of the point of view:

> La realidad cósmica es tal, que sólo puede ser vista bajo una determinada perspectiva. *La perspectiva es uno de los componentes de la realidad.* Lejos de ser su deformador, es su organización. Una realidad que vista desde cualquier punto resultase siempre idéntica es un concepto absurdo. [73]

This way of thinking, he notes, must lead to a radical reform of philosophy. The individuality of each observer had been the insurmountable obstacle for intellectual tradition, since it was thought that two different individuals would reach divergent truths.

> Ahora vemos que la divergencia entre los mundos de dos sujetos no implica la falsedad de uno de ellos. Al contrario, precisamente porque lo que cada cual ve es una realidad y no una ficción, tiene que ser su aspecto distinto del que otro percibe. Esa divergencia no es una contradicción sino

---

[71] *Obras Completas,* III, 187.
[72] *Obras Completas,* III, 187.
[73] *Obras Completas,* III, 199.

complemento. Si el universo hubiese presentado una faz idéntica a los ojos de un griego socrático que a los de un yanqui, deberíamos pensar que el universo no tiene verdadera realidad, independiente de los sujetos.

Cada vida es un punto de vista sobre el universo. En rigor, lo que ella ve no lo puede ver otra. Cada individuo —persona, pueblo, época— es un órgano insustituible para la conquista de la verdad. [74]

Reality is conceived, like a landscape, as having innumerable perspectives, all of them equally authentic. The only false perspective, concludes Ortega, is one which pretends to be the *only* one; false is the "truth" seen from nowhere in particular. This in essence was the error of rationalism, and of philosophy in general heretofore, for each different system pretended to be true for all times and all men. They lacked the vital, historical dimension or perspective.

La doctrina del punto de vista exige, en cambio, que dentro del sistema vaya articulada la perspectiva vital de que ha emanado, permitiendo así su articulación con otros sistemas futuros o exóticos. *La razón pura tiene que ser sustituida por una razón vital, donde aquélla se localice y adquiera movilidad y fuerza de transformación.* [75]

Thus Ortega has arrived at last at his famous doctrine of vital reason, which is a doctrine of the truth of the individual perspective, in that each sees a different, equally valid aspect of reality. He has resolved, at least to his own apparent satisfaction, the problem of the inacceptability of rationalism and relativism, which existentialism in general has recognized as a problem but has not devoted itself to resolving. The same solution may be implicit in the existentialist view of the subjective nature of truth, but Ortega was certainly first to work out a theoretical statement and relate it to the multifaceted nature of reality.

There are several appendices to *El tema de nuestro tiempo* which deal with aspects intrinsically prior to the conclusions above. They are largely historical meditations, and while they could be related

---

[74] *Obras Completas,* III, 200.
[75] *Obras Completas,* III, 201.

to the problems of life and reality outlined above, this would add little of value.

La deshumanización del arte e ideas sobre la novela is less closely related to Ortega's philosophy of life than are the philosophical meditations of *El tema de nuestro tiempo,* but his aesthetics, as part of his total philosophy, should also reflect his attitudes toward life. A few examples will serve to illustrate this.

Ortega's point of departure is modern art, and he is concerned in particular with the purely photographic and with the abstract or non-representational. At times he uses art in the broader sense of culture, at others to include all of the fine arts, and yet others with respect to painting alone. He first relates art to society at large, to contemporary life:

> Se acerca el tiempo en que la sociedad, desde la política al arte, volverá a organizarse, según es debido, en dos órdenes o rangos: el de los hombres egregios y el de los hombres vulgares. Todo el malestar de Europa vendrá a desembocar y curarse en esa nueva y salvadora escisión. La unidad indiferenciada, caótica, informe, sin arquitectura anatómica, sin disciplina regente en que se ha vivido por espacio de ciento cincuenta años, no puede continuar. Bajo toda la vida contemporánea late una injusticia profunda e irritante: el falso supuesto de la igualdad real entre los hombres. [76]

Ortega points out a few pages later that the artistic public (at least where modern art is concerned) is divided into two groups, those who understand and those who do not.

> Si el arte nuevo no es inteligible para todo el mundo, quiere decirse que sus resortes no son los genéricamente humanos. No es un arte para los hombres en general, sino para una clase muy particular de hombres que podrán no valer más que los otros, pero que evidentemente son distintos. [77]

People understand or appreciate art which concerns human destinies, loves, hates, joys and sorrows. Works are judged good when they

---

[76] *Obras Completas,* III, 356.
[77] *Obras Completas,* III, 356.

succeed in producing the amount of illusion necessary so that the imaginary personages seem real.

> Esto quiere decir que para la mayoría de la gente el goce estético no es una actitud espiritual diversa de la que habitualmente adopta en el resto de su vida. Sólo se distingue de ésta en calidades adjetivas: es, tal vez, menos utilitaria, más densa y sin consecuencias penosas. Pero, en definitiva, el objeto de que en el arte se ocupa, lo que sirve de término a su atención, y con ella a las demás potencias, es el mismo que en la existencia cotidiana: figuras y pasiones humanas. [78]

Thus neither art nor its enjoyment can be separated from daily, individual existence.

Ortega uses "human" in relation to art to mean the degree of intensity of human experience which is involved. This is directly related to his doctrine of point of view. He illustrates with the example of the case of the death of a public figure, witnessed by four persons: his doctor, his wife, a newspaper correspondent, and an artist who accidentally happened to be present. Ortega points out that they are there for different reasons, they see the event in entirely different ways, experiencing it with varying intensity. The difference between what it represents for the grief-stricken wife and the impassive painter is such that it can truly be said they are witnessing different events.

> Resulta, pues, que una misma realidad se quiebra en muchas realidades divergentes cuando es mirada desde puntos de vista distintos. Y nos ocurre preguntarnos: ¿cuál de esas múltiples realidades es la verdadera, la auténtica? Cualquiera decisión que tomemos será arbitraria. Nuestra preferencia por una u otra sólo puede fundarse en el capricho. Todas esas realidades son equivalentes, cada una la auténtica para su congruo punto de vista. Lo único que podemos hacer es clasificar estos puntos de vista y elegir entre ellos el que prácticamente parezca más normal o más espontáneo. Así llegaremos a una noción nada absoluta, pero, al menos, práctica y normativa de la realidad. [79]

---

[78] *Obras Completas,* III, 357.
[79] *Obras Completas,* III, 361.

It is clear that Ortega is using precisely the same concepts in his treatise on aesthetics as in the primarily epistemological sections of *El tema de nuestro tiempo*. He emphasizes that "our" reality is always the most vivid:

> Quiere decir esto que en la escala de las realidades corresponde a la realidad vivida una peculiar primacía que nos obliga a considerarla como "la" realidad por excelencia. En vez de realidad vivida, podíamos decir realidad humana. El pintor que presencia impasible la escena de agonía parece "inhumano." Digamos, pues, que el punto de vista humano es aquel en que "vivimos" las situaciones, las personas, las cosas. Y viceversa, son humanas todas las realidades —mujer, paisaje, peripecia— cuando ofrecen el aspecto bajo el cual suelen ser vividas. [80]

It is in this sense that the concept of "dehumanization" of art is used. The point of reference is clearly the individual existence; as with his philosophy of history, and of knowledge, the framework is life itself.

The mission of art, as Ortega conceives it, is to represent life in its most human form, the form under which it is experienced. It is for this reason that he finds fault with art in its modern manifestations:

> Lejos de ir el pintor más o menos torpemente hacia la realidad, se ve que ha ido contra ella. Se ha propuesto denodadamente deformarla, romper su aspecto humano, deshumanizarla. Con las cosas representadas en el cuadro tradicional podríamos ilusoriamente convivir. De la Gioconda se han enamorado muchos ingleses. Con las cosas representadas en el cuadro nuevo es imposible la convivencia: al extirparles su aspecto de realidad vivida, el pintor ha cortado el puente. ... Nos deja encerrados en un universo abstruso, nos fuerza a tratar con objetos con los que no cabe tratar humanamente. Tenemos, pues, que improvisar otra forma de trato por completo distinta del usual vivir las cosas; hemos de crear e inventar actos inéditos que sean adecuados a aquellas figuras insólitas. Esta nueva vida, esta vida inventada previa anulación de la espontánea,

---

[80] *Obras Completas*, III, 363.

es precisamente la comprensión y el goce artísticos. No faltan en ella sentimientos y pasiones, pero evidentemente estas pasiones y sentimientos pertenecen a una flora psíquica muy distinta de la que cubre los paisajes de nuestra vida primaria y humana. [81]

Ortega observes that the new art forms are dominated by a repugnance for what is human, and inquires into the cause and implications.

> ¿Qué significa ese asco a lo humano en el arte? ¿Es, por ventura, asco a lo humano, a la realidad, a la vida, o es más bien todo lo contrario: respecto a la vida y una repugnancia a verla confundida con el arte, con una cosa tan subalterna como es el arte? [82]

His meditations are thoroughly colored by the tendency to refer everything to life or existence as the standard, and attempts to understand the new sensibility are made in terms of the attitude toward life which it represents.

Further examples could be adduced to illustrate how Ortega's philosophy of life has infused his aesthetics, but they would hardly be more conclusive than the foregoing. The articles of literary criticism examined earlier might be added here as further evidence.

The foregoing pages have provided an introduction to Ortega's themes and major ideas. Those which follow present a closer interrelation of these major themes with those of existentialism. Ortega's most important works are considered in the light of this question: Can they be fitted into the framework of an existentialist philosophy?

As was suggested in the introduction, the idea of God is not a primary consideration. Existentialist philosophy is characterized, not by its idea of God, which varies, but rather by its idea of man. Therefore Ortega's references to God, which might be relevant in a more general philosophic context, are omitted. They are not too numerous.

---

[81] *Obras Completas,* III, 365.
[82] *Obras Completas,* III, 370.

Ortega's ideas of life and of man continue to evolve, and the following pages contain numerous attributes of *la realidad radical.*

La rebelión de las masas has been considered by many as Ortega's masterpiece, although there is little indication that the author shared this opinion. Both because of its timeliness and because of its controversial title, it has been more widely translated and is better known than Ortega's other works. The book has been interpreted as primarily political, although the writer insists that his purpose is not political. It is true that the book deals with many political themes and concepts and can be said to embody a certain political philosophy. Ortega himself was for a period active in politics, and stated upon a number of occasions that the circumstances of modern life oblige everyone to take a part in politics.

The most frequent interpretations of *La rebelión de las masas,* considering the book as a political treatise, have been that the book is aristocratic, conservative or even reactionary. Critics speak of Ortega's aristocratic disdain for the masses, his pride, his scorn for the proletariat, and so on. These opinions are based on the simple error of not reading Ortega's definitions of his terms. He explicitly and repeatedly states that the concepts of mass and minority or elite are not political. Ortega gives extensive explanations and illustrations of the sense in which he means to employ the terms. Those critics who have simply taken the concepts out of context and quoted them at random, recasting the meaning in the traditional sense, are guilty either of deliberately altering the authors' meaning, or of careless or incomplete scholarship. [83]

In the "Prólogo para franceses" published in the Revista de Occidente edition (*Obras Completas,* IV) of *La rebelión de las masas,* Ortega explains that the material was first published in a Madrid daily and its subject is "too human" not to be affected by the intervening passage of time. He is further worried that the effect of his words may be quite different for foreign audiences: "¿No es sobremanera improbable que mis palabras, cambiando ahora de destinatario, logren decir a los franceses lo que ellas pretenden

---

[83] For a fuller treatment, see my master's thesis, "The Political Philosophy of Ortega y Gasset" (Duke University, 1957).

enunciar?"[84] This is of course best understood in the light of the doctrine of the point of view.

> Ni este volumen ni yo somos políticos. El asunto de que aquí se habla es previo a la política y pertenece a su subsuelo. Mi trabajo es oscura labor subterránea de minero. La misión del llamado "intelectual" es, en cierto modo, opuesta a la del político. La obra intelectual aspira, con frecuencia en vano, a aclarar un poco las cosas, mientras que la del político suele, por el contrario, consistir en confundirlas más de lo que estaban.[85]

Having stated emphatically that the book is not political, nor its author a politician, Ortega clarifies his purpose in writing on this ostensibly political subject:

> Hay obligación de trabajar sobre las cuestiones del tiempo. Esto, sin duda. Y yo lo he hecho toda mi vida. He estado siempre en la brecha. Pero una de las cosas que ahora *se* dicen —una "corriente"— es que, incluso a costa de la claridad mental, todo el mundo tiene que hacer política *sensu stricto*. Lo dicen, claro está, los que no tienen otra cosa que hacer.[86]

Taking sides politically is a form of idiocy; labeling or pigeonholing according to parties is meaningless to the philosopher.

> Cuando alguien nos pregunta qué somos en política, o, anticipándose con la insolencia que pertenece al estilo de nuestro tiempo, nos adscribe a una, en vez de responder debemos preguntar al impertinente qué piensa él que es el hombre y la naturaleza y la historia, qué es la sociedad y el individuo, la colectividad, el Estado, el uso, el derecho.[87]

The concepts of human nature, of history, of society, of individual, of the State, of reality—all are more important than the political label. An what is necessary is that contemporary thought give these new clarity.

---

[84] *Obras Completas,* IV, 113.
[85] *Obras Completas,* IV, 130.
[86] *Obras Completas,* IV, 130.
[87] *Obras Completas,* IV, 131

Este volumen no pretende, ni de muy lejos, nada parecido. Como sus últimas palabras hacen constar, es sólo una primera aproximación al problema del hombre actual.

Una vez que hemos hecho bien cargo de cómo es este tipo humano hoy dominante, y que he llamado el hombre-masa, es cuando se suscitan las interrogaciones más fértiles y más dramáticas: ¿Se puede reformar este tipo de hombre? [88]

It is clear from the foregoing citations that Ortega's principal concern is contemporary life, the problems of the individual in his *social* circumstance. Thus political aspects are secondary, even though they ostensibly receive primary scrutiny.

After having inquired if the mass-man is subject to betterment, or can be reformed, Ortega generalizes the question to the mass as a whole:

La otra pregunta decisiva, de la que, a mi juicio, depende toda posibilidad de salud, es ésta: ¿pueden las masas, aunque quisieran, despertar a la vida personal? No cabe desarrollar aquí el tremebundo tema, porque está demasiado virgen. Los términos en que hay que plantearlo no constan en la conciencia pública. Ni siquiera está esbozado el estudio del distinto margen de individualidad que cada época del pasado ha dejado a la existencia humana. Porque es pura inercia mental del "progresismo" suponer que conforme avanza la historia crece la holgura que se concede al hombre para poder ser individuo personal. ... [89]

It is interesting in this context to remember that Ortega's disciple, collaborator and continuer, Julián Marías, has used *personal* as equivalent with *existencial*. There seems to be little doubt that in the context above, Ortega is using *personal* in the sense of that awareness of life and circumstance which existentialists denote by existence in its fullest sense.

The idea is certainly related to personal and individual authenticity and creativity, for Ortega continues:

---

[88] *Obras Completas*, IV, 131.
[89] *Obras Completas*, IV, 132.

¿Puede hoy un hombre de veinte años formarse un proyecto de vida que tenga figura individual y que, por tanto, necesitaría realizarse mediante sus iniciativas independientes, mediante sus esfuerzos particulares? Al intentar el despliegue de esta imagen en su fantasía, ¿no notará que es, si no imposible, casi improbable, porque no hay a su disposición espacio en que poder alojarla y en que poder moverse según su propio dictamen? Pronto advertirá que su proyecto tropieza con el prójimo, como la vida del prójimo aprieta la suya. El desánimo le llevará, con la facilidad de adaptación propia de su edad, a renunciar no sólo a todo acto, sino hasta a todo deseo personal, y buscará la solución opuesta: imaginará para sí una vida *standard,* compuesta de *desiderata* comunes a todos y verá que para lograrla tiene que solicitarla o exigirla en colectividad con los demás. De aquí la acción en masa.
La cosa es horrible. ... [90]

This, then, is the real danger which has inspired Ortega to write *La rebelión de las masas*: it is the loss of individuality. He envisions the world converted into an anthill and reflects that individualism has enriched the world and the human species. The first step in a solution of the present situation is to realize its importance, gravity, and difficulty. Revolution *per se* is no solution:

En las revoluciones intenta la abstracción sublevarse contra lo concreto: por eso es consustancial a las revoluciones el fracaso. Los problemas humanos no son, como los astronómicos o los químicos, abstractos. Son problemas de máxima concreción porque son históricos. Y el único método de pensamiento que proporciona alguna probabilidad de acierto en su manipulación es la "razón histórica." [91]

By "razón histórica" Ortega means the same as "razón vital," or the doctrine of perspectivism: the application of the subjective truth of each individual.

Tres siglos de experiencia "racionalista" nos obligan a recapacitar sobre el esplendor y los límites de aquella prodigiosa *raison* cartesiana. Esa *raison* es sólo matemática,

---

[90] *Obras Completas,* IV, 132.
[91] *Obras Completas,* IV, 134.

física, biológica. Sus fabulosos triunfos sobre la naturaleza, superiores a cuanto pudiera soñarse, subrayan tanto más su fracaso ante los asuntos propiamente humanos e invitan a integrarla en otra razón más radical, que es la "razón histórica." [92]

The introductory treatment of the problem of the "revolt of the masses" is clearly more than political. The philosopher once more makes this explicit in the closing words of his explanatory foreword:

Haciéndome a mí mismo violencia he aislado en este casi-libro, del problema total que es para el hombre y aun especialmente para el hombre europeo su inmediato porvenir, un solo factor: la caracterización del hombre medio que hoy va adueñándose de todo. ... He medido al hombre medio actual en cuanto a su capacidad para continuar la civilización moderna y en cuanto a su adhesión a la cultura. Cualquiera diría que esas dos cosas —la civilización y la cultura— no son para mí cuestión. La verdad es que ellas son precisamente lo que pongo en cuestión casi desde mis primeros escritos. [93]

Ortega's definition of culture is particularly relevant in view of the words above. He defines it some time later, in "Pidiendo un Goethe desde dentro":

La vida es en sí misma y siempre un naufragio. Naufragar no es ahogarse. El pobre humano, sintiendo que se sumerge en el abismo, agita los brazos para mantenerse a flote. Esa agitación de los brazos con que reacciona ante su propia perdición, es la cultura —un movimiento natatorio. Cuando la cultura no es más que eso, cumple su sentido y el humano asciende sobre su propio abismo. [94]

It is difficult to imagine a more existentialist context in which to define culture. Life is always "shipwreck" and culture is a swimming motion, the frantic motions of the drowning man to keep himself afloat in life. And it is this culture which Ortega says is his concern

---

[92] *Obras Completas*, IV, 135.
[93] *Obras Completas*, IV, 138-139.
[94] *Obras Completas*, IV, 397.

in *La rebelión de las masas* and which has always been the problem for him since his earliest writings.

In the book's opening paragraphs, Ortega reiterates that the work is not to be interpreted as primarily political:

> Para la inteligencia del formidable hecho conviene que se evite dar, desde luego, a las palabras "rebelión," "masas," "poderío social," etcétera, un significado exclusiva o primariamente político. La vida pública no es sólo política, sino, a la par y aun antes, intelectual, moral, económica, religiosa; comprende los usos todos colectivos e incluye el modo de vestir y el modo de gozar. [95]

If one adds up the intellectual, moral, economic, and religious functions listed as primarily characteristic of public life, the total can be none other than culture, understood both in its conventional sense and the special meaning which Ortega gives it. The Spanish thinker then proceeds to define the particular and restricted sense in which he will use mass and minority:

> En rigor, la masa puede definirse, como hecho psicológico, sin necesidad de esperar a que aparezcan los individuos en aglomeración. Delante de una sola persona podemos saber si es masa o no. Masa es todo aquel que no se valora a sí mismo —en bien o en mal— por razones especiales, sino que se siente como "todo el mundo," y sin embargo, no se angustia, se siente a sabor al sentirse idéntico a los demás. [96]

It may be particularly significant that Ortega uses the words *no se angustia*; the mass-man feels no anguish at the realization that he is just like the crowd. The quality of mass-man is a mental attitude, the attitude of the individual toward his own merits or defects. One does not have to *be* excellent in order to belong to the minority; one only has to feel special concern about excellence:

> Imagínese un hombre humilde que al intentar valorarse por razones especiales —al preguntarse si tiene talento para

---

[95] *Obras Completas,* IV, 143.
[96] *Obras Completas,* IV, 146.

esto o lo otro, si sobresale en algún orden— advierte que no posee ninguna calidad excelente. Este hombre se sentirá mediocre y vulgar, mal dotado; pero no se sentirá "masa." [97]

There is more than simple desire involved in belonging to Ortega's elite, however; one must also make a particular effort to excel. The select man expects more of himself, and disciplines himself to obtain it:

> Cuando se habla de "minorías selectas," la habitual bellaquería suele tergiversar el sentido de esta expresión, fingiendo ignorar que el hombre selecto no es el petulante que se cree superior a los demás, sino el que se exige más que los demás, aunque no logre cumplir en su persona esas exigencias superiores. Y es indudable que la división más radical que cabe hacer en la humanidad es ésta, en dos clases de criaturas: las que se exigen mucho y acumulan sobre sí mismas dificultades y deberes y las que no se exigen nada especial, sino que para ellas vivir es ser en cada instante lo que ya son, sin esfuerzo de perfección sobre sí mismas, boyas que van a la deriva. [98]

Ortega specifies that the division of society in mass and minority is *not* a division in social classes, but that in each social class there are authentic masses and minorities. It is difficult to see how any critic, after even a superficial reading of the first chapter of *La rebelión de las masas* in which these statements are made, could possibly interpret the book as a defense of colonialism (as did Canto), a Fascist proclamation (as did Sánchez Villaseñor), or a rallying cry for conservatives and reactionaries (as have Barja and numerous others).

After having explained the sense in which he is using his terms, Ortega applies his concepts to the contemporary scene. The outstanding characteristic of the intellectual arena of our day is the presence of the mass-man.

> *Lo característico del momento es que el alma vulgar, sabiéndose vulgar, tiene el denuedo de afirmar el derecho de la vulgaridad y lo impone dondequiera.* Como se dice

---

[97] *Obras Completas,* IV, 146.
[98] *Obras Completas,* IV, 146.

en Norteamérica: ser diferente es indecente. La masa arrolla todo lo diferente, egregio, individual, calificado y selecto. Quien no sea como todo el mundo, quien no piense como todo el mundo, corre riesgo de ser eliminado. Y claro está que ese "todo el mundo" no es "todo el mundo." "Todo el mundo" era, normalmente, la unidad compleja de masa y minorías discrepantes, especiales. Ahora todo el mundo es sólo la masa.

Este es el hecho formidable de nuestro tiempo, descrito sin ocultar la brutalidad de su apariencia. [99]

There can be no doubt that the work is a defense of individualism in the best existentialist tradition. The major theme of *La rebelión de las masas* is the threat to individuality, the danger of conformism and self-annihilation posed by present-day society. It is the menace of becoming production-line personalities, a principal theme with Jaspers and Sartre, studied only slightly less by Kierkegaard and Heidegger.

The historical level of life has risen, inasmuch as numerous benefits of technically advanced democracies are available to large segments of the world population. Ortega sees this as a good; he is far from suggesting that the comforts of life should be reserved for the select few. "El imperio de las masas presenta una vertiente favorable en cuanto significa una subida de todo el nivel histórico, y revela que la vida media se mueve hoy en altura superior a la que ayer pisaba." [100] This, however, is not fulness of life in its best sense. Plenitude of life consists in struggle and progress toward a goal:

> Según he dicho, lo esencial para que exista "plenitud de los tiempos" es que un deseo antiguo, el cual venía arrastrándose anheloso y querulante durante siglos, por fin un día queda satisfecho. Y en efecto, esos tiempos plenos son tiempos satisfechos de sí mismos; a veces, como en el siglo XIX, archisatisfechos. Pero ahora caemos en la cuenta de que esos siglos tan satisfechos, tan logrados, están muertos por dentro. *La auténtica plenitud vital no consiste en la satisfacción, en el logro, en la arribada.* Ya decía

---

[99] *Obras Completas,* IV, 148.
[100] *Obras Completas,* IV, 156.

Cervantes que "el camino es siempre mejor que la posada." [101]

In finding life's meaning in progress toward a goal, rather than any transcendent goal itself, Ortega has struck another note characteristic of existentialist philosophy as a whole.

Ortega next observes that while the world may have grown smaller in a certain sense, the world of the individual has grown larger —the possibilities of the average individual's life now embrace a much larger sphere. He is concerned with events in the world as a whole, as at no time in the past. "Es sencillamente, que el mundo, de pronto, ha crecido, y con él y en él, la vida." [102] Ortega is led further to define his concept of life:

> Cuando se habla de nuestra vida suele olvidarse esto, que me parece esencialísimo: nuestra vida es en todo instante y antes que nada conciencia de lo que nos es posible. Si en cada momento no tuviéramos delante más que una sola posibilidad, carecería de sentido llamarla así. Sería más bien pura necesidad. Pero ahí está: este extrañísimo hecho de nuestra vida posee la condición radical de que siempre encuentra ante sí varias salidas, que por ser varias adquieren el carácter de posibilidades entre las que hemos de decidir. Tanto vale decir que vivimos como decir que nos encontramos en un ambiente de posibilidades determinadas. A este ámbito suele llamarse "las circunstancias." Toda vida es hallarse dentro de la "circunstancia" o mundo. [103]

In a footnote to the text quoted above, Ortega notes that in *Las Atlántidas,* he uses *horizonte* in the same sense as circumstances. Circumstances constitute our life potential, which has increased with the expansion of individual horizons. Ortega feels that in another sense the human potential has increased; he observes that in modern times all sorts of records are broken, and apparently the performance potential has expanded. This does not mean, even so, that life in its most human sense is better than in other times; it has merely grown

---

[101] *Obras Completas,* IV, 159.
[102] *Obras Completas,* IV, 163.
[103] *Obras Completas,* IV, 165.

in terms of possibilities. Such expansion has had its effect on the contemporary psychology:

> *Vivir no es más que tratar con el mundo.* .... Mientras en el pretérito vivir significaba para el hombre medio encontrar en derredor dificultades, peligros, escaseces, limitaciones de destino y dependencia, el mundo nuevo aparece como un ámbito de posibilidades prácticamente ilimitadas, seguro, donde no se depende de nadie. ... Y si la impresión tradicional decía: "Vivir es sentirse limitado y, por lo mismo, tener que contar con lo que nos limita," la voz novísima grita: "Vivir es no encontrar limitación alguna; por tanto, abandonarse tranquilamente a sí mismo. Prácticamente nada es imposible, nada es peligroso y, en principio, nadie es superior a nadie." [104]

It is due to this attitude, and because living costs him so little effort, that we have the increase in the mass-man. "*El hombre que analizamos se habitúa a no apelar de sí mismo a ninguna instancia fuera de él.*" [105] The typical mass-man is satisfied with himself as he is, and would never have considered anything beyond himself if not forced to it by circumstances. Circumstances now do not require him to seek any self-transcendent norm. "Conforme se avanza por la existencia, va uno hartándose de advertir que la mayor parte de los hombres son incapaces de otro esfuerzo que el estrictamente impuesto como reacción a una necesidad externa." [106] It is because of this prevalent attitude that Ortega has denominated the present *la época del "señorito satisfecho."* He analyzes the personality of the mass-man as analagous to that of the spoiled child:

> Este personaje, que ahora anda por todas partes y dondequiera impone su barbarie íntima, es, en efecto, el niño mimado de la historia humana. El niño mimado es el heredero que se comporta exclusivamente como heredero. Ahora la herencia es la civilización —las comodidades, la seguridad, en suma, las ventajas de la civilización... hereda, es decir, encuentra atribuidas a su persona unas condiciones de vida que él no ha creado, por tanto, que no se

---

[104] *Obras Completas,* IV, 180.
[105] *Obras Completas,* IV, 181.
[106] *Obras Completas,* IV, 183.

producen orgánicamente unidas a su vida personal y propia. Se halla al nacer instalado, de pronto y sin saber cómo, en medio de su riqueza y de sus prerrogativas. Él no tiene, íntimamente, nada que ver con ellas, porque no vienen de él. Son el caparazón gigantesco de otra persona, de otro ser viviente, su antepasado. Y tiene que vivir *como* heredero, esto es, tiene que usar el caparazón de otra vida. ... Está condenado a *representar* al otro, por tanto, a *no ser* ni el otro ni él mismo. Su vida pierde, inexorablemente, autenticidad, y se convierte en pura representación o ficción de otra vida. La sobra de medios que está obligado a manejar no le deja vivir su propio y personal destino, atrofia su vida. *Toda vida es lucha, el esfuerzo por ser sí misma.* [107]

To resume, the life which is not creative is not authentic, and those who content themselves with a passive role, with merely living as the heirs or recipients of a civilization created by their ancestors, are inauthentic. They are merely imitating their forebears. In order to be oneself, to live *personally,* one must fight. Ortega's concern with the mass-man is therefore the concern of the altruistic existentialist for those who are not aware, who are not really living in the best sense of the word.

The philosopher includes another special mentality in the category of mass-man: the specialist. He calls him the partially qualified man, the one who feels himself an expert in his narrow field, and believes himself qualified thereby as an expert in all others. In this psychology he sees another of the dangers of contemporary civilization. There is, however, yet a greater menace:

Me refiero al peligro mayor que hoy amenaza a la civilización europea. Como todos los demás peligros que amenazan a esta civilización, también éste ha nacido de ella. Más aún: constituye una de sus glorias; es el Estado contemporáneo. Nos encontramos, pues, con una réplica de lo que en el capítulo anterior se ha dicho sobre la ciencia: la fecundidad de sus principios la empuja hacia un fabuloso progreso; pero éste impone inexorablemente la especialización, y la especialización amenaza con ahogar a la ciencia. Lo mismo acontece con el Estado. [108]

---

[107] *Obras Completas,* IV, 208.
[108] *Obras Completas,* IV, 222-223.

In our day, the state has become a formidable machine which, says Ortega, is admired by the mass-man, without his actually being aware that it is a human creation invented by certain men and sustained by certain virtues and presuppositions which may disappear. The *hombre-masa* sees in the state an anonymous power, just as he feels himself anonymous, and identifies himself with the state, believing it to be his own. It is in the potential absorption of individual personality that the state constitutes a danger.

> Este es el mayor peligro que hoy amenaza a la civilización: la estatificación de la vida, el intervencionismo del Estado, la absorción de toda espontaneidad social por el Estado; es decir, la anulación de la espontaneidad histórica, que en definitiva sostiene, nutre y empuja los destinos humanos. [109]

On this note of warning Ortega ends *La rebelión de las masas.* Rather than a plea for totalitarian government, it is exactly the opposite: it is a warning of the dangers to individual personality and life inherent in "too much" government. Ortega's concern throughout the book is first with the individual *qua* individual, and second with the individual obligation to *be* an individual, to be authentic, and to choose an external standard of excellence.

In *Pidiendo un Goethe desde dentro,* Ortega again seeks a definition of life or existence:

> La vida es una operación que se hace hacia adelante. Se vive *desde* el porvenir, porque vivir consiste inexorablemente en un hacer, en un hacerse la vida de cada cual a sí misma. Es envaguecer la terrible realidad de que se trata llamar "acción" a ese "hacer." La "acción" es sólo el comienzo del "hacer." Es sólo el momento de decidir lo que se va a hacer, de decidirse. Pero la vida no es sólo comienzo. El comienzo es ya el *ahora.* Y la vida es continuación, es pervivencia en el instante que va a llegar más allá del ahora. Por eso va angustiada bajo un imperativo ineludible de realización. [110]

---

[109] *Obras Completas,* IV, 225.
[110] *Obras Completas,* IV, 396.

Ortega turns to the already mentioned concept of life as *naufragio,* or shipwreck and despair, in which he visualized culture as the motions of a drowning man.

> La conciencia de nufragio, al ser la verdad de la vida, es ya la salvación. Por eso yo no creo más que en los pensamientos de los náufragos. Es preciso citar a los clásicos ante un tribunal de náufragos para que allí respondan ciertas preguntas perentorias que se refieren a la vida auténtica. [111]

The consciousness of drowning (what could this be but anguish?) is salvation. Certainly the above passage is Ortega's expression of the existentialist tenet that life begins on the "far side of despair."

The philosopher questions what sort of figure Goethe would present to the *tribunal de náufragos.* There should be a Goethe for "the drowning," *un Goethe desde dentro.*

> ¿Desde dentro de quién? ¿De Goethe? Pero... *quién* es Goethe? No sé si entiende usted bien mi pregunta. Si usted se pregunta a sí mismo, con rigor y perentoriedad: ¿Quién soy yo?— no ¿qué soy yo?, sino ¿quién es ese *yo* de que hablo a todas horas en mi existencia cotidiana?—, caerá usted en la cuenta del increíble descarrío en que ha caminado siempre la filosofía al llamar "yo" las cosas más extravagantes, pero nunca a eso que usted llama "yo" en su existencia cotidiana. Ese yo que es usted, amigo mío, no consiste en su cuerpo, pero tampoco en su alma, conciencia o carácter. ... Usted no es *cosa* ninguna, es simplemente el que tiene que vivir *con* las cosas, *entre* las cosas, el que tiene que vivir no una vida cualquiera, sino una vida determinada. No hay un vivir abstracto. Vivir significa la inexorable forzosidad de realizar el proyecto de existencia que cada cual es. Este proyecto en que consiste el yo no es una idea o plan ideado por el hombre y libremente elegido. ... Sin embargo, es nuestro auténtico *ser,* es nuestro destino. Nuestra voluntad es libre para *realizar o no* ese proyecto vital que últimamente somos, pero no puede corregirlo, cambiarlo, prescindir de él o sustituirlo. Somos indeleblemente ese único personaje programático que necesita realizarse. ... La vida es constitutivamente un drama,

---

[111] *Obras Completas,* IV, 397-398.

porque es la lucha frenética con las cosas y aun con nuestro
carácter por conseguir ser de hecho el que somos en proyecto. [112]

There is probably not a better or more concise statement anywhere of the existentialist concepts of human nature, of man as the
sum of his vital possibilities, and of life as a struggle, a drama,
the necessity of realizing one's projected existence. Also in the passage just quoted are the ideas of one's being necessarily free, and at
the same time limited by circumstances, and *forced* to realize a
particular destiny.

Despite the importance of consciousness and of the psychological
aspects of living, life is much more than what goes on inside the
individual:

> Es preciso superar el error por el cual venimos a pensar
> que la vida de un hombre pasa dentro de él y que, conse-
> cuentemente, se la puede reducir a pura psicología. ¡Bueno
> fuera que nuestra vida pasase dentro de nosotros! Entonces
> el vivir sería la cosa más fácil que se puede imaginar:
> sería flotar en el propio elemento. Pero la vida es lo más
> distante que puede pensarse de un hecho subjetivo. Es la
> realidad más objetiva de todas. Es encontrarse el yo del
> hombre sumergido precisamente en lo que no es él, en el
> puro *otro* que es su circunstancia. Vivir es ser fuera de sí
> —realizarse. [113]

Ortega amplifies his explanation of individual destiny and liberty:

> El hombre —esto es, su alma, sus dotes, su carácter, su
> cuerpo— es la suma de aparatos con que se vive, y equivale,
> por tanto, a un actor encargado de representar aquel perso-
> naje que es su auténtico yo. Y aquí surge lo más sorpren-
> dente del drama vital: el hombre posee un amplio margen
> de libertad con respecto a su yo o destino. Puede negarse
> a realizarlo, puede ser infiel a sí mismo. Entonces su vida
> carece de autenticidad. Si por vocación no se entendiese
> solo, como es sólito, una forma genérica de la ocupación
> profesional y del *curriculum* civil, sino que significase un
> programa íntegro e individual de existencia, sería lo más

---

[112] *Obras Completas,* IV, 399-400.
[113] *Obras Completas,* IV, 400.

claro decir que nuestro yo es nuestra vocación. Pues bien, podemos ser más o menos fieles a nuestra vocación y, consecuentemente, nuestra vida más o menos auténtica. [114]

The most interesting thing is not man's struggle with the external world, but with his vocation, and how he behaves when confronted with it. Perhaps the most tragic aspect of the human condition is that man can falsify his life in this sense. How, exactly, does man recognize his true self, his vocation?

El hombre no reconoce su yo, su vocación singularísima, sino por el gusto o el disgusto que en cada situación siente. La infelicidad le va avisando, como la aguja de un aparato registrador, cuándo su vida efectiva realiza su programa vital, su entelequia, y cuándo se desvía de ella. [115]

This explanation of the ego's concept of its destiny and its awareness of degree of authenticity through the pleasure or pain produced by various actions is almost mystical.

Ortega returns once more to the place and function of ideas, of the abstract in the individual existence:

El caso es que *no hay* tal *species aeternitatis.* Y no por casualidad. Lo que verdaderamente *hay* es lo real, lo que *integra* el destino. Y lo real no es nunca *species, aspecto, espectáculo,* objeto para un contemplador. Todo esto precisamente es lo irreal. Es nuestra idea, no nuestro ser. Europa necesita curarse de su "idealismo" —única manera de superar también todo materialismo, positivismo, utopismo. Las ideas están siempre demasiado cerca de nuestro capricho, son dóciles a él —son siempre revocables. Tenemos, sin duda, y cada vez más, que vivir *con* ideas —pero tenemos que dejar de vivir *desde* nuestras ideas y aprender a vivir *desde* nuestro inexorable, irrevocable destino. Esto tiene que decidir sobre nuestras ideas y no al revés. [116]

The major works contained in the fifth volume of Ortega's *Obras Completas* are *En torno a Galileo, Ensimismamiento y alteración,*

---

[114] *Obras Completas,* IV, 401.
[115] *Obras Completas,* IV, 406.
[116] *Obras Completas,* IV, 416.

and *Ideas y creencias*. The first is primarily historical, being an amplification of the theories of history introduced in *El tema de nuestro tiempo*, particularly the concept of the generation. There are, however, two relevant chapters, "La estructura de la vida, sustancia de la historia," and "La verdad como coincidencia del hombre consigo mismo."

Ensimismamiento y alteración deals with the relationship of the individual to others, and contains much which is sociological. In several aspects it anticipates *El hombre y la gente,* and portions may be omitted in favor of a fuller treatment of the latter book.

Ideas y creencias deals not, as one might expect from the title, with Ortega's personal beliefs but with the technical distinction between ideas and beliefs, and contains his reflections on the nature of thought, reason, and doubt. Ideas expressed here are better presented in *¿Qué es Filosofía? Ideas y creencias* is one of the most esoteric and abstract of all of Ortega's works, and while it is certainly a part of his total philosophy, it is perhaps less closely related than others of the philosopher's works to his philosophy of existence.

En torno a Galileo represents at least a partial continuation of Ortega's effort to define human nature:

> Lo esencial del hombre es no tener más remedio que esforzarse en conocer, en hacer ciencia, mejor o peor, en resolver el problema de su propio ser y para ello el problema de lo que son las cosas, entre las cuales inexorablemente tiene que ser. Esto, que necesita saber, que necesita —quiera o no— afanarse con sus medios intelectuales, es lo que constituye indubitablemente la condición humana. [117]

Life is again defined as a task, a vital project, and Ortega emphasizes the element of decision, of human freedom in deciding "human nature" itself.

> Esa faena —según dijimos—, se llama "vivir" y consiste el vivir en que el hombre está siempre en una circunstancia, proyectado en un orbe o contorno incanjeable, es éste de ahora.

---

[117] *Obras Completas,* V, 22.

> El hombre, cada hombre tiene que decidir en cada ins-
> tante lo que va a hacer, lo que va a ser en el siguiente.
> Esta decisión es intransferible: nadie puede sustituirme en
> la faena de decidirme, de decidir mi vida. Cuando me pongo
> en manos de otro, soy yo quien ha decidido y sigue deci-
> diendo que él me dirija: no transfiero, pues, la decisión,
> sino tan sólo su mecanismo. [118]

There is no way of understanding what human life is, according to
Ortega, if one does not realize that the world or universe is the intellectual solution with which man reacts in the face of given problems planted by his circumstance. This has its consequences for the
nature of reality:

> Hemos visto cómo la idea del mundo o universo es el
> plano que el hombre se forma, quiera o no, para andar
> entre las cosas y realizar su vida, para orientarse en el caos
> de la circunstancia. Pero esa idea le es, por lo pronto, dada
> por su contorno humano, es la idea dominante en su tiempo.
> Con ella tiene que vivir sea aceptándola, sea polemizando
> en tal o cual punto contra ella. [119]

The philosopher distinguishes the life of man today from that of
his paleolithic counterparts in that material problems no longer beset
and perplex him in the same way; he has other problems. His life,
then, is of an identical fundamental structure, but the perspective
of problems is different. Life is always preoccupation, but in each
epoch we are preoccupied more by some things than by others.

> Sin haber hecho más que asomarnos al asunto nos en-
> contramos, pues, con estas verdades claras: 1.º, toda vida
> de hombre parte de ciertas convicciones radicales sobre lo
> que es el mundo y el puesto del hombre en él —parte de
> ellas y se mueve dentro de ellas—; 2.º, toda vida se en-
> cuentra en una circunstancia con más o menos técnica o
> dominio sobre el contorno material.
> He aquí dos funciones permanentes, dos factores esen-
> ciales de toda vida humana —que, además, se influyen
> mutuamente: ideología y técnica. [120]

---

[118] *Obras Completas*, V, 23.
[119] *Obras Completas*, V, 26.
[120] *Obras Completas*, V, 26.

Ortega's statement that all human life takes as its point of departure certain radical convictions about the nature of the world and man's place in it, makes clear his reasons for entitling the series of essays "En torno a Galileo."

In the same series, Ortega returns once more to his reflections on the nature of truth and of knowledge:

> Vivimos, en efecto, de la ciencia, se entiende, de nuestra fe en la ciencia. Y esta fe no es más ni menos fe que otra cualquiera —con lo cual, conste, yo no quiero decir que no sea, tal vez, más justificada y en tal o cual sentido superior a toda otra fe. Lo único que digo es que se trata de una fe, que la ciencia es una fe, una creencia en que se está, como se puede estar en la creencia religiosa. [121]

Man is interested in the nature of things because he must live with them, and must form a program of conduct with reference to each thing, that is, what he can do with each thing, and what he cannot do, and what he can expect from each.

> En efecto, yo necesito saber a qué atenerme con respecto a las cosas de mi circunstancia. Este es el sentido verdadero, originario del saber: saber yo a qué atenerme. El ser de las cosas consistiría, según esto, en la fórmula de mi atenimiento con respecto a ellas. [122]

Knowledge of reality is important with respect to the future, says Ortega; the present does not preoccupy me because I am already existing *in it*. The immediate future, on the other hand, is not *here*, it is not a thing, but I must invent it, imagine it, construct an intellectual scheme of belief about it.

> Una vez que sé a qué atenerme con respecto a la tierra —sea cual sea el contenido de mi creencia, aunque sea el más pesimista— me sentiré tranquilo porque me adoptaré a lo que creo inevitable. El hombre se adapta a todo, a lo mejor y a lo peor; sólo a una cosa no se adapta: a no estar en claro consigo mismo respecto a lo que cree de las cosas. [123]

---

[121] *Obras Completas*, V, 82.
[122] *Obras Completas*, V, 85.
[123] *Obras Completas*, V, 85.

The writer holds that one of man's beliefs can be the conviction that everything is doubtful, that nothing can be positively determined about the nature of things. But even in this extreme case, man will feel himself as tranquil as when he enjoys more positive beliefs. In this sense, scepticism is a form of human adaptation like any other. So long as the sceptic is sure of his doubt, his orientation is adequate for his daily business of living.

> Lo esencial es que el escéptico esté plenamente convencido de su escepticismo, esto es, que sea, en efecto, su auténtico pensamiento; en suma, que al pensar coincida consigo mismo, que no dude respecto a cómo atenerse frente a las cosas. Lo malo es si el escéptico duda de si duda, porque esto significa que no sabe no ya lo que las cosas son, sino cuál es su auténtico pensamiento. Y esto, esto es lo único a que el hombre no se adapta, lo que la realidad radical, que es la vida, no tolera. [124]

This, then, is what Ortega means by defining truth as *coincidencia del hombre consigo mismo*: truth for each individual is his authentic thought or attitude with respect to a given problem. A given object is problematical for me, not because I am in doubt as to the nature of its being, but because when I search within myself, I do not know what is my authentic attitude with respect to it, what I truly believe, what coincides with my ego with respect to a given problem. "El problema sustancial, originario y en este sentido único, es encajar yo en mí mismo, coincidir conmigo, encontrarme a mí mismo." [125]

Ortega examines several concrete attitudes or beliefs with regard to reality, giving particular attention to Christianity and rationalism. Without devoting further time and space to the details of his investigation, we may note that neither of these vital attitudes coincides with his "authentic ego"; they do not represent his "authentic" thought.

Leaving *Ensimismamiento y alteración* for the time being (since as already noted, it is repeated in *El hombre y la gente*) and omitting *Ideas y creencias* for the reasons earlier alleged, there remains

---

[124] *Obras Completas,* V, 86.
[125] *Obras Completas,* V, 86.

the sixth and last volume of Ortega's *Obras Completas* containing *Historia como sistema, Del Imperio Romano, Teoría de Andalucía,* and a number of miscellaneous prologues and essays. Enough of Ortega's essays on various subjects have been examined to indicate that there is usually some relation (though at times not a clear one) to his life philosophy, and that they are inspired, if not by a concept of system, at least by the same underlying attitudes which persist over many years. We will therefore omit much of this miscellaneous material in volume VI in order to allow a fuller treatment of two major posthumous works, and glance only briefly at *Historia como sistema* and *Del Imperio Romano.*

The opening paragraphs of *Historia como sistema* make it clear that, in keeping with Ortega's frequent practice, the title bears a remote and almost symbolic relationship to the basic subject matter. (Other cases in point are *Meditaciones del Quijote, En torno a Galileo, Pidiendo un Goethe desde dentro.*) The true subject of *Historia como sistema* is human life or existence:

> La vida humana es una realidad extraña de la cual lo primero que conviene decir es que es la realidad radical, en el sentido de que a ella tenemos que referir todas las demás, ya que las demás realidades, efectivas o presuntas, tienen de uno u otro modo que aparecer en ella. [126]

Life is not only the radical reality, but it is in addition a task, project or activity; Ortega has matured and polished his definition of this aspect of life, but his meaning is essentially the same:

> La nota más trivial, pero a la vez más importante de la vida humana, es que el hombre no tiene otro remedio que estar haciendo algo para sostenerse en la existencia. La vida nos es dada, puesto que no nos la damos a nosotros mismos, sino que nos encontramos en ella de pronto y sin saber cómo. Pero la vida que nos es dada no nos es dada hecha, sino que necesitamos hacérnosla nosotros, cada cual la suya. La vida es quehacer. ... Antes que hacer algo, tiene cada hombre que decidir, por su cuenta y riesgo, lo que va a hacer. Pero esta decisión es imposible si el hombre no posee algunas convicciones sobre lo que son las cosas en su

---

[126] *Obras Completas,* VI, 13.

> derredor, los otros hombres, él mismo. Sólo en vista de ellas
> puede preferir una acción a otra, puede, en suma, vivir. [127]

The foregoing passage effectively summarizes and relates the ideas
presented in *En torno a Galileo*. Ortega has neatly tied the threads
together, and the result is very existentialist, indeed.

Ortega continues to be preoccupied with the nature of knowledge, of philosophy, of beliefs and their role in man's existence:

> Las creencias constituyen el estrato básico, el más pro-
> fundo de la arquitectura de nuestra vida. Vivimos de ellas
> y, por lo mismo, no solemos pensar en ellas. Pensamos en
> lo que nos es más o menos cuestión. Por eso decimos que
> *tenemos* estas o las otras ideas; pero nuestras creencias,
> más que tenerlas, las somos. [128]

In the following two excerpts, the writer contrasts the reality
we designate by "nature" and the radical reality which is human
existence:

> La naturaleza es una cosa, una gran cosa, que se com-
> pone de muchas cosas menores. Ahora bien: cualesquiera
> que sean las diferencias entre las cosas, tienen todas ellas
> un carácter radical común, el cual consiste simplemente
> en que las cosas *son,* tienen un ser. Y esto significa no sólo
> que existen, que las hay, que están ahí, sino que poseen
> una estructura o consistencia fija y dada. Cuando hay una
> piedra hay ya, está ahí, lo que la piedra es. ... Esta consis-
> tencia fija y dada de una vez para siempre es lo que sole-
> mos entender cuando hablamos del ser de una cosa. Otro
> nombre para expresar lo mismo es la palabra naturaleza. [129]
> La vida humana, por lo visto, no es una cosa, no tiene
> una naturaleza y, en consecuencia, es preciso resolverse a
> pensarla con categorías, con conceptos radicalmente dis-
> tintos de los que nos aclaran los fenómenos de la materia. [130]

Several subsequent chapters deal in more detail with Ortega's
concept of life as possibility, and as *quehacer*. They contain nothing

---

[127] *Obras Completas,* VI, 13.
[128] *Obras Completas,* VI, 18.
[129] *Obras Completas,* VI, 23-24.
[130] *Obras Completas,* VI, 25.

fundamental not already quite clearly explained in earlier writings. The consideration which inspired the series of essays and the idea of "history as a method" is this: while various possibilities of being lie before us, all that we have been lies behind us and acts negatively upon what we can be in the future.

> La experiencia de la vida no se compone sólo de las experiencias que yo personalmente he hecho, de mi pasado. Va integrada también por el pasado de los antepasados que la sociedad en que vivo me transmite. La sociedad consiste primariamente en un repertorio de usos intelectuales, morales, políticos, técnicos, de juego y placer. Ahora bien: para que una forma de vida —una opinión, una conducta— se convierta en uso, en vigencia social, es preciso "que pase tiempo" y con ello que deje de ser una forma espontánea de la vida personal. El uso *tarda* en formarse. Todo uso es viejo. ... La determinación de *lo que* la sociedad en cada momento *va a ser* depende de lo que ha sido, lo mismo que la vida personal. [131]

In this concept which relates the past of an individual or a nation to both present and future, history becomes much more than a collection of facts about the past. One can see in the present all of humanity's past. "La historia es un sistema —el sistema de las experiencias humanas, que forman una cadena inexorable y única. De aquí que nada pueda estar verdaderamente claro en historia mientras no está toda ella clara." [132]

Up until now, says Ortega, history has been the opposite of reason. Man needs a "new revelation."

> El hombre necesita una nueva revelación. Porque se pierde dentro de su arbitraria e ilimitada cabalística interior cuando no puede contrastar ésta y disciplinarla en el choque con algo que sepa a auténtica e inexorable realidad. Esta es el único verdadero pedagogo y gobernante del hombre. Sin su presencia inexorable y patética, ni hay en serio cultura, ni hay Estado, ni hay siquiera —y esto es lo más terrible— realidad en la propia vida personal. Cuando el hombre se queda o cree quedarse solo, sin otra realidad,

---

[131] *Obras Completas*, VI, 37-38.
[132] *Obras Completas*, VI, 43.

> distinta de sus ideas, que le limite crudamente, pierda la sensación de su propia realidad, se vuelve ante sí mismo entidad imaginaria, espectral, fantasmagórica. Sólo bajo la presión formidable de alguna transcendencia se hace nuestra persona compacta y sólida y se produce en nosotros una discriminación entre lo que, en efecto, somos y lo que meramente imaginamos ser. [133]

Until now, according to Ortega, history was contrary to reason. And thus hardly anyone has searched in history for its rational substance. The Spanish thinker declares his purpose is to find in history itself that reason, *razón histórica*. (It will be remembered that in *El tema de nuestro tiempo*, Ortega used *razón vital* and *razón histórica* as equivalent concepts.) Its essence consists in being "no una razón extrahistórica que parece cumplirse en la historia, sino literalmente, *lo que al hombre le ha pasado, constituyendo la sustantiva razón*, la relevación de una realidad trascendente a las teorías del hombre y que es él mismo por debajo de sus teorías." [134]

Much of *Del Imperio Romano* is, in fact, as the title would indicate, a more or less historical meditation about life, beliefs and social practices (*usos*) in the days of the Roman Empire. There are chapters, however, such as "Vida como libertad y vida como adaptación" which clearly relate the series of essays to the overall philosophy and betray preoccupations not indicated by the title. Since passages illustrating Ortega's ideas of liberty and of life as adaptation have already been quoted, however, it would add little to repeat these concepts. Others of his reflections on collective life are more fully presented in *El hombre y la gente*.

In addition to the six volumes of his collected *Obras Completas*, five books by Ortega appeared in the first five years following his death. They are the following:

El hombre y la gente (Madrid, 1957).

La idea de principio en Leibniz y la evolución de la teoría deductiva (Buenos Aires, 1957).

¿Qué es Filosofía? (Madrid, 1957).

Idea del teatro (Madrid, 1958).

---

[133] *Obras Completas*, VI, 47-48.
[134] *Obras Completas*, VI, 49.

Meditación del pueblo joven (Buenos Aires, 1958).
Of these, the first is probably the most important, and may be
Ortega's masterpiece. *La idea de principio en Leibniz* is, contrary
to Ortega's frequent practice, actually about the philosophy of
Leibniz, and while it has obviously been colored by Ortega's own
thought, it is basically an expository work, or what his editors call
docente.

Idea del teatro repeats and develops many of the ideas implicit
and explicit in *La deshumanización del arte,* and since the integra-
tion of Ortega's aesthetics in his total philosophy has already been
demonstrated, no detailed treatment of this work is included.

Meditación del pueblo joven is undoubtedly the least valuable
of the posthumous works, and falls below the standard of Ortega's
writings in general. It is a collection of "occasional" essays, or lectures delivered more or less as command performances before the
legislature of Chile, to the Institución Cultural Española in Buenos
Aires, to the first Congress of the Union of Latin Nations, etc. It
contains phrases which unmistakably relate the volume to the main
current of Ortega's thought, such as this one: "No hay vivir si no
se acepta la circunstancia dada, y no hay buen vivir si nuestra
libertad no la plasma en el camino de la perfección." [135] There is
otherwise no unifying thread in the book, aside from the fact that
all the lectures were directed to Latin Americans, the *pueblo joven.*
Therefore, the two most important of Ortega's posthumous works,
and the only two of real relevance for this study are *El hombre y
la gente* and *¿Qué es filosofía?*

El hombre y la gente purports to be Ortega's sociology. The
actual contents of the book cover only approximately half of the
topics listed in the index; the editors note that the philosopher was
still working on the last chapters at the time of his death. Thus,
the greater part of the book deals with *el hombre*; the book ends
after barely having introduced *la gente.*

Ortega gave a course with the same title in Argentina, and
before beginning it the second time, circulated a synopsis, which
covered most important points made in the book. The editors have
included this summary by way of introduction. A fairly detailed

---

[135] *Meditación del pueblo joven,* p. 25.

consideration of the condensation will eliminate the necessity for a good deal of repetition, and so a smaller number of quotations will suffice to give the flavor of *El hombre y la gente.*

The Spanish writer observes that the concepts used by the sociologist often increase the confusion created by contemporary society, rather than alleviate it:

> Partí de afirmar que buena parte de las angustias históricas actuales procede de la falta de claridad sobre problemas que sólo la sociología puede aclarar, y que esta falta de claridad en la conciencia del hombre medio se origina, a su vez, en el estado deplorable de la teoría sociológica. La insuficiencia del doctrinal sociológico que hoy está a disposición de quien busque, con buena fe, orientarse sobre lo que es la política, el Estado, el derecho, la colectividad y su relación con el individuo, la nación, la revolución, la guerra, la justicia, etc., estriba en que los sociólogos mismos no han analizado suficientemente en serio, esto es, yendo a la raíz, los fenómenos sociales y elementales. [136]

It must first be clarified just what society is, if any of these other concepts are to have clear meaning. One must not assume that society is a reality in itself; it may be only the combination of other realities, an association of realities. "Si la sociedad no es más que una 'asociación,' la sociedad no tiene propia y auténtica realidad y no hace falta una sociología. Bastará con estudiar el individuo." [137] Therefore we must first verify whether there is in the repertory of authentic realities anything which corresponds to what we call "social facts" or "social realities." "Para eso tenemos que partir de la realidad fundamental en que todas las demás, de uno u otro modo, tienen que aparecer. Esa realidad fundamental es nuestra vida, la de cada cual." [138]

Ortega does just that, using individual life as his point of departure.

> En el área de nuestra vida —prescindiendo del problema trascendente que es Dios— hallamos minerales, vegeta-

---

[136] *El hombre y la gente,* pp. 21-22.
[137] *El hombre y la gente,* p. 22.
[138] *El hombre y la gente,* pp. 22-23.

les, animales y los otros hombres, realidades irreductibles entre sí y, por tanto, auténticas. Lo social nos aparece adscrito sólo a los hombres. ...

Lo social consiste en acciones o comportamientos humanos —es un hecho de la vida humana. Pero la vida humana es siempre la de cada cual, es la vida individual o personal y consiste en que el yo que cada cual es se encuentra teniendo que existir en una circunstancia sin seguridad de existir en el instante inmediato, teniendo siempre que estar haciendo algo —material o mentalmente— para asegurar esa existencia. [139]

Our life is the total of these tasks and ways of behavior. The strictly human, says Ortega, is only that which I wish, feel, and do with my body, am the subjective creator of, or which happens to *me*. It follows that human is only that which I do because it has a meaning for me, or because I understand it. In every human action, there is a subject which originates it, and who is responsible for it. Consequently life is essentially solitude, for that which *I* do or think, *I* must do alone. The act is not transferable.

Mas el hecho social no es un comportamiento de nuestra vida humana como soledad, sino que aparece en tanto en cuanto estamos en relación con otros hombres. No es, pues, vida humana en sentido estricto y primario; es lo social un hecho, no de la vida humana, sino algo que surge en la humana convivencia. Por convivencia entendemos la relación o trato entre dos vidas individuales. [140]

The philosopher distinguishes between actions which are human, specific, and individual on the one hand, and those which, on the other hand, do not originate in the individual personality but in social mores (*usos*). Their author is everybody and nobody, *la gente,* society, the collectivity. The individual action, the authentic action is rational (in terms of *la razón vital*) while those actions which result from social convention are irrational, the products of social pressures and expectations.

---

[139] *El hombre y la gente,* p. 23.
[140] *El hombre y la gente,* p. 24.

> Y como la "vida social o colectiva" consiste en los usos, esa vida no es humana, es algo intermedio entre la naturaleza y el hombre, es una casi-naturaleza, y, como la naturaleza, irracional, mecánica y brutal. No hay un "alma colectiva." La sociedad, la colectividad es la gran desalmada —ya que es lo humano naturalizado, mecanizado y como mineralizado. Por eso está justificado que a la sociedad se la llame "mundo" social. No es, en efecto, tanto "humanidad" como "elemento inhumano" en que la persona se encuentra. [141]

Society is nonetheless a formidable machine for the molding of personalities. *Usos* produce several effects in the individual. They permit us to foresee (at least to a limited extent) the conduct of individuals unknown to us; by imposing a certain repertory of ideas, norms, and techniques, they oblige the individual to live at the "height of his times" through the transmission of the accumulated heritage of the past. "Gracias a la sociedad el hombre es progreso e historia. La sociedad atesora el pasado." [142] Finally, by rendering automatic a large part of conduct and determining much of what the individual must do (socially), *usos* permit him to concentrate his personal, creative and truly human activities in other directions. "La sociedad sitúa al hombre en cierta franquía frente al porvenir y le permite crear lo nuevo, racional y más perfecto." [143]

Ensimismamiento y alteración, previously published as a book, is included as the first chapter of *El hombre y la gente.* The first question has to do with the nature of society, of which Ortega concludes that little or nothing is known. It is therefore necessary to search for clear ideas, or truths, about it. He observes that in the world's present state, few peoples enjoy the tranquility necessary for searching for, or recognizing the truth.

> Casi todo el mundo está alterado, y en la alteración el hombre pierde su atributo más esencial: la posibilidad de meditar, de recogerse dentro de sí mismo para ponerse consigo mismo de acuerdo y precisarse qué es lo que cree; lo que de verdad estima y lo que de verdad detesta. La altera-

---

[141] *El hombre y la gente,* p. 27.
[142] *El hombre y la gente,* p. 28.
[143] *El hombre y la gente,* p. 28.

ción le obnubila, le ciega, le obliga a actuar mecánicamente en un frenético sonambulismo. [144]

Almost the entire remainder of the essay is devoted to evolving definitions of *ensimismamiento* and *alteración,* and to giving examples and descriptions of their operation. *Alteración* is preoccupation with that which is outside of oneself, that which is other than oneself; rather than directing one's own existence, one is manipulated, puppet-like, by that which one is not. *Ensimismamiento* is turning one's back on the world, listening to one's inner voice, being preoccupied with oneself and not with externals. The basic difference between man and animal, as Ortega sees it, is that only man is capable of *ensimismamiento.* "El animal es pura alteración. No puede ensimismarse." [145] On the other hand, the capacity of directing attention inward, of reflection, of meditation, is the most human characteristic, or in Darwinian parlance, the most highly evolved trait.

> Esa atención hacia dentro, que es el ensimismamiento, es el hecho más antinatural, más ultrabiológico. El hombre ha tardado miles y miles de años en educar un poco —nada más que un poco— su capacidad de concentración. Lo que le es natural es dispersarse, distraerse hacia fuera, como el mono en la selva. . . . [146]

It is *ensimismamiento,* reflection, which leads to authentic action. For Ortega the three (*alteración, ensimismamiento, acción*) form an ever more complicated cycle in the course of human history, a process which he relates in thoroughly existentialist terms:

> El hombre se siente perdido, náufrago en las cosas; es *la alteración.* El hombre, con un enérgico esfuerzo, se retira a su intimidad para formarse ideas sobre las cosas y su posible dominación; es el *ensimismamiento,* la *vita contemplativa* que decían los romanos. El hombre vuelve a sumergirse en el mundo para actuar en él conforme a un plan preconcebido; es la *acción,* la vida *activa.* [147]

---

[144] *El hombre y la gente,* p. 36.
[145] *El hombre y la gente,* p. 39.
[146] *El hombre y la gente,* p. 42.
[147] *El hombre y la gente,* p. 43.

The Spanish thinker refuses to admit that thought itself is characteristic of man, taking exception to the definition of man as a rational animal. This is an overly optimistic position, he asserts, which assumes that man possesses the gift of thought and is sure of being rational just as the fish is sure of being a fish:

> Este es un error formidable y fatal. El hombre no está nunca seguro de que va a poder ejercitar el pensamiento, se entiende, de una manera adecuada; y sólo si es adecuada, es pensamiento... el hombre no está nunca seguro de que va a estar en lo cierto, de que va a acertar. Lo cual significa nada menos que esta cosa tremenda: que, a diferencia de todas las demás entidades del universo, el hombre no está, no puede nunca estar seguro de que es, en efecto, hombre, como el tigre está seguro de ser tigre y el pez de ser pez. [148]

Rather than thought's being a gift, it has had to be created little by little through discipline and cultivation over thousands of years, without having been nearly completed.

> Y aun esa porción ya lograda, a fuer de cualidad adquirida y no constitutiva, está siempre en riesgo de perderse y en grandes dosis se ha perdido, muchas veces de hecho, en el pasado y hoy estamos a punto de perderla otra vez. ¡Hasta ese grado, a diferencia de los demás seres del universo, el hombre no es nunca seguramente *hombre,* sino que ser hombre significa, precisamente, estar siempre a punto de no serlo, ser viviente problema. ... [149]

This is true, not only in a generic sense, but also with reference to the individual existence; each person is constantly in danger of not being himself, by which Ortega means the unique and authentic and intransferable self. "La mayor parte de los hombres traiciona de continuo a ese sí mismo que está esperando ser, y para decir toda la verdad, es nuestra individualidad personal un personaje que no se realiza nunca del todo." [150]

---

[148] *El hombre y la gente,* p. 44.
[149] *El hombre y la gente,* pp. 44-45.
[150] *El hombre y la gente,* p. 45.

Ortega blames the false security of believing thought and progress to be inevitable human attributes for the problems of contemporary society. Man has never known what he needed to know.

> Conste, pues, que el hombre no ejercita su pensamiento porque se lo encuentra como un regalo, sino porque no teniendo más remedio que vivir sumergido en el mundo y bracear entre las cosas, se ve obligado a organizar sus actividades psíquicas, no muy diferentes de las del antropoide, en forma de pensamiento —que es lo que no hace el animal. [151]

We do not live in order to think, but rather think in order to subsist or survive. "Era necesaria esta advertencia sobre el pensamiento para comprender mi enunciado anterior, según el cual el hombre es primaria y fundamentalmente acción." [152] Authentic action must spring from a personal truth, arrived at through meditation and reflection, *ensimismamiento*. "Hay hoy una gran cosa en el mundo que está moribunda, y es la verdad. Sin cierto margen de tranquilidad, la verdad sucumbe." [153] The Ortegan doctrine of *ensimismamiento* is related to his doctrine of the point of view, for he observes that oriental *ensimismamiento*, for example, differs from the occidental.

There is in this insistence upon the importance of reflection a striking similarity to José Enrique Rodó's message in *Ariel*. There are other points of convergence in the thought of the two men (for example, the rather utopian idea of a "superstate"—one a "United States of Europe," the other a hemispheric federation) which suggest that some interesting parallels could be drawn.

Ortega devotes several pages to the idea of human life as the radical reality, and then asserts that all knowledge must begin with the individual existence as its point of departure. This point, of course, is basic existentialist doctrine. The following excerpt makes it clear that the Spaniard uses "living" in the sense in which existentialists use "existing." It also clarifies his use of *existir*, and suggests his reasons for not employing this verb:

---

[151] *El hombre y la gente*, p. 48.
[152] *El hombre y la gente*, p. 48.
[153] *El hombre y la gente*, p. 55.

De aquí que ningún conocimiento de algo es suficiente
—esto es—, suficientemente profundo, radical, si no co-
mienza por descubrir y precisar el lugar y modo, dentro
del orbe que es nuestra vida, donde ese algo hace su apari-
ción, asoma, brota y surge, en suma, existe. Porque eso
significa propiamente *existir* —vocablo, presumo, origina-
riamente de lucha y beligerancia que designa la situación
vital en que súbitamente aparece entre nosotros, como bro-
tando del suelo, un enemigo que nos cierra el paso, esto es,
nos resiste y se afirma a sí mismo ante y contra nosotros.
En el existir va incluido el resistir y, por tanto, el afirmarse
el existente si nosotros pretendemos suprimirlo, anularlo o
tomarlo como irreal. Por eso lo existente o surgente es realidad, ya que realidad es todo aquello con que, queramos o
no, tenemos que contar, porque, queramos o no, *está ahí*,
ex-iste, re-siste. Una arbitrariedad terminológica que raya
en lo intolerable ha querido desde hace unos años emplear
los vocablos "existir" y "existencia" con un sentido abstru-
so e incontrolable que es precisamente inverso del que por
sí la palabra milenaria porta y dice.
  Algunos quieren hoy designar así el modo de ser del
hombre, pero el hombre, que es siempre *yo*, es lo único
que no existe, sino que *vive* o es viviendo. Son precisamente todas las demás cosas que no son el hombre, yo, las
que *existen*, porque aparecen, surgen, saltan, me resisten,
se afirman dentro del ámbito que es mi vida. [154]

The reference is clearly to the existentialists, but Ortega avoids
using the word. This is the only place in his philosophy where he
is clearly at variance with other existentialists over terminology.
Here it is clear beyond all doubt that he and the existentialists are
talking about the same thing, although each individual philosopher,
with a certain petulance, maintains the superiority of his own choice
of words. It is also interesting that on the following page Ortega
makes this statement:

De pronto y sin saber cómo ni por qué, sin anuncio previo,
el hombre se descubre y sorprende teniendo que ser en un
ámbito impremeditado, imprevisto, en este de ahora, en
una coyuntura de determinadísimas circunstancias. *Tal vez
no es ocioso hacer notar que esto —base de mi pensamiento*

---

[154] *El hombre y la gente,* p. 64.

filosófico— fue ya enunciado, tal y como ahora lo he hecho, en mi primer libro, publicado en 1914. [155]

The reference, clearly, is again to existentialism; Ortega is asserting the priority of his ideas. What he states at the same time as the nucleus of his philosophy is a basic tenet of existentialism. His contention that his basic ideas are the same as in 1914 would indicate that, at least to his personal satisfaction, Ortega considers his own philosophy coherent and systematic.

Before leaving the last quotations, it should be noted that Ortega's description of the things which exist is essentially the same as Sartre's concept of the *En-soi,* and of Heidegger's description of Being. Also, the distinction which the three make between the individual personality and the rest of the world is identical.

Existentialism has been called "the literature of possibility" because of its insistence on the fact that man is continually faced with the necessity of choosing between different vital possibilities. The identical concept occurs over and over in Ortega's works, although perhaps he insists a little more on the ethical dimension. Choice is seen both as necessity and as responsibility. In any case, Ortega and other existentialists coincide in seeing man as free in all respects except that he is forced to choose:

> La circunstancia, el aquí y ahora dentro de los cuales estamos inexorablemente inscritos y prisioneros, no nos impone en cada instante una acción o hacer, sino varias posibles y nos deja cruelmente entregados a nuestra iniciativa e inspiración; por tanto, a nuestra responsabilidad.
> ... ...
> Esta forzosidad de tener que elegir y, por tanto, estar condenado, quiera o no, a ser libre, a ser por su propia cuenta y riesgo, proviene de que la circunstancia no es nunca unilateral, tiene siempre varios y a veces muchos lados. Es decir, nos invita a diferentes posibilidades de hacer, de ser. ... La vida es multilateral. Cada instante y cada sitio abre ante nosotros diversos caminos. Como dice el viejísimo libro indio: "Dondequiera que el hombre pone la planta, pisa siempre cien senderos." De aquí que la vida sea permanente encrucijada y constante perplejidad. [156]

---

[155] *El hombre y la gente,* p. 65. Italics mine.
[156] *El hombre y la gente,* pp. 66-68.

The same idea of man's being condemned to freedom is found in Sartre.

In much of the remainder of the book, the philosopher further explains the attributes of life as radical reality and radical solitude. He analyzes reality as divided basically into individual and circumstances. The latter exist on several planes: the thing or things which are immediately next to us, those things included in our visible horizon and therefore present or patent, and the things which we know exist but cannot see, those things which are latent.

Ortega points out that where "I" am is always "here," and that therefore the ideas are inseparable. This he calls the third structural law of the world, and points out that it means that the world is a perspective. With several examples, he repeats the idea that we never apprehend more than a single aspect of a given reality at once, although several aspects may be observed in turn and stored in memory. Having thus defined life, reality, the individual and his circumstances, Ortega is at last ready to introduce the Other. "Desde el fondo de radical soledad que es propiamente nuestra vida, practicamos, una y otra vez, un intento de interpenetración, de *de-soleda-dizarnos* asomándonos al otro ser humano, deseando darle nuestra vida y recibir la suya." [157]

The author points out that inter-individual life always takes place in the framework of *nosotros,* between a *tú* and a *yo.* With the progress of intimacy, the Other becomes a *Tú.* In the sense in which he means it, the Other can only be one who is capable of responding to me in the same measure as I to him; thus animals, for example, are excluded from this sort of relationship. It is at this point that the generic Man appears:

> Yo, en mi soledad, no podría llamarme con un nombre genérico tal como "hombre." La realidad que este nombre representa sólo me aparece cuando hay otro ser que me responde o reciproca. Muy bien lo dice Husserl: "El sentido del término hombre implica una existencia recíproca del uno para el otro; por tanto, *una comunidad de hombres, una sociedad.*" [158]

---

[157] *El hombre y la gente,* p. 120.
[158] *El hombre y la gente,* p. 133.

Thus, Man is the Other, never the individual self. Since one is from birth surrounded with others, he is of necessity altruistic. This applies even to one's idea of self: we learn to know ourselves from the ideas which others have of us, and from the differences which we note between ourselves and others.

Ortega's concept of the stranger resembles Sartre's ideas of the other and of human relationships as conflict:

> ante el puro y desconocido Otro, yo tengo que ponerme en lo peor y anticipar que su reacción puede ser darme una puñalada. Y como esto, innúmeras otras reacciones adversas. El puro Otro, en efecto, es por lo pronto e igualmente mi amigo en potencia que un potencial enemigo." [159]
>
> El otro Hombre es esencialmente peligroso, y este carácter que se acusa superlativamente cuando se trata del por completo desconocido, en gradación menguante perdura cuando se nos convierte en Tú y —si hablamos rigurosamente— no desaparece nunca. Todo *otro* ser humano nos es peligroso —cada cual a su modo y en su peculiar dosis. [160]

The greatest danger of the Other is not the possibility of his hostility, but the simple fact that he is the Other, that he has his own peculiar way of being which does not coincide with mine:

> Del *tú,* en efecto, emergen frecuentemente negaciones de mi ser —de mi modo de pensar, de sentir, de querer. A veces la negación consiste precisamente en que tú y yo queremos lo mismo y esto implica que tenemos que luchar por ello. ... Mi mundo está todo él impregnado de mí. Tú mismo antes de serme el preciso Tú que ahora me eres, no me eras extraño: creía que eras como yo —*alter*— pero yo, *ego* —*alter ego.* Mas ahora frente a ti y los otros *tús,* veo que en el mundo hay más que aquel vago, indeterminado *yo: hay anti-yos.* [161]

Ortega proceeds from here to his concept of the ego as *alter-tú,* in which he has, I believe, gone beyond Sartre. The concepts with which the two began were, however, almost identical, and the threat

---

[159] *El hombre y la gente,* p. 182.
[160] *El hombre y la gente,* pp. 190-191.
[161] *El hombre y la gente,* pp. 193-194.

which the Other poses as negation of the ego is explained in essentially the same way by both philosophers.

In the small remaining portion, Ortega devotes himself to what might be called sociological theory and observations, concentrating primarily on social conventions or *usos*.

In *¿Qué es Filosofía?* the primary concern is the relating of vital reason to philosophy as a whole. (This does not emerge in any clear fashion until the closing pages.) The author begins with the announcement that the book is a monograph on a "hypertechnical" question. He observes that for us today philosophy is a very different thing than it was for the preceding generation, to admit which is to recognize that truth changes. Ortega prefers to represent changes in thought not as changes by which yesterday's truth becomes today's error, but rather a change in man's orientation which leads him to see before him different truths than those of yesteryear. Thus, it is not truth which changes, but men.

This leads to some historical digression and a new introduction of the concept of generations, after which are presented the historical background of the philosophic conflict between realism and idealism, and long meditations on the meaning of "science" and the nature and origin of knowledge.

A chapter called "Conocimiento del Universo o Multiverso" leads again to the doctrine of perspectivism, and this remark on the scope of philosophy: "De suerte, que no sólo el problema filosófico es ilimitado en extensión, puesto que abarca todo y no tiene confines, sino que lo es también en intensidad problemática. No sólo es el problema de lo absoluto, sino que es absolutamente problema." [162]

A subsequent chapter deals with the necessity of philosophy, of which Ortega has this to say:

> Parece, decía yo, una loca empresa. ¿Por qué intentarla?
> ¿Por qué no contentarse con vivir y excusar el filosofar?
> Si no es probable el logro de su empeño, la filosofía no sirve
> de nada, no hay necesidad de ella. Perfectamente; mas,
> por lo pronto, es un hecho que hay hombres para quienes
> lo superfluo es lo necesario. ... La filosofía no brota por

---

[162] *¿Qué es Filosofía?*, p. 88.

razón de utilidad, pero tampoco por sinrazón de capricho. Es constitutivamente necesaria al intelecto. [163]

He defines philosophy as the knowledge of the universe, of all that there is, but points out that the philosopher's problem is always the *unknown*; what is known is no longer a problem.

The philosopher's next chapters deal with the difference between belief and theory, with intuition, with doubt, with the philosophic discovery of subjectivity, and what he calls the roots of modern subjectivity. Ortega returns to the ideas of *El tema de nuestro tiempo* and the necessity of a radical reform of philosophy, emphasizing once more the distinction between individual and circumstances, and the definition of human life as radical reality.

There follows a chapter devoted to the new idea of reality, to life as finding oneself in the world, and the concept of life as constantly deciding what we are going to be. Much of this is repetition of what has been said in essence or in fact in several other works, and thus requires no closer scrutiny. One passage, however, is worth special attention, for in it Ortega recognizes the similarity of his idea of life and Heidegger's:

> Vivir es encontrarse en el mundo. ... Heidegger, en un recentísimo y genial libro, nos ha hecho notar todo el enorme significado de esas palabras. No se trata principalmente de que encontremos nuestro cuerpo entre otras cosas corporales y todo ello dentro de un gran cuerpo o espacio que llamaríamos mundo. Si sólo cuerpos hubiese, no existiría el vivir, los cuerpos ruedan los unos sobre los otros, sin que se sepan ni importen. ... Mundo es *sensu stricto* lo que nos afecta. Y vivir es hallarse cada cual a sí mismo en un ámbito de temas, de asuntos que le afectan. Así, sin saber cómo, la vida se encuentra a sí misma a la vez que descubre el mundo. ... [164]

Other attributes of life are adduced, including once again the idea of possibility, of liberty, of necessity of choice, of action, and ending with the concept of life as futurity:

---

[163] *¿Qué es Filosofía?*, pp. 103-104.
[164] *¿Qué es Filosofía?*, pp. 230-231.

> Nuestra vida es ante todo toparse con el futuro. He aquí otra paradoja. No es el presente o el pasado lo primero que vivimos, no; la vida es una actividad que se ejecuta hacia adelante, y el presente o el pasado se descubren después, en relación con ese futuro. La vida es futurición, es lo que aún no es. [165]

The work's final chapter again presents life as the radical reality, asserting that it is apprehended under certain categories:

> "Encontrarse," "enterarse de sí," "ser transparente" es la primera categoría de nuestra vida, y una vez más no se olvide que aquí el sí mismo no es sólo el sujeto, sino también el mundo. Me doy cuenta de mí en el mundo, de mí y del mundo —esto es, por lo pronto, "vivir." [166]

Ortega returns to the original question of the book, and states his conviction that the question has been answered more radically than ever before, since philosophic doctrine has now been defined, and "life" discovered. Philosophic doctrine, that found in books, Ortega calls the abstraction of the authentic reality, "philosophy"; it is its half-dead body. The "being" of philosophy is the activity of the philosopher; philosophy is a form of life. In the closing pages, then, Ortega has returned to the idea of the importance of the contemplative life, of the importance of meditation and reflection in deciding our future actions.

> Hemos visto que el vivir consiste en estar decidiendo lo que vamos a ser. Muy finamente, Heidegger dice: entonces la vida es "cuidado," cuidar —Sorge— lo que los latinos llaman cura, de donde viene procurar, curar, curiosidad, etc. En antiguo español la palabra "cuidar" tenía exactamente el sentido que nos conviene. ... [167]

Life is preoccupation. To attempt to live otherwise is falsification, an attempt which characterizes the *hombre-masa* and relates him to this part of Ortega's philosophy.

---

[165] *¿Qué es Filosofía?*, pp. 236-237.
[166] *¿Qué es Filosofía?*, p. 250.
[167] *¿Qué es Filosofía?*, p. 261.

> Cuando creemos no preocuparnos en nuestra vida, en cada instante de ella la dejamos flotar a la deriva, como una boya sin amarras, que va y viene empujada por las corrientes sociales. Y esto es lo que hace el hombre medio y la mujer mediocre, es decir, la inmensa mayoría de las criaturas humanas. Para ellas vivir es entregarse a lo unánime, dejar que las costumbres, los prejuicios, los usos, los tópicos se instalen en su interior, los hagan vivir a ellos y tomen sobre sí la tarea de hacerlos vivir. [168]

Like the mass-man, this sort of individual attempts to escape the responsibility of life, of decision, of being himself, by doing what everybody else does. He tries to substitute the anonymous social collectivity for himself, and, says Ortega, so to defraud the powers of life and beyond life.

> No hay modo de escaparse a la condición esencial del vivir, y siendo ella la realidad, lo mejor, lo más discreto es subrayarlo con ironía, repitiendo el gesto elegante del hada Titania que en la selva encantada de Shakespeare acaricia la cabeza de asno. [169]

But it is not on this note of irony which Ortega ends, but rather on one of optimism, of acceptance, and of duty:

> Los sacerdotes japoneses maldicen de lo terreno, siguiendo este prurito de todos los sacerdotes, y para denigrar la inquietante futilidad de nuestro mundo, lo llaman "mundo de rocío." En un poeta, Isa, aparece un sencillo hai-kai, al cual me atento, y dice así: "Un mundo de rocío no es más que un mundo de rocío. Y ¡sin embargo! ..." Sin embargo... aceptemos ese mundo de rocío como materia para hacer una vida más completa. [170]

[168] ¿Qué es Filosofía?, p. 263.
[169] ¿Qué es Filosofía?, p. 264.
[170] ¿Qué es Filosofía?, p. 264.

Chapter IV

SUMMARY AND CONCLUSIONS

The major theme of existentialism is, as the term indicates, existence, the word being understood as a "standing out" from the mere biological vitality by which all subhuman forms of existence are characterized. Life, which is Ortega's major theme, is unquestionably used by him in the same sense.

Let us take a concrete example for purposes of comparison. Heidegger distinguished between three different modes in which existents are or have their being: things are given or exist as objects of human knowledge; things are given or exist as tools or means of human activity, deriving meaning from the practical use which man makes of them; man stands out from all other modes of existence in that man *is,* not simply and statically like minerals, plants, and animals, but has constantly and dynamically to affirm and actualize his existence in self-knowledge and self-realization.

We have seen numerous examples of the first case, in which circumstances are given in Ortega's writings; the second case was not quoted, but the concept occurs in Chapters IX and X of *¿Qué es Filosofía?* in which Ortega points out that things are defined in terms of the use man makes of them. There are, of course, differences in the examples and explanations given by the two philosophers, but it is an entirely fair and accurate summary of Ortega's concept of human nature to say that man is a being who must constantly affirm his existence in self-realization. Life, according to Ortega, is given in a similar sense as *quehacer.*

The existentialists hold that man is a being suspended between nothingness and the plenitude of being. Ortega never states it in just these terms; the concept of nothingness is relatively neglected in his philosophy. The idea of plenitude of being, however, occurs repeatedly, beginning with *El tema de nuestro tiempo* and continuing through *El hombre y la gente* and *¿Qué es Filosofía?*

One of the critics cited in Chapter I has this to say about existentialist philosophy:

> Existentialism in its modern and particularly its contemporary form concentrates critical reflection on the individual human self. It confronts this individual human existence with those collective claims and forces which threaten to submerge or pulverize individuality and personality in abstract, ideal essences or in such pseudo-absolutes as "the nation," "the fatherland," "the race," "the international proletariat." Existentialism has risen in modern Europe because the steadily increasing pressures of collectivism and abstract idealism have forced the individual to a resolute and radical self-affirmation. [1]

All of the above is equally true of Ortega's philosophy, if taken as a whole; it applies in particular to *La rebelión de las masas* and *El hombre y la gente*.

"Existentialism is a translation of the abstract to the concrete, an ethical appropriation of the ideal, an active practice and realization rather than any doctrinal knowledge; a 'how' rather than a 'what.'" [2]

Ortega in every case rejects the abstract for the concrete; there is no doubt that his philosophy is ethical, or that it concentrates on practice rather than doctrine; it is truly a "how," not a "what."

Existentialism emphasizes the idea of alternative or choice (a case in point is the title of Kierkegaard's great book, *Either/Or*).

Existentialism (in the case of all four philosophers examined in Chapter I) emphasizes the element of human freedom in choice or decision, emphasizes the risk of incertitude involved in decision, and especially in the case of Sartre, emphasizes the necessity or inescapability of decision. Ortega repeatedly states that man is free in all choices save that of *not* choosing (cf. Sartre in that even a

---

[1] Kurt F. Reinhardt, *The Existentialist Revolt* (Milwaukee, 1951), p. 14.
[2] Reinhardt, p. 39.

decision not to decide is a decision). Ortega's philosophy mentions the element of insecurity, but does not emphasize risk to the extent that other existentialists do.

"The existing individual is constantly in the process of becoming". [3] Ortega's philosophy emphasizes that human life consists in a striving toward what it is not, a constant effort to reduce the gap between what we are and what we want or believe ourselves to be.

"Existential thinking is not yet moral action, but it is pregnant with the possibility of moral action. It makes sense to speak of virtue in thought and sin in thought, because the external act is related to an internal moral decision." [4] This is precisely what Ortega means by *ensimismamiento*. The concept can be equated with "existential thinking" since both lead to action, in the sense of meaningful, goal-directed activity.

"What, then, is the supreme ethical task of the individual? No more and no less than to become 'an entire man.' " [5] The Ortegan concept of man implies human in the highest sense, and can fairly be equated with the above.

"Existential despair expresses the *reductio ad absurdum* of the sensual mode of life. But this 'sickness unto death' may bear within itself its own cure. The shipwreck of the aesthetic life may mean the emergence and growth of the *ethical* life." [6] Ortega's concept of *náufrago* is not only comparable; in this case, even his term coincides.

"Kierkegaard had started out with the contention that the deadly disease of the modern age was the divorce of thought and life." [7] Ortega's concern in *El tema de nuestro tiempo* is one and the same—the separation which exists between life and culture.

"Existential thinking calls for the unity of thought and life." [8] This is exactly what Ortega does in *la razón vital*. His meaning is different, for example, than that of Kierkegaard, who saw the pat-

---

[3] Reinhardt, p. 44.
[4] Reinhardt, p. 50.
[5] Reinhardt, p. 50.
[6] Reinhardt, p. 55.
[7] Reinhardt, p. 57.
[8] Reinhardt, p. 58.

tern of this unity in Christ, but there can be no doubt that the definition applies.

> The existential themes, discussed by various authors in the terminology coined by Heidegger, include among others: the contingency, insecurity, self-estrangement, and dereliction of human existence; its ultimate meaning; its "temporality," "historicity," and "authenticity"; its "care," its "dread," and its "freedom-toward-death"; the interrelation of "being" and "existence," "being" and "truth," "being" and "nothing." The connotations implied in these philosophical concepts and the conclusions educed from them vary according to the theological and metaphysical convictions of individual authors, but the questions and problems to which they refer are essentially the same. [9]

Ortega philosophy contains equivalents for all or nearly all of the above terms: *contingencia, inseguridad, alteración, náufrago,* the concept of *verdad radical,* the concept of life as futurity, *circunstancia, autenticidad, preocupación,* and the idea of one's being able to choose the manner (and often the time) of one's death. The major difference lies in that Ortega did not use the concepts of "being" and "existence" in the same apposition as have other existentialists; however, his distinction between *yo* and *circunstancia* is comparable.

An extensive or detailed comparison of Ortega's ideas with those of the several individual existentialists would be considerably beyond the scope of this study. Obviously, a number of differences and similarities would emerge. Some have already been indicated. For example, Ortega gives almost no consideration to the idea of nothingness. Death is mentioned only a few times in Ortega's writings, being emphasized much less than is the case with the usual existentialist Ortega's use of *náufrago* appears to cover the concepts of shipwreck, anguish, and despair, but there is no clear parallel of the idea of nausea. While most existentialists take some fairly decisive metaphysical stance, whether atheistic or Christian or otherwise, Ortega has almost completely ignored God as an issue. He has treated Christianity as ethic and as epistemological orientation

---

[9] Reinhardt, p. 122.

and found it lacking in each case; God, when mentioned, has been called a transcendental problem and dismissed in favor of dealing with the problem of life. This was ruled out in the beginning as a ground for determining the presence or absence of existentialism, however, since there is no one typically existentialist solution.

Ortega's adherents, and particularly Marías, have maintained that he has gone beyond existentialism in his development of the doctrine of vital reason. Ortega's emphasis on the responsibility of the individual is also greater than the emphasis of Sartre or Heidegger, for example. While there is no doubt that existentialism is an ethic, this seems to be even more true of the philosophy of Ortega. He has given more time and thought to the problems faced by the existential individual in relating to society, which may be a practical extension of existentialist ethics. All of the differences just mentioned can be explained by one fundamental difference in attitude. The average existentialist (if there is an average existentialist!) is concerned with the individual to the virtual exclusion of society; Ortega would not sacrifice either. This may explain his minimizing of personal or individual themes such as nausea and death, while giving relatively greater importance to ethics and the social sphere.

Undoubtedly other parallels and contrasts might be drawn. On the basis of the study just completed, I believe that the similarities would outweigh the differences. Our purpose has been to compare Ortega's major themes with those of the four philosophers conceded by a majority of critics to be existentialists, and to attempt to place Ortega's works in the context of a philosophy of existence. The major themes coincide in an overwhelming majority of cases. At times it appeared at first glance that Ortega's topic was history or sociology or aesthetics, but his underlying concern proved to be with life or the individual existence. In addition, Ortega's terminology often coincides with, or is highly comparable to, that of other existentialists. Ortega's important works fit easily and neatly into a framework of existence philosophy.

In view of this extensive coincidence of Ortega's themes and tenets with those of existentialism, it is even more puzzling that major critics should have so avoided the mention of any existential element. While Ortega never aligned himself with the existentialists publicly, he was not reluctant to own that many ideas now con-

sidered existentialist were originally his. He recognized that he and
Heidegger, for example, were dealing with the same subjects in
the same way. This was indicated clearly by his remarks quoted
in Chapter III. The apparent conspiracy of silence regarding existentialism in Spain is difficult to explain. It can only be speculated,
as suggested earlier, that since the Catholic critics have used the
word in an exclusively condemnatory sense, Ortega's disciples have
decided to avoid the appearance of evil.

If the ideas herein expressed have served to clarify the thought
of this important philosopher, or to open other avenues of interpretation of his work, this study will have achieved its purpose.

APPENDIX

A. Homenajes

This section contains articles which were written primarily as tributes to Ortega after his death, and a number of other non-critical articles containing miscellaneous anecdotes and biographical incidents. Articles which might be helpful are annotated.

ALONSO, MARÍA ROSA. "En la muerte de Don José Ortega y Gasset," *Revista Nacional de Cultura*, XVIII, No. 114 (Jan.-Feb. 1956), 44-47.

ÁLVAREZ, V. A. "Introducción al coloquio *Nuestra imagen de Ortega*," *Cultura Universitaria* (Caracas), No. 41 (1954). Recounts personal contacts with Ortega.

ARAQUISTÁIN, LUIS. "En defensa de un muerto profanado," *Sur*, No. 241 (July-Aug. 1956), 120-130.

Deals in part with the critical controversies over whether Ortega was or was not a philosopher, and whether his philosophy was systematic.

BALBÉ, RAÚL R. "Repetición de Ortega," *Sur*, No. 241 (July-Aug. 1956), 156-165.

BARGA, CORPUS. "Un aspecto de Ortega. El refractario," *Sur*, No. 241 (July-Aug. 1956), 170-179.

Deals with *El Espectador* as reflection of contemporary scene.

BATAILLON, M. "José Ortega y Gasset," *Revue de Littérature Comparée*, XXIX, No. 4 (Oct.-Dec. 1955), 449-452.

This major French critic comments on Ortega's influence in France, his significance, and laments his loss.

BELAUNDE, VÍCTOR ANDRÉS. "Ortega y Gasset," *Mercurio peruano*, XXXVI, No. 345 (Dec. 1955), 839-845.

BENÍTEZ, JAIME. "Recuerdo de Ortega," *Sur*, No. 241 (July-Aug. 1956), 192-199.

Recounts personal acquaintaince, some biography.

BURCKHARDT, CARL J. "Encuentro con Ortega," *Sur*, No. 241 (July-Aug. 1956), 179-187.

Reminiscences of a single meeting with Ortega.

CAILLOIS, ROGER. "Juegos y sociedades," *La Torre*, XV-XVI (July-Dec. 1956), 477-499.

Original work of the author dedicated to Ortega because he feels it part of Ortega's "spiritual legacy."

CASTELLET, JOSÉ MARÍA. "Poder irse tranquilo," *Ínsula*, X, No. 119 (Nov. 15, 1955).

Sustains point of view held by Marías and others that Ortega lived authentically, lived up to his own philosophy.

CASSOU, JEAN. "José Ortega y Gasset," *Sur*, No. 241 (July-Aug. 1956), 131-135.

DÍEZ DEL CORRAL, LUIS. "Saber y personalidad de Ortega," *La Torre*, XV-XVI (July-Dec. 1956), 45-58.

Deals with several critics' impressions of Ortega, and the controversy regarding Ortega's system or lack of system.

FRANCO DE MARÍAS, DOLORES. "El brillo de su ausencia," *La Torre*, XV-XVI (July-Dec. 1956), 59-64.

GARAGORRI, PAULINO. "Complementos a un artículo sobre Ortega," *Suplemento de Ínsula*, No. 121 (Dec. 15, 1955).

Completes thoughts of same author in article listed below.

——. "La realidad de la muerte," *Ínsula*, X, No. 119 (Nov. 15, 1955).

JIMÉNEZ, JUAN RAMÓN. "Recuerdo a Ortega y Gasset," *Clavileño*, IV, No. 24 (Nov.-Dec. 1953), 44-49.

Remembrance of youth; mostly personal reflections. Has some reference to the philosophic system controversy; Jiménez feels it is unimportant to true personal philosophy.

LAFUENTE FERRARI, ENRIQUE. "En memoria de Ortega: Recuerdos y deberes," *Ínsula*, X, No. 119 (Nov. 15, 1955).

LARA MÍNGUEZ, DIONISIO DE. "Ortega: Recuento y epílogo," *Revista Cubana de Filosofía*, IV, No. 13 (Jan.-June 1956), 52-61.

Attempts to answer unflattering allusions to Ortega's lack of system; alleges "perfect symmetry," "perfect harmony" in systematic thought.

MANENT, ALBERT. "Mi Don José Ortega y Gasset," *Suplemento de Ínsula*, No. 121 (Dec. 15, 1955).

MINDÁR, M. "Ortega y Gasset, o Homen e o Filósofo," *Revista Portuguesa de Filosofía*, XII, No. 2 (1956).

OCAMPO, VICTORIA. "Entre Dakar y Barcelona (Recordando a Ortega)," *La Torre*, XV-XVI (July-Dec. 1956), 79-83.

————. "Mi deuda con Ortega," *Sur*, No. 241 (July-Aug. 1956), 206-220.

PIÑERA LLERA, HUMBERTO. "Ortega y Gasset: el filósofo," *Boletín*, VIII, No. 2 (Feb. 1955), 1-7.
    Disagrees with those who contend Ortega was not a philosopher.

POZZI, HÉCTOR. "Ortega como nosotros," *Sur*, No. 241 (July-Aug. 1956), 141-151.

PRESA, FERNANDO DE LA. "Perfil humano de D. José Ortega y Gasset," *Revista Cubana de Filosofía*, IV, No. 13 (Jan.-Feb. 1956), 90-103.
    Much physical description, in detail, combined with small incidents; gives a feeling for the man and his personality. Enjoyable reading.

REYES, ALFONSO. "Treno para José Ortega y Gasset," *Cuadernos Americanos*, LXXXV, No. 1 (1956), 65-67.
    The Mexican philosopher reminisces about personal contacts with Ortega; a reference to the controversy over Ortega's philosophic "system."

ROA, RAÚL. "Dichos y hechos de Ortega y Gasset," *Cuadernos Americanos*, LXXXV, No. 1 (1956), 120-131.
    Mostly biography and personal recollections.

RODRÍGUEZ HUÉSCAR, ANTONIO. "Relato personal," *La Torre*, XV-XVI (July-Dec. 1956), 85-92.

ROF CARBALLO, J. "Un recuerdo de Ortega," *Ínsula*, X, No. 119 (Nov. 15, 1955).

ROMERO, FRANCISCO. "Ortega y el ausentismo filosófico español," *Sur*, No. 241 (July-Aug. 1956), 24-29.

SANSEVERRA DE ELEZALDE, ELENA. "Mi amistad con Ortega," *Sur*, No. 241 (July-Aug. 1956), 187-192.

TREND, J. B. "Boceto de memoria," *Sur*, No. 241 (July-Aug. 1956), 199-206.
    The British critic recalls a meeting with Ortega.

VÁZQUEZ, JUAN ADOLFO. "Ortega como circunstancia," *Sur,* No. 241 (July-Aug. 1956), 29-32.
Sees Ortega as a cultural, philosophical and intellectual monument.
VELA, FERNANDO. "Evocación de Ortega," *Sur,* No. 241 (July-Aug. 1956), 3-12.
The story of a life-long admiration for Ortega.

ZAMBRANO, MARÍA. "Don José," *Ínsula,* X, No. 119 (Nov. 15, 1955).
Recollections of a former student.
———. "Ortega y Gasset, filósofo español," *Asomante,* V, Nos. 1-2 (1949), 5-17, 6-15.
Part of the *filósofo-literato* argument.

B. AESTHETICS

This section contains articles as well as chapters from a number of histories of literature, manuals, and reference works. The unifying approach is a common concentration on Ortega's aesthetics, style, or literary criticism. Certain articles of miscellaneous literary criticism, largely expository in nature, are also included. Where titles are not self-explanatory, notations have been added to clarify the subjects covered.

AMADOR SÁNCHEZ, LUIS. "Ortega y Gasset y el nuevo misterio de Velázquez," *Atenea,* XCIX, No. 304 (Oct. 1950), 71-83.
A study of Ortega's ideas on Velázquez and art.

BAQUERO GOYANES, MARIANO. "La novela como tragicomedia: Pérez de Ayala y Ortega," *Ínsula,* X, No. 110 (Feb. 15, 1955).
Compares Pérez de Ayala's technique with Ortega's ideas on the novel.
BALSEIRO, JOSÉ A. "Ortega y Gasset, el artista," *Clavileño,* IV, No. 24 (Nov.-Dec. 1953), 75-76.
Ortega's essays as artistic creations.
BAREO, ARTURO. "The Conservative Critics: Ortega and Madariaga," *University Observer,* No. 1 (Winter 1947), 29-36.
Interprets Ortega as an intellectual aristocrat, political conservative.
BERGES, CONSUELO. "Ortega, Stendhal y el Amor," *Ínsula,* VIII, No. 90 (June 15, 1953).
Compares Ortega's ideas on love with those of Stendhal.

Bo, Carlo. "Ortega y *El Espectador*," *Clavileño,* IV, No. 24 (Nov.-Dec. 1953), 77-80.

Views the book as a diary, Ortega's "most sincere."

Botín Polanco, Antonio. "El estilo de Ortega," *Clavileño,* IV, No. 24 (Nov.-Dec. 1953), 81.

Brenan, Gerald. *The Literature of the Spanish People.* New York, 1957. See pp. 419-421.

A concise, conventional review of Ortega's best-known books.

Canito, Enrique. "Ortega en las '*Recontres,*'" *Ínsula,* VII, No. 73 (Aug. 15, 1953).

Chacel, Rosa. "Respuesta a Ortega. La novela no escrita," *Sur,* No. 241 (July-Aug. 1956), 97-119.

Analyzes several "novelistic" characters who recur in Ortega's writings.

Clemente, José Edmundo. *Ortega y Gasset. Estética de la razón vital.* Buenos Aires, 1956.

A brief monograph which relates Ortega's aesthetic ideas to *la razón vital,* showing how Ortega used life as his yardstick for measuring art.

Conelia, Edmundo. "El estilo en José Ortega y Gasset," *Atenea,* CXXIV, Nos. 367-368 (1957), 73-81.

On Ortega's choice of words, idea of good writing. Emphasis on variety, brilliance of Ortega's style.

Córdova de Braschi, Julia. "Dos paisajes españoles: Castilla y Asturias," *La Torre,* XV-XVI (July-Dec. 1956), 95-101.

A study of Ortega's treatment of nature, and particularly of the Castilian and Asturian landscapes.

———. "La psicología española vista por Ortega y Gasset," *Asomante,* No. 4 (1954).

Cruz Ocampo, Luis David. "La intelectualización del arte," *Revista Atenea* (1927), pp. 12-85.

Primarily a review and exposition of Ortega's ideas on this subject, with some misunderstanding and hostility; sees Ortega as against art, especially the contemporary.

Curtius, Ernst R. "Ortega," *Partisan Review,* XVII (Jan.-April 1950), 262-271.

del Río, Ángel, and M. J. Bernadete. *El Concepto contemporáneo de España.* Buenos Aires, 1956. See pp. 491-532.

Brief biography, and a view of Ortega as somewhat conservative. Selections from his works.

Fernández Suárez, Álvaro. "El viajero antiguo," *Sur,* No. 241 (July-Aug. 1956), 74-79.

GAOS, JOSÉ. "Alfonso Reyes, el escritor," *Cuadernos Americanos,* CXII, No. 5 (Sept.-Oct. 1960).
Compares style of Reyes to Ortega's.

GARCÍA MORENTE, MANUEL. *Lecciones Preliminares de filosofía.* 3d ed. Buenos Aires, 1943. See pp. 366-368.
Brief reference to Ortega.

GARCÍA TUDURI, ROSAURA. "Ideas estéticas de Ortega y Gasset," *Revista Cubana de Filosofía,* IV, No. 13 (Jan.-June 1956), 28-32.

GULLÓN RICARDO. "Ortega, crítico literario," *Sur,* No. 241 (July-Aug. 1956), 89-97.

HUERTA, ELEAZAR. "La prosa de Ortega," *Atenea,* CXXIV, Nos. 367-368 (1956), 48-72.
Expresses the idea that Ortega's particular circumstances forced him to a special media and form of expression. Sees Ortega as *engagé.* Information on Ortega's political activities and general biography.

―――. "Lenguaje y literatura en la filosofía de Ortega," *Revista Nacional de Cultura,* XVIII, No. 114 (Jan.-Feb. 1956), 37-43.
Language is conceived as *prefilosofía.* Many philosophers write badly, obscurely, but Ortega wrote beautifully, using everyday words. Sees him not as both *filósofo* and *literato,* but as a philosopher conscious of the common roots of human activity and language.

ILDEFONSO, MANUEL GIL. "Sobre el arte de escribir novelas," *Cuadernos Hispanoamericanos,* No. 121 (Jan. 1960), 39-47.
Cites Ortega and several others.

INGENIEROS, JOSÉ. *La cultura filosófica en España,* Buenos Aires, 1939.
Published as volume 22 of his *Obras completas,* this book contains a brief reference to Ortega as head of a *krausista* group.

LAFUENTE FERRARI, ENRIQUE. "Las artes visuales y su historia en el pensamiento de Ortega," *La Torre,* XV-XVI (July-Dec. 1956), 167-247.

LAÍN ENTRALGO, P. *Vestigios.* Madrid, 1948. See pp. 333-348.
Portraits of several of the generation of '98, including Ortega, by means of personal anecdotes and superficial literary impressions.

LÓPEZ-MORILLAS, JUAN. "Ortega y Gasset y la crítica literaria," *Cuadernos Americanos,* XCIII, No. 3 (1957), 72-86.
Sees an instrumental use of literature for the systematic analysis of a phase in the history of culture. Thus literature for Ortega serves as an "ancillary function of cultural psychology."

MAEZTU, MARÍA DE. *Antología — Siglo XX, Prosistas Españoles.* Buenos Aires, 1943. See pp. 86-92.

A chapter on Ortega is largely the author's reminiscence of Ortega's first class as professor of philosophy in the Escuela de Estudios Superiores del Magisterio; a description of Ortega's *oposiciones* for chair of Metaphysics, and early literary production.

MARQUINA, RAFAEL. "Ortega y Gasset y la crítica de arte," *Revista Cubana de Filosofía,* IV, No. 13 (Jan.-June 1956), 62-71.

MCDONALD, E. CORDELL. "The Modern Novel as Viewed by Ortega," *Hispania,* XLII, No. 4 (1959), 475-481.

Straight exposition and summary of Ortega's *Ideas sobre la novela.*

ROGGIANO, ALFREDO. "Estética y crítica literaria en Ortega y Gasset," *La Torre,* XV-XVI (July-Dec. 1956), 337-359.

ROMERA, ANTONIO R. "Ortega y Velázquez," *Atenea,* CXXIV, Nos. 367-368 (1956), 94-106.

Velázquez is seen as an obsessive theme with Ortega. The critic theorizes that this is because of a concept of realism somehow shared by the painter and Ortega, and the importance to both of them of what he classifies as *temas fugaces.* Romera also takes a stand in the critical controversy over Ortega's "system": he calls his philosophy coherent and systematic.

SALAVERRÍA, J. M. *Retratos.* Madrid, 1926. See pp. 173-221.

Contains a superficial and noticeably hostile personality sketch of Ortega; some minor biographical information.

TORRE, GUILLERMO DE. "Las ideas estéticas de Ortega," *Sur,* No. 241 (July-Aug. 1956), 79-89.

———. "Ortega, escritor y teórico de la literatura," *Cursos y conferencias,* LI, No. 278 (Sept. 1957), 185-202.

———. "Ortega, teórico de la literatura," *Papeles de son Armadans,* XIX (Oct. 1957), 22-46.

Believes Ortega was *literato* before filósofo, and stresses the artist and critic more than the thinker. The article deals with light, the *leit-motiv* of Ortega's writings, and mentions that the periodicals Ortega founded bore the names of *Sol, Crisol, Luz,* and *Faro.*

———. "Ortega y su palabra viva," *Atenea,* CXXIV, Nos. 367-368 (1956), 19-26.

Relates Ortega's writings to his vocation as lecturer; all essays planned to be delivered, so conceived in terms of spoken word.

TORRE, GUILLERMO DE. "Ortega y su palabra viva," *Revista Nacional de Cultura,* XVIII, No. 115 (March-April 1956), 33-38.
Essentially same as above.
TORRENTE BALLESTER, G. *Literatura española contemporánea.* Madrid, 1949. See pp. 327-341.

VALBUENA PRAT, A. *Historia de la literatura española,* vol. III. Barcelona, 1940.

WARREN, L. A. *Contemporary Spanish Literature.* London, 1929. See pp. 669-676.
Very early—sees Ortega as "promising."

C. ORTEGA'S HISTORY, SOCIOLOGY, AND POLITICAL THEORIES

This section contains articles primarily concerned with Ortega's theories of history, his sociology, his politics and political theories, and a few which refer to his ideas on education.

ARMANDO NÚÑEZ, FÉLIX. "Ortega y Gasset o la Jerarquía, *Revista Nacional de Cultura,* XVIII, No. 114 (Jan.-Feb. 1956), 11-26.
The article deals with Ortega's historical ideas in *El tema de nuestro tiempo* in a predominantly hostile fashion.
ARTOLA, MIGUEL. "En torno al concepto de historia," *Revista de estudios políticos,* LXII, No. 99 (1958), 145-183.
The article refers to Ortega's concept of the generation and to Marías's work on the same concept. (Deals primarily with Dilthey, to whom Ortega is related.)
ARSENIO TORRES, JOSÉ. "Supuestos filosóficos de la reconstrucción social en Ortega y Gasset," *La Torre,* XV-XVI (July-Dec. 1956), 401-432.

BARALDI DE MARSAL, SONIA. "Vida, generación e historia en Ortega," *Universidad,* No. 34 (April 1957), 195-209.
A conventional exposition and summary.

CIARLO, HÉCTOR OSCAR. "Los dos 'hoy' de la historia," *Sur,* No. 241 (July-Aug. 1956), 62-69.
CONANGLA FONTANILLES, JOSÉ. *Espíritu humano y social del arte,* conferencia dada en el "Círculo de bellas artes" de La Habana, el 28 de marzo de 1936.
Objects to Ortega's *La deshumanización del arte* because of what may be its social or practical effects.

DAIRLA QUINTERO, JOSÉ RAFAEL. "Sobre Ortega y Gasset," *Revista Nacional de Cultura*, XIX, Nos. 121-122 (Jan.-June 1957), 178-182.
Deals with historical and social concepts as basis for *la razón vital*.

FINCK, EUGEN. "El problema del modo de ser de la comunidad humana," *La Torre*, XV-XVI (July-Dec. 1956), 501-524.
FUERTES, RODOLFO. "El tema de nuestro tiempo, *Estudios*, No. 89 (Nov.-Dec. 1957).

GARCÍA ASTRADA, A. "Filosofía social y sociología en Ortega," *Humanitas*, VII, No. 2 (1959).
———. "Historia, ciencia histórica e historiología en Ortega y Gasset," *Humanitas*, III, No. 9 (1957).

HELMAN, EDITH. "On Humanizing Education: Ortega's Institute of Humanities," *Hispania*, XXXIV (1951).

IZQUIERDO QUINTANA, FRANCISCO. "El estado como piel," *Revista Cubana de Filosofía*, IV, No. 13 (Jan.-June 1956), 86-89.
Sees institutions, politics, social order, State as abstractions of reason, and their problems due to the absence of reason. Relates to Ortega's observations of divorce of reason and life.

LAMANA, MANUEL. "Ortega y la juventud," *Revista de la Universidad de Buenos Aires*, II, No. 2 (April-June 1957).
Vaguely related to Ortega's ideas on education, influence on present generation of scholars.
LARA MÍNGUEZ, DIONISIO DE. "Ortega y Gasset y el bibliotecario," *Boletín de la Asociación cubana de bibliotecarios*, VII, No. 4 (Dec. 1955), 140-143.
LÓPEZ-MORILLAS, JUAN. "Ortega y Gasset: Historicism versus Classicism," *Yale French Studies*, VI (Dec. 1950), 63-74.
Deals primarily with the concept of mass and minority.

MANTOVANI, JUAN. "Ortega y la idea de la Universidad," *Sur*, No. 241 (July-Aug. 1956), 136-141.
MARAVALL, JOSÉ ANTONIO. "La historia del pensamiento político, la ciencia política y la historia," *Revista de estudios políticos*, No. 84 (1955).
Refers to Ortega.
———. "La situación actual de la ciencia y la ciencia de la historia," *Revista de estudios políticos*, LXII, No. 97 (1958), 33-55.
Cites Ortega as contributing to advance of the "science of history."

MARAVALL, JOSÉ ANTONIO. "Testimonio de Ortega," *La Torre,* XV-XVI (July-Dec. 1956), 65-78.

On the historicity of *la razón vital* and the relation of Ortega's philosophy to the national history and social scene.

PERRIAUX, JAIME. "Nota sobre la sociología de Ortega," *Sur,* No. 241 (July-Aug. 1956), 166-169.

RECASÉNS SICHES, LUIS. "José Ortega y Gasset. Su metafísica, su sociología y su filosofía social," *La Torre,* XV-XVI (July-Dec. 1956), 305-335.

Actually a summary exposition of Ortega's major themes, but emphasizes *razón histórica* more than *razón vital*; relates philosophy to society and social relations, and stresses the importance of the social dimension in life, and in Ortega's thought.

———. "Sociología, filosofía social y política en el pensamiento de José Ortega y Gasset," *Cuadernos Americanos,* LXXXV, No. 1 1956), 86-119.

The subtitle, "El tema de la sociedad en la obra de Ortega y Gasset" clarifies the focus of the article. The author defines Ortega's basic sociological notions, and discusses the relation of individual and state. The article could well serve as a topical summary for *El hombre y la gente.*

ROMERO, FRANCISCO. "Al margen de *La rebelión de las masas," Sur,* I, No. 2 (1931), 192-205.

SANDOVAL C., JUAN. "Ortega y Gasset y la pedagogía," *Atenea,* CXXIV, Nos. 367-368 (1956), 82-93.

Deals mostly with faults of the educational system, emphasizing Ortega's idea of educating the "whole child" with attention to *circunstancia interior.*

D. MISCELLANEOUS PHILOSOPHICAL CRITICISM

This section contains articles and books in which the approach to Ortega is predominantly literary rather than philosophical, and some remaining articles which cannot be fitted into the other categories employed. As has been the practice heretofore, articles of particular interest are annotated, and identifying notes added to those whose titles are not self-explanatory.

ARCINIEGAS, GERMÁN. "Ortega, el tema de nuestro tiempo," *Sur,* No. 241 (July-Aug. 1956), 151-156.

ASTI VERA, ARMANDO. "Teología y mística en la obra de Ortega," *Sur*, No. 241 (July-Aug. 1956), 57-62.

BARAHONA, JAVIER DE. "Ortega y Zubiri, o la trascendencia," *Revista Cubana de Filosofía*, IV, No. 13 (Jan.-June 1956), 126-127.
  Mentions life as radical reality, but says the problem of man's relation to the totality of his existence has been no more than stated. Sees the idea of man's *necessary* freedom as key to an idea of transcendence (God) which determines the relationship between person, life, and being. Thus, a "rebirth of the idea of transcendence" is made possible by Ortega's discovery of *la realidad radical*.

BARJA, CÉSAR. *Libros y autores contemporáneos*. Madrid, 1935. See pp. 98-263.
  Interprets Ortega's work as largely political philosophy of an aristocratic, conservative and even reactionary nature.

BASAVE FERNÁNDEZ DEL VALLE, AGUSTÍN. "La ruta filosófica de José Ortega y Gasset," *Armas y letras*, VII, No. 11 (Nov. 1955), 2-5.
  Deals with the development or evolution and direction of Ortega's thought.

BERENGUER CARISOMO, ARTURO. "Ortega y la Argentina," *Cuadernos Hispanoamericanos*, CXXI (Jan. 1960), 5-16.
  Concerned largely with Ortega's influence on the intellectual life of the present generation in Argentina.

BITURRO, JORGE. "El relativismo de Ortega," *Estudios*, No. 89 (Nov.-Dec. 1957).

CASTRO TURBIANO, MÁXIMO. "Ortega y el tema de la razón," *Revista Cubana de Filosofía*, IV, No. 13 (Jan.-June 1956), 72-85.
  Proposes to define vital reason and the function it is destined to exercise, the motives which inspired it, and the problems which it attempts to resolve. However, the author indulges in a long sketch of the history of the problem of reason, gets lost in Aristotelian logic, and doesn't return to Ortega until his closing paragraphs. His only conclusion is that Ortega has not left a systematic treatise of vital reason in the manner of Aristotle's books on logic. He clearly interprets vital reason with the accent on reason, and blames the ills of the world on *irracionalismo*.

CHABÁS, JUAN. *Literatura española contemporánea*. Havana, 1952. See pp. 347-379.
  This critic, like Barja, interprets Ortega's work largely as reactionary political philosophy, but writes from a strongly Communistic standpoint.

COBIÁN Y MACHIAVELLO, ALFONSO. "Una obra inédita de Ortega: ¿Qué es filosofía?" Mercurio peruano, XXXIX, No. 375 (July 1958), 376-379.

Consists of a topical summary of the posthumous book, but so sketchily that there is some doubt that the author had actually seen a copy of Ortega's recently published work.

DE KALB, COURTENAY. "The Spiritual Law of Gravitation," Hispania, XIV (1931), 81-90.

Deals primarily with the relationship of mass and minority and the social dynamics involved.

DURÁN MANUEL. "Dos filósofos de la simpatía y el amor: Ortega y Max Scheler," La Torre, XV-XVI (July-Dec. 1956), 103-118.

FERRATER MORA, J. "Una fase en el pensamiento de Ortega, el objetivismo," Clavileño, VII, No. 40 (1956), 11-15.

Covers essentially the same ground as the first part of his book, Ortega y Gasset. Also in La Torre.

GÁNDARA, CARMEN. "Claridad sobre las cosas," Sur, No. 241 (July-Aug. 1956), 69-74.

Deals with Ortega's concept of truth as aletheia, or discovery, and his intellectual love of truth.

GARCÍA ASTRADA, ARTURO. "Ortega y Gasset desde dentro," Humanitas, II, No. 6 (1955), 245-255.

Proceeds from Ortega's concept of life as drama to characterize the "topography" of great zones or regions of the personality as the first step toward intimidad humana. In other words, self-knowledge precedes self-realization in the life-drama.

GARCÍA BACCA, JUAN DAVID. "El estilo filosófico de Ortega y Gasset," Revista Nacional de Cultura, XVIII, No. 114 (Jan.-Feb. 1956), 27-36.

Concerned with Ortega's manner of approaching his philosophical themes, putting each thought in place. Describes it as conscience acting upon original chaos.

GRANELL, MANUEL. "Ortega y el transfondo filosófico de la microfísica," La Torre, XV-XVI (July-Dec. 1956), 141-165.

The orientation of the article is epistemological, and aside from a mention of the ideas of certain physicists in this area, deals little with microphysics; the relation to Ortega is nebulous.

HUERTA, ELEAZAR. "Dinamismo del ser en Ortega," Humanitas, III, No. 8 (1956-57), 155-164.

IRIARTE, JOAQUÍN. "La novísima visión de la filosofía de Ortega y Gasset," Razón y Fe, CXXVII, No. 107 (1943).

JOBIT, PIERRE. "De la esencial nobleza del hombre," *Clavileño,* IV, No. 24 (Nov.-Dec. 1953), 50-54.
Concerned with the idea of natural goodness in man as this critic sees it in Ortega. Several comparisons to Peguy are made, and a tribute to Marías for his work on *la razón vital.*

LAÍN ENTRALGO, PEDRO. "Ortega y el futuro," *La Torre,* XV-XVI (July-Dec. 1956), 249-270.
Studies Ortega's various expressions of the future.

LIZASO, FÉLIX. "José Ortega y Gasset," *Revista Cubana de Filosofía,* IV, No. 13 (Jan.-June 1956), 45-51.
On values of meditation, observation, and perspective. Many mythological allusions.

LLOPES, VICENTE. "Realidad y metáfora, meditación metafísica acerca de las relaciones entre la realidad y la metáfora," *Cuadernos Hispanoamericanos,* CXXIII (March 1960), 298-304.
Studies metaphor in Ortega, Zubiri, Scheler, and Jaspers.

MADARIAGA, SALVADOR DE. "Nota sobre Ortega," *Sur,* No. 241 (July-Aug. 1956), 13-15.
Considers Ortega not a philosopher, but something more: a journalist, *captador de la realidad viva.*

MÁRQUEZ DE LA CERRA, MIGUEL F. "Nuestro tiempo en el pensamiento de Ortega y Gasset," *Revista Cubana de Filosofía,* IV, No. 13 (Jan.-June 1956), 34-44.
Reviews early articles of Ortega; notes that he is not well understood, but does not explain. Recounts many conflicting comments by disciples of Ortega and by Catholic critics.

MARRERO, DOMINGO. "Crítica de la ciencia y concepto de la filosofía en Ortega," *La Torre,* XV-XVI (July-Dec. 1956), 285-303.

MASÓ FERNÁNDEZ, FAUSTO. "Ortega y los malentendidos," *Revista Cubana de Filosofía,* IV, No. 13 (Jan.-June 1956), 128-130.
Concerned with misinterpretations of Ortega, which he sees as the price the philosopher paid for not turning away from his circumstances. This critic views the postwar period as one which doesn't believe in reason or culture, so it isn't the *momento de Ortega.* Explains misunderstandings of Ortega's works on the grounds that he belongs to a vital and dynamic, unfinished period.

MEREGALLI, FRANCO. "Ortega en busca de sí mismo," *Clavileño,* IV, No. 24 (Nov.-Dec. 1953), 60-66.
―――. "Ortega y Gasset," *Studi filosofici* (Jan.-March 1953), p. 55.

ORTEGA RODRIGO, ELISEO. "En las coordenadas de la filosofía orteguiana," *La Torre,* XV-XVI (July-Dec. 1956), 525-551.

Ideas for an outline of the ontological problem, and an attempt to interrelate Ortega's various theories.

PAITA, JORGE A. "Dos aspectos en la filosofía de Ortega," *Sur,* No. 241 (July-Aug. 1956), 49-57.

An attempt to solve the controversy over Ortega's system or lack thereof through compromise: views his work as a-systematic, on the one hand, and systematic on the other, with order underlying disorder.

QUILES, ISMAEL. "Actitud filosófico de Ortega y Gasset," *Estudios,* No. 89 (Nov.-Dec. 1957), 1-34.

Written from the point of view of the orthodox Catholic critic.

ROJO, ROBERTO. "La posibilidad de una lógica vital en Ortega," *Humanitas,* III, No. 8 (1954), 151-154.

Razón vital is a-logical because logic presupposes generalizing, which cannot be done on the basis of one life.

ROMANELL, PATRICK. "Ortega in Mexico: A Tribute to Ramos," *Journal of the History of Ideas,* XXI, No. 4 (Oct.-Dec. 1960), 600-608.

ROMERO, FRANCISCO. "Ortega y la circunstancia española," *La Torre,* XV-XVI (July-Dec. 1956), 361-369.

Relates Ortega's activities to his national circumstances in much the manner of Marías and Salmerón.

ROSENBLATT, ÁNGEL. "Ortega y Gasset: ¿Filósofo o poeta?," *Revista Nacional de Cultura,* XIX, No. 123 (July-Aug. 1957), 28-32.

Basically a word analysis study. "Typical words" are viewed as manifestations of Ortega's philosophy. His terminology is classified as pictorial and perspectivist, on the one hand, and geometric or rational, on the other.

SÁNCHEZ LATORRE, MARIO. "El problema del humanismo en Ortega y Gasset," *Atenea,* CXXIV, Nos. 367-368 (1956), 44-47.

SERRANO PONCELA, SEGUNDO. "Ortega en el Finisterrae," *Sur,* No. 241 (July-Aug. 1956), 32-39.

TORRE, GUILLERMO DE. "Sobre una deserción de Ortega y Gasset," *Cuadernos Americanos,* I, No. 4 (1942).

URIARTE, FERNANDO. "La lectura problemática de Ortega," *Atenea,* CXXIV, Nos. 367-368 (1956), 27-33.

Begins with problems of interpretation of Ortega, but deals mostly with the "system"—believes total philosophy anticipated, can be foreseen, in *Meditaciones del Quijote.*

VAN HORNE, J. "Ortega en los Estados Unidos," *Clavileño,* IV, No. 24 (Nov.-Dec. 1953), 55-59.

Concerned principally with Ortega's influence in the United States, and the extent to which he is known.

VELA, FERNANDO. "La 'fantasía' en la filosofía de Ortega," *La Torre,* XV-XVI (July-Dec. 1956), 433-453.

Concerned with Ortega's concept of the role of the imagination.

ZAMBRANO, MARÍA. "Apuntes sobre la acción de la filosofía," *La Torre,* XV-XVI (July-Dec. 1956), 553-576.

———. "Unidad y sistema en la filosofía de Ortega," *Sur,* No. 241 (July-Aug. 1956), 40-49.

Takes the affirmative in answering the question as to whether Ortega's philosophy is systematic.

ZARAGÜETA, JUAN. "El vitalismo de Ortega," *La Torre,* XV-XVI (July-Dec. 1956), 455-466.

ZEA, LEOPOLDO. "Medio siglo de filosofía en México," *Filosofía y Letras,* XXI, No. 41, 111-131.

Deals with the influence of Ortega and Gaos in Mexico.

———. "Ortega el Americano," *Cuadernos Americanos,* LXXXV, No. 1 (1956), 132-145.

Historical background, much reference to Latin American philosophy. Considers Ortega more "modern" than Spanish, and because of the importance of his work in the history of Latin American culture, he calls Ortega *americano.*

BIBLIOGRAPHY OF WORKS CONSULTED

ALONSO, MARÍA ROSA. "En la muerte de Don José Ortega y Gasset," *Revista Nacional de Cultura*, XVIII, No. 114 (Jan.-Feb. 1956), 44-47.

ALONSO-FUELLO, SABINO. *Existencialismo y existencialistas*. Valencia, 1949.

ÁLVAREZ, VALENTÍN ANDRÉS. "Introducción al coloquio *Nuestra imagen de Ortega*," *Cultura Universitaria*, No. 41 (1954).

———. "Teoría e historia o Apolo y Dionisio," *La Torre*, XV-XVI (July-Dec. 1956), 469-476.

AMADOR SÁNCHEZ, LUIS. "Ortega y Gasset y el nuevo misterio de Velázquez," *Atenea*, XCIX, No. 304 (Oct. 1950), 71-83.

ARANGUREN, JOSÉ LUIS. "Ferrater Mora y el pensamiento de la crisis," *Ínsula*, X, No. 109 (Jan. 15, 1955).

ARAQUISTÁIN, LUIS. "En defensa de un muerto profanado," *Sur*, No. 241 (July-Aug. 1956), 120-130.

ARCINIEGAS, GERMÁN. "Ortega, el tema de nuestro tiempo," *Sur*, No. 241 (July-Aug. 1956), 151-156.

ARMANDO NÚÑEZ, FÉLIX. "Ortega y Gasset o la jerarquía," *Revista Nacional de Cultura*, XVIII, No. 114 (Jan.-Feb. 1956), 11-26.

ARSENIO TORRES, JOSÉ. "Supuestos filosóficos de la reconstrucción social en Ortega y Gasset," *La Torre*, XV-XVI (July-Dec. 1956), 401-432.

ARTOLA, MIGUEL. "En torno al concepto de historia," *Revista de estudios políticos*, LXII, No. 99 (1958), 145-183.

ASTI VERA, ARMANDO. "Teología y mística en la obra de Ortega," *Sur*, No. 241 (July-Aug. 1956). 57-62.

BALBÉ, RAÚL R. "Repetición de Ortega," *Sur*, No. 241 (July-Aug. 1956), 156-165.

BALSEIRO, JOSÉ A. "Ortega y Gasset, el artista," *Clavileño*, IV, No. 24 (Nov.-Dec. 1953), 75-76.

BAQUERO GOYANES, MARIANO. "La novela como tragicomedia: Pérez de Ayala y Ortega," *Ínsula*, X, No. 110 (Feb. 15, 1955).

BARAHONA, JAVIER DE. "Ortega y Zubiri, o la trascendencia," *Revista Cubana de Filosofía*, IV, No. 13 (Jan-June 1956), 126-127.

BARALDI DE MARSAL, SONIA. "Vida, generación e historia en Ortega," *Universidad*, No. 34 (April 1957), 195-209.

BAREO, ARTURO. "The Conservative Critics: Ortega and Madariaga," *University Observer*, I (Winter 1947), 29-36.

BARGA, CORPUS. "Un aspecto de Ortega. El refractario," *Sur*, No. 241 (July-Aug. 1956), 170-179.

BARJA, CÉSAR. *Libros y autores contemporáneos.* Madrid, 1935. See pp. 98-263.

BASAVE FERNÁNDEZ DEL VALLE, AGUSTÍN. "La ruta filosófica de José Ortega y Gasset," *Armas y letras,* VII, No. 11 (Nov. 1955), 2-5.

——. *Miguel de Unamuno y Ortega y Gasset.* Madrid, 1950.

BATAILLON, M. "José Ortega y Gasset," *Revue de Littérature Comparée,* XXIX, No. 4 (Oct.-Dec. 1955), 449-452.

BELAUNDE, VÍCTOR ANDRÉS. "Ortega y Gasset," *Mercurio peruano,* XXXVI, No. 345 (Dec. 1955), 839-845.

BENÍTEZ, JAIME. "Recuerdo de Ortega," *Sur,* No. 241 (July-Aug. 1956), 192-199.

BERENGUER CARISOMO, ARTURO. "Ortega y la Argentina," *Cuadernos Hispano-americanos,* CXXI (Jan. 1960) 5-16.

BERGES, CONSUELO. "Ortega, Stendhal y el Amor," *Ínsula,* VIII, No. 90 (June 15, 1953).

BITURRO, JORGE. "El relativismo de Ortega," *Estudios,* No. 89 (Nov.-Dec. 1957).

BLACKHAM, H. J. *Six Existentialist Thinkers.* New York, 1959.

BO, CARLO. "Ortega y *El Espectador,*" *Clavileño,* IV, No. 24 (Nov.-Dec. 1953), 77-80.

BOREL, JEAN-PAUL. *Raison et vie chez Ortega y Gasset,* Neuchâtel, 1959.

BOTÍN POLANCO, ANTONIO. "El estilo de Ortega," *Clavileño,* IV, No. 24 (Nov.-Dec. 1953), 81.

BRENAN, GERALD. *The Literature of the Spanish People.* New York, 1957. See pp. 419-421.

BRIGGS, MICHAEL H. *Handbook of Philosophy.* New York, 1959.

BRÜNING, WALTHER. "Existencialismo, irracionalismo, transcendentalismo," *Humanitas,* II, No. 5 (1955), 215-226.

BUBER, MARTIN. *Between Man and Man,* trans. Ronald G. Smith. Boston, 1957.

BURCKHARDT, CARL J. "Encuentro con Ortega," *Sur,* No. 241 (July-Aug. 1956), 179-187.

CAILLOIS, ROGER. "Juegos y sociedades," *La Torre,* XV-XVI (July-Dec. 1956), 477-499.

CANITO, ENRIQUE. "Ortega en las 'Recontres,'" *Ínsula,* VII, No. 73 (Aug. 15, 1952).

CANTO, PATRICIO. *El caso Ortega y Gasset.* Buenos Aires, 1958.

CASIRRER, ERNST. "Kant y el problema de la metafísica," *Humanitas,* III, No. 8 (1956-57), 167-193.

CASSOU, JEAN. "José Ortega y Gasset," *Sur,* No. 241 (July-Aug. 1956), 131-135.

CASTELLET, JOSÉ MARÍA. "Poder irse tranquilo," *Ínsula,* X, No. 119 (Nov. 15, 1955).

CASTRO TURBIANO, MÁXIMO. "Ortega y Gasset y el tema de la razón," *Revista Cubana de Filosofía,* IV, No. 13 (Jan.-June 1956), 72-85.

CEPLECHA, CHRISTIAN. *The Historical Thought of José Ortega y Gasset.* Washington, D. C., 1958.

CHABÁS, JUAN. *Literatura española contemporánea.* Havana, 1952. See pp. 347-379.

CHACEL, ROSA. "Respuesta a Ortega. La novela no escrita," *Sur,* No. 241 July-Aug. 1956), 97-119

CIARLO, HÉCTOR OSCAR. "Los dos 'hoy' de la historia,' *Sur*, No. 241 (July-Aug. 1956), 62-69.

CLEMENTE, JOSÉ EDMUNDO. *Ortega y Gasset. Estética de la razón vital.* Buenos Aires, 1956.

COLLINS, JAMES. *The Existentialists.* Chicago, 1951.

COBIÁN Y MACHIAVELLO, ALFONSO. "Una obra inédita de Ortega: ¿Qué es filosofía?," *Mercurio peruano*, XXXIX, No. 375 (July 1958), 376-379.

CONANGLA FONTANILLES, JOSÉ. *Espíritu humano y social del arte.* Conferencia dada en el "Círculo de Bellas Artes" de La Habana, el 28 de marzo de 1936.

CONELIA, EDMUNDO. "El estilo en José Ortega y Gasset," *Atenea*, CXXIV, Nos. 367-368 (1956), 73-81.

CÓRDOVA DE BRASCHI, JULIA. "Dos paisajes españoles: Castilla y Asturias," *La Torre*, XV-XVI (July-Dec. 1956), 95-101.

————. "La psicología española vista por Ortega y Gasset," *Asomante*, No. 4 (1954).

CRUZ OCAMPO, LUIS DAVID. "La intelectualización del arte," *Revista Atenea* 1927), 12-85.

CURTIUS, ERNST R. "Ortega," *Partisan Review*, XVII (Jan.-April 1950), 262-271.

DAIRLA QUINTERO, JOSÉ RAFAEL. "Sobre Ortega y Gasset," *Revista Nacional de Cultura*, XIX, Nos. 121-122 (Jan.-June 1957), 178-182.

DE KALB, COURTENAY. "The Spiritual Law of Gravitation," *Hispania*, XIV (1931), 81-90.

DEL CAMPO, ALBERTO. "Crítica y rehacimiento de la razón en la filosofía de Ortega y Gasset," *Escritura*, III, No. 7 (June 1949).

DEL RÍO, ÁNGEL, and M. J. BERNADETE. *El concepto contemporáneo de España.* Buenos Aires, 1956. See pp. 491-532.

DÍEZ DEL CORRAL, LUIS. "Saber y personalidad de Ortega," *La Torre*, XV-XVI (July-Dec. 1956), 45-58.

DURÁN, MANUEL. "Dos filósofos de la simpatía y el amor: Ortega y Max Scheler," *La Torre*, XV-XVI (July-Dec. 1956), 103-118.

Enciclopedia filosofica. Roma, 1957.

FASEL, OSCAR A. "Observations on Unamuno and Kierkegaard," *Hispania*, XXXVIII, No. 4 (Dec. 1955), 443-450.

FERNÁNDEZ SUÁREZ, ÁLVARO. "El viajero antiguo," *Sur*, No. 241 (July-Aug. 1956), 74-79.

FERRATER MORA, JOSÉ. "De la filosofía a la 'filosofía,' " *Sur*, No. 241 (July-Aug. 1956), 21-24.

————. *Diccionario de filosofía.* Buenos Aires, 1938.

————. "Dos obras maestras españolas," *Cuadernos del Congreso por la libertad de la cultura*, No. 42 (May-June 1960), 47-54.

————. "Idea del teatro," *Cuadernos del Congreso por la libertad de la cultura*, No. 38 (Sept.-Oct. 1959), 108-109.

————. *Filósofos de hoy en España.* Madrid, 1951.

————. *La Filosofía en el mundo de hoy.* Madrid, 1959.

————. *Ortega y Gasset: An Outline of his Philosophy.* New Haven, 1957.

————. "Ortega y la idea de la sociedad," *Humanitas*, III, Nos. 7-9 (1956-57), 13-20.

FERRATER MORA, JOSÉ. "Ortega y la idea de la sociedad," *Ínsula*, X, No. 119 (Nov. 15, 1955).

——. "Una fase en el pensamiento de Ortega, el objetivismo," *Clavileño*, VII, No. 40 (1956), 11-15.

——. "Una fase en el pensamiento de Ortega: El objetivismo," *La Torre*, XV-XVI (July-Dec. 1956), 119-126.

FINCK, EUGEN. "El problema del modo de ser de la comunidad humana," *La Torre*, XV-XVI (July-Dec. 1956), 501-524.

FRANCO DE MARÍAS, DOLORES. "El brillo de su ausencia," *La Torre*, XV-XVI (July-Dec. 1956), 59-64.

FRUTOS, EUGENIO. "El existencialismo jubiloso de Jorge Guillén," *Cuadernos Hispanoamericanos*, V-VI, No. 18 (Nov.-Dec. 1950).

FUERTES, RODOLFO. "El tema de nuestro tiempo," *Estudios*, No. 89 (Nov.-Dec. 1957).

GÁNDARA, CARMEN. "Claridad sobre las cosas," *Sur*, No. 241 (July-Aug. 1956), 69-74.

GAOS, JOSÉ. "Alfonso Reyes, el escritor," *Cuadernos Americanos*, CXII, No. 5 (Sept.-Oct. 1960).

——. "De paso por *El historicismo y existencialismo*," *Cuadernos Americanos*, No. 2 (March-April 1951).

——. "De paso por *El historicismo y existencialismo*," *Filosofía y letras*, XXI, Nos. 41-42 (Jan.-June 1951).

——. *La filosofía en España*. México, 1953.

——. "Los dos Ortegas," *La Torre*, XV-XVI (July-Dec. 1956), 127-140.

——. "Salvación de Ortega," *Cuadernos Americanos*, LXXXV, No. 1 (1956), 68-85.

——. *Sobre Ortega y Gasset*. México, 1957.

GARAGORRI, PAULINO. "Albert Camus y su generación," *Cuadernos del Congreso por la libertad de la Cultura*, No. 43 (July-Aug. 1960), 81-85.

——. "Complementos a un artículo sobre Ortega," *Suplemento de Ínsula*, No. 121 (Dec. 15, 1955).

——. "La realidad de la muerte," *Ínsula*, X, No. 119 (Nov. 15, 1955).

GARCÍA ASTRADA, ARTURO. "Aspectos metafísicos en el pensamiento de Unamuno...," *Humanitas*, III, No. 7 (1956-57), 37-47.

——. "Filosofía social y sociología en Ortega," *Humanitas*, VII, No. 2 (1959).

——. "Historia, ciencia histórica e historiología en Ortega y Gasset," *Humanitas*, III, No. 9 (1957) 107-115.

——. "Ortega y Gasset desde dentro," *Humanitas*, II, No. 6 (1955), 245-255.

GARCÍA BACCA, JUAN DAVID. "El estilo filosófico de Ortega y Gasset," *Revista Nacional de Cultura*, XVIII, No. 114 (Jan.-Feb. 1956), 27-36.

GARCÍA MORENTE, MANUEL. *Lecciones preliminares de filosofía*. Buenos Aires, 1943.

GARCÍA TUDURI, MERCEDES. "Valor de la circunstancia en la filosofía de Ortega y Gasset," *Revista Cubana de Filosofía*, IV, No. 13 (Jan.-June 1956), 7-14.

GARCÍA TUDURI, ROSAURA. "Ideas estéticas de Ortega y Gasset," *Revista Cubana de Filosofía*, IV, No. 13 (Jan.-June 1956) 28-32.

GRANELL, MANUEL. "Ortega y el transfondo filosófico de la microfísica," *La Torre*, XV-XVI (July-Dec. 1956), 141-165.

GRENE, MARJORIE. *Introduction to Existentialism*. Chicago, 1959.

Gullón, Ricardo. "Ortega, crítico literario," *Sur*, No. 241 (July-Aug. 1956), 89-97.

Heinemann, F. H. *Existentialism and the Modern Predicament.* New York, 1958.

Helman, Edith. "On Humanizing Education: Ortega's Institute of Humanities," *Hispania*, XXXIV (Nov. 1951), 267-270.

Huerta, Eleazar. "Dinamismo del ser en Ortega," *Humanitas*, III, No. 8 (1956-57), 155-164.

———. "La prosa de Ortega," *Atenea*, CXXIV, Nos. 367-368 (1956), 48-72.

———. "Lenguaje y literatura en la filosofía de Ortega," *Revista Nacional de Cultura*, XVIII, No. 114 (Jan.-Feb. 1956), 37-43.

Ildefonso, Manuel Gil. "Sobre el arte de escribir novelas," *Cuadernos Hispanoamericanos*, CXXI (Jan. 1960), 39-47.

Ingenieros, José. *La cultura filosófica en España.* Buenos Aires, 1939.

Iriarte, Joaquín. "La novísima visión de la filosofía de Ortega y Gasset," *Razón y Fe*, CXXVII (1943), 107.

———. *La ruta mental de Ortega.* Madrid, 1949.

———. *Ortega y Gasset, su persona y su doctrina.* Madrid, 1942.

Izquierdo Quintana, Francisco. "El estado como piel," *Revista Cubana de Filosofía*, IV, No. 13 (Jan.-June 1956), 86-89.

Jaspers, Karl. *Reason and Existenz*, trans. William Earle. New York, 1955.

Jiménez, Juan Ramón. "Recuerdo a Ortega y Gasset," *Clavileño*, IV, No. 24 (Nov.-Dec. 1953), 44-49.

Jiménez Grullón, Juan Isidro. *Al margen de Ortega y Gasset.* Havana, 1957.

Jobit, Pierre. "De la esencial nobleza del hombre," *Clavileño*, IV, No. 24 (Nov.-Dec. 1953), 50-54.

Kaufmann, Walter. *Existentialism from Dostoevsky to Sartre.* New York, 1957.

King-Farlow, John. "Existentialism and the Humanist's Choice," *The Humanist*, No. 3 (May-June 1960).

Kogan Albert, J. "El concepto de experiencia en Hegel y en Heidegger," *Cuadernos Americanos*, LXXXVIII, No. 4 (July-Aug. 1956), 98-118.

Lafuente Ferrari, Enrique. "En memoria de Ortega; Recuerdos y deberes," *Insula*, X, No. 119 (Nov. 15, 1955).

———. "Las artes visuales y su historia en el pensamiento de Ortega," *La Torre*, XV-XVI (July-Dec. 1956), 167-247.

Lagos Matus, Gustavo. *El pensamiento social de Ortega y Gasset.* Santiago, Chile, 1956.

Laín Entralgo, Pedro. "Ortega y el futuro," *La Torre*, XV-XVI (July-Dec. 1956), 249-270.

———. *Vestigios.* Madrid, 1948. See pp. 333-348.

Lamana, Manuel. "Ortega y la juventud," *Revista de la Universidad de Buenos Aires*, II, No. 2 (April-June 1957).

Lara Mínguez, Dionisio de. "Ortega: Recuento y epílogo," *Revista Cubana de Filosofía*, IV, No. 13 (Jan.-June 1956) 52-61.

———. "Ortega y Gasset y el bibliotecario," *Boletín de la Asociación cubana de bibliotecarios*, VII, No. 4 (Dec. 1955), 140-143.

Lázaro Ros, Armando. "Unamuno, filósofo existencialista," in Mildred Grene, *El sentimiento trágico de la existencia*, Madrid, 1952.

Lizaso, Félix. "José Ortega y Gasset," *Revista Cubana de Filosofía*, IV, No. 13 (Jan.-June 1956), 45-51.

LLOPES, VICENTE. "Realidad y metáfora, meditación metafísica acerca de las relaciones entre la realidad y la metáfora," *Cuadernos Hispanoamericanos,* CXXIII (March 1960), 298-304.

LÓPEZ-MORILLAS, JUAN. "Ortega y Gasset. Historicism vs. Classicism," *Yale French Studies,* VI (Dec. 1950), 63-74.

———. "Ortega y Gasset y la crítica literaria," *Cuadernos Americanos,* XCIII, No. 3 (1957), 72-86.

MADARIAGA, SALVADOR DE. "Nota sobre Ortega," *Sur,* No. 241 (July-Aug. 1956), 13-15.

MAEZTU, MARÍA DE. *Antología — Siglo XX, Prosistas Españoles.* Buenos Aires, 1943. See pp. 86-92.

MAÑACH, JORGE. "Imagen de Ortega y Gasset," *Revista Cubana de Filosofía,* IV, No. 13 (Jan-June 1956).

MANENT ALBERT. "Mi Don José Ortega y Gasset," *Suplemento de Ínsula,* No. 121 (Dec. 15, 1955).

MANTOVANI, JUAN. "Ortega y la idea de la Universidad," *Sur,* No. 241 (July-Aug. 1956), 136-141.

MARAVALL, JOSÉ ANTONIO. "La historia del pensamiento político, la ciencia política y la historia," *Revista de estudios políticos,* No. 84 (1955), 49.

———. "La situación actual de la ciencia y la ciencia de la historia," *Revista de estudios políticos,* LXII, No. 97 (1958), 33-55.

———. "Testimonio de Ortega," *La Torre,* XV-XVI (July-Dec. 1956), 65-78.

MARÍAS Y AGUILERA, JULIÁN. "El futuro de Ortega," *Sur,* No. 241 (July-Aug. 1956), 15-20.

———. "*El hombre y la gente*: el lugar de la teoría de la vida social en la filosofía de Ortega," *Revista de Ciencias Sociales,* I (March 1957).

———. *El método histórico de las generaciones.* Madrid, 1949.

———. "El primer libro de Ortega," *La Torre,* XV-XVI (July-Dec. 1956), 271-283.

———. *Ensayos de teoría.* Barcelona, 1954.

———. *Filosofía actual y existencialismo en España.* Madrid, 1955.

———. *La escuela de Madrid.* Buenos Aires, 1959.

———. *Meditaciones del Quijote: Comentario.* Madrid, 1957.

———. *Obras.* 4 vols. Madrid, 1959.

———. *Ortega: I, Circunstancia y vocación.* Madrid, 1960.

———. "Ortega: Historia de una amistad," *Ínsula,* X, No. 119 (Nov. 15, 1955).

———. *Ortega y la idea de la razón vital.* Madrid, 1948.

———. *Ortega y tres antípodas.* Madrid, 1951.

———. "Realidad y ser en la filosofía 'española,' " *Ínsula,* X, No. 117 (Sept. 15, 1955).

MÁRQUEZ DE LA CERRA, MIGUEL F. "Nuestro tiempo en el pensamiento de Ortega y Gasset," *Revista Cubana de Filosofía,* IV, No. 13 (Jan.-June 1956), 34-44.

MARQUINA, RAFAEL. "Ortega y Gasset y la crítica de arte," *Revista Cubana de Filosofía,* IV, No. 13 (Jan.-June 1956), 62-71.

MARRERO, DOMINGO. *El centauro: persona y pensamiento de Ortega y Gasset.* Santurce, P. R., 1951.

———. "Crítica de la ciencia y concepto de la filosofía en Ortega," *La Torre,* XV-XVI (July-Dec. 1956), 285-303.

MASÓ F., FAUSTO. "Ortega y los malentendidos," *Revista Cubana de Filosofía,* IV, No. 13 (Jan.-June 1956) 128-130.

McDonald, E. Cordell. "The Modern Novel as Viewed by Ortega," *Hispania*, XLII, No. 4 (1959), 475-481.

Mengod, Vicente. "El tema de las ideas en Ortega," *Atenea*, CXXIV, Nos. 367-368 (1956), 34-43.

Meregalli, Franco. "Ortega en busca de sí mismo," *Clavileño*, IV, No. 24 (Nov.-Dec. 1953), 60-66.

———. "Ortega y Gasset," *Studi filosofici* (Jan.-March 1953), 53.

Mesnard, P. "Kierkegaard aux prises avec la conscience française...," *Revue de Littérature Comparée*, XXIX, No. 4 (Oct.-Dec. 1955), 453-477.

Meyer, F. "Kierkegaard et Unamuno," *Revue de Littérature Comparée*, XXIX, No. 4 (Oct.-Dec. 1955), 478-492.

Mindar, M. "Ortega y Gasset, o Homen e o Filósofo," *Revista Portuguesa de Filosofía*, XII, No. 2 (1956).

Moreno, Julio E. *Filosofía de la existencia*. Quito, 1940.

Nagley, Winfield E. "Kierkegaard on Liberation," *Ethics*, LXX, No. 1 (Oct. 1959), 47-58.

Nicol, Eduardo. *Historicismo y existencialismo*. Mexico, 1950.

Niedermayer, Franz. "Ortega y Gasset y su relación con Alemania," *Clavileño*, IV, No. 24 (Nov.-Dec. 1953), 67-74.

Ocampo, Victoria. "Entre Dakar y Barcelona (Recordando a Ortega)," *La Torre*, XV-XVI (July-Dec. 1956), 79-83.

———. "Mi deuda con Ortega," *Sur*, No. 241 (July-Aug. 1956), 206-220.

Ortega Rodrigo, Eliseo. "En las coordenadas de la filosofía orteguiana," *La Torre*, XV-XVI (July-Dec. 1956), 525-551.

Ortega y Gasset, José. *El hombre y la gente*. Madrid, 1957.

———. *Idea del teatro*. Madrid, 1958.

———. *La idea de principio en Leibniz y la evolución de la teoría deductiva*. Buenos Aires, 1957.

———. *Meditación del pueblo joven*. Buenos Aires, 1958.

———. *Obras Completas*. 6 vols. Madrid, 1946.

———. *¿Qué es Filosofía?* Madrid, 1957.

Paita, Jorge A. "Dos aspectos en la filosofía de Ortega," *Sur*, No. 241 (July-Aug. 1956), 49-57.

Perriaux, Jaime. "Nota sobre la sociología de Ortega," *Sur*, No. 241 (July-Aug. 1956), 166-169.

Piñera Llera, Humberto. "Ortega y Gasset: el filósofo," *Boletín*, VIII, No. 2 (Feb. 1955), 1-7.

———. "Ortega y la idea de la vida," *Revista Cubana de Filosofía*, IV, No. 13 (Jan.-Jun. 1956), 15-25.

Pozzi, Héctor. "Ortega como nosotros," *Sur*, No. 241 (July-Aug. 1956), 141-151.

Presa, Fernando de la. "Perfil humano de D. José Ortega y Gasset," *Revista Cubana de Filosofía*, IV, No. 13 (Jan.-June 1956), 90-103.

Quiles, Ismael. "Actitud filosófica de Ortega y Gasset," *Estudios*, No. 89 (Nov.-Dec. 1957), 1-34.

Recaséns Siches, Luis. "José Ortega y Gasset: Su metafísica, su sociología y su filosofía social," *La Torre*, XV-XVI (July-Dec. 1956), 305-355.

———. "Sociología, filosofía social, y política en el pensamiento de José Ortega y Gasset," *Cuadernos Americanos*, LXXXV, No. 1 (1956), 86-119.

Reinhardt, Kurt F. *The Existentialist Revolt*. Milwaukee, 1951.

REYES, ALFONSO. "Treno para José Ortega y Gasset," *Cuadernos Americanos,* LXXXV, No. 1 (1956), 65-67.

ROA, RAÚL. "Dichos y hechos de Ortega y Gasset," *Cuadernos Americanos,* LXXXV, No. 1 (1956), 120-131.

RODRÍGUEZ ALCALÁ, HUGO. "Existencia y destino del hombre según Ortega y Gasset y Jean-Paul Sartre," *Cuadernos Americanos,* CX, No. 3 (May-June 1960).

RODRÍGUEZ HUÉSCAR, ANTONIO. "Relato personal," *La Torre,* XV-XVI (July-Dec. 1956), 85-92.

ROF CARBALLO, J. "Un recuerdo de Ortega," *Insula,* X, No. 119 (Nov. 15, 1955).

ROGGIANO, ALFREDO. "Estética y crítica literaria en Ortega y Gasset," *La Torre,* XV-XVI (July-Dec. 1956), 337-359.

ROJO, ROBERTO. "La posibilidad de una lógica vital en Ortega," *Humanitas,* III, No. 8 (1954), 151-154.

ROMANELL, PATRICK. "Ortega in Mexico: A Tribute to Ramos," *Journal of the History of Ideas,* XXI, No. 4 (Oct.-Dec. 1960), 600-608.

ROMERA, ANTONIO R. "Ortega y Velázquez," *Atenea,* CXXIV, Nos. 367-368 (1956), 94-106.

ROMERO, FRANCISCO. "Al margen de la *Rebelión de las masas,*" *Sur,* I, No. 2 (1931), 192-205.

———. "Ortega y el ausentismo filosófico español," *Sur,* No. 241 (July-Aug. 1956), 24-29.

———. "Ortega y la circunstancia española," *La Torre,* XV-XVI (July-Dec. 1956), 361-369.

ROSENBLATT, ÁNGEL. "Ortega y Gasset: ¿Filósofo o poeta?," *Revista Nacional de Cultura,* XIX, No. 123 (July-Aug. 1957), 28-32.

RUNES, DAGOBERT D., ed. *Dictionary of Philosophy.* New York, n.d.

SAÍZ BARBERÁ, JUAN. *Ortega y Gasset ante la crítica.* Madrid, 1950.

SALAVERRÍA, JOSÉ MARÍA. *Retratos.* Madrid, 1926. See pp. 173-221.

SALMERÓN, FERNANDO. "Las mocedades de Ortega y Gasset," *La Torre,* XV-XVI (July-Dec. 1956), 369-383.

———. *Las Mocedades de Ortega y Gasset.* Mexico, 1959.

SÁNCHEZ AGESTA, LUIS. "Crisis de la política como ciencia moral," *Revista de estudios científicos,* LVII, No. 89 (1956), 3-18.

SÁNCHEZ BARBUDO, A. *Estudios sobre Unamuno y Machado.* Madrid, 1959.

SÁNCHEZ LATORRE, MARIO. "El problema del humanismo en Ortega y Gasset," *Atenea,* CXXIV, Nos. 367-368 (1956), 44-47.

SÁNCHEZ VILLASEÑOR, J. *Ortega y Gasset. Existentialist.* Chicago, 1949.

SANDOVAL C., JUAN. "Ortega y Gasset y la pedagogía," *Atenea,* CXXIV, Nos. 367-368 (1956), 82-93.

SANSEVERRA DE ELEZALDE, ELENA. "Mi amistad con Ortega," *Sur,* No. 241 (July-Aug. 1956), 187-192.

SARMIENTO, EDUARDO. "Orteguianismo y Cristianismo," *Atlante,* III, No. 4 (1955), 167-170.

SCHWARTZ, KESSEL. "Ortega y Gasset and Goethe," *Hispania,* XLIII, No. 3 (Sept. 1960), 320-327.

SEPICH, JUAN R. "Situación de M. Heidegger en la filosofía," *Humanitas,* II, No. 4 (1955), 15-113.

SERIS, HOMER. *Manual de bibliografía de la literatura española.* Syracuse, 1948.

Serrano Poncela, Segundo. "Ortega en el Finisterre," *Sur*, No. 241 (July-Aug. 1956), 32-39.

Stern, Alfredo. "¿Ortega, existencialista o esencialista?," *La Torre*, XV-XVI (July-Dec. 1956), 385-399.

Thrall, William F., et. al., eds. *A Handbook to Literature*. New York, 1960.

Torre, Guillermo de. "Las ideas estéticas de Ortega," *Sur*, No. 241 (July-Aug. 1956), 79-89.

————. "Ortega escritor y teórico de la literatura," *Cursos y conferencias*, LI, No. 278 (Sept. 1957), 185-202.

————. "Ortega, teórico de la literatura," *Papeles de son Armadans*, XIX (Oct. 1957), 22-46.

————. "Ortega y su palabra viva," *Atenea*, CXXIV, Nos. 367-368 (1956), 19-26.

————. "Ortega y su palabra viva," *Revista Nacional de Cultura*, XVIII, No. 115 (March-April 1956), 33-38.

————. "Sobre una deserción de Ortega y Gasset," *Cuadernos Americanos*, I, No. 4 (1942).

Torrente Ballester, G. *Literatura española contemporánea*. Madrid, 1949. See pp. 327-341.

Trend, J. B. "Boceto de memoria," *Sur*, No. 241 (July-Aug. 1956), 199-206.

Uriarte, Fernando. "La lectura problemática de Ortega," *Atenea*, CXXIV, Nos. 367-368 (1956), 27-33.

Valbuena Prat, Ángel. *Historia de la literatura española*. 3 vols. Barcelona, 1940.

Van Horne. J. "Ortega en los Estados Unidos," *Clavileño*, IV, No. 24 (Nov.-Dec. 1953), 55-59.

Vázquez, Juan Adolfo. "Ortega como circunstancia," *Sur*, No. 241 (July-Aug. 1956), 29-32.

Vela, Fernando. "Evocación de Ortega," *Sur*, No. 241 (July-Aug. 1956), 3-12.

————. "La 'fantasía' en la filosofía de Ortega," *La Torre*, XV-XVI (July-Dec. 1956), 433-453.

Ventura Chumillas, B. *¿Es D. José Ortega y Gasset un filósofo propiamente dicho?* Buenos Aires, 1940.

————. *Filósofos y literatos*. Buenos Aires, 1941.

Vitier, Medardo. *José Ortega y Gasset*. Havana, 1936.

Warren, L. A. *Contemporary Spanish Literature*. London, 1929. See pp. 669-676.

Zambrano, María. "Apuntes sobre la acción de la filosofía," *La Torre*, XV-XVI (July-Dec. 1956), 553-576.

————. "Don José," *Ínsula*, X, No. 119 (Nov. 15, 1955).

————. "Ortega y Gasset, filósofo español," *Asomante*, V, Nos. 1-2 (1949), 5-17, 6-15.

————. "Unidad y sistema en la filosofía de Ortega," *Sur*, No. 241 (July-Aug. 1956), 40-49.

Zaragüeta, Juan. "El vitalismo de Ortega," *La Torre*, XV-XVI (July-Dec. 1956), 455-466.

Zea, Leopoldo. "Medio siglo de filosofía en México," *Filosofía y Letras*, XXI, No. 41 (1957), 111-131.

————. "Ortega el Americano," *Cuadernos Americanos*, LXXXV, No. 1 (1956), 132-145.